Babette

The Many Lives,

Two Deaths and

Double Kidnapping

of Dr. Ellsworth

Ross Eliot

Babette: The Many Lives, Two Deaths and Double Kidnapping of Dr. Ellsworth / Ross Eliot.

Printed in the United States of America

On the cover: Albert J. Ellsworth as a child in France with nun, 1930s, photographer unknown. (author's collection) For additional documentation please visit:

www.profellsworth.com

www.rosseliot.wordpress.com

The main text in this book is printed with Times New Roman, a completely typical, yet highly readable serif typeface dating from 1931. The cover is Cochin, a slightly more interesting transitional serif font from 1912 and named after the French copperplate engraver Nicolas Cochin.

Author's Note:

Writers often take great liberties when recounting political histories, personal memoirs or other allegedly non-fictional works. I have not found such embellishments necessary. This tale is easily verifiable, even in most remarkable elements, and requires no sensationalism. To the best of my knowledge, I am passing on accurate information of legitimate public interest.

Names, localities and characteristics of certain people have been changed because they participated in acts that may not have been entirely legal or to protect them from embarrassment. Some timeframes were also distorted for the sake of coherence. Beyond those exceptions, my account is entirely factual, notwithstanding the unavoidable bias of a single perspective and intimate involvement in many unusual circumstances. Some individuals may remember events differently. Cases where I recount dialogue are based on memory of specific conversations and bolstered by extensive diary entries. In other places, I have presented the essential content of what were often quite unforgettable interactions. If there is any contradiction, it is unintentional and not through any malicious intent on my part.

Lastly, many quotations in this book come from antiquated publications. I have preserved spelling, capitalization and grammatical idiosyncrasies as they appeared originally. Specific sources and additional details can be found in the endnotes section.

R.E.

No Book Writes Itself, No Writer Writes Alone

I extend special appreciation to those whose instrumental contributions made this project a reality: Lane Browning for editing genius, Kristin Cleveland for feedback and technology assistance, Ken Gengler for website design, Lisa Kendall for critiques and enthusiasm, Nikki Lev for promotion and Craig Snyder for generous information on the Brown family.

Great thanks to my literary comrades for their experience and encouragement: Tele Aadsen, Katie Ash, Jenn Benton, Kimi Boylan, Cricket Corleone, Susan Finesman, Raaja Gharbi, Chris Gustafson, Kimberlee Conway Ireton, Cassandra Koslen, Matt Siegel, Cappy Spruance, Michael Tomlinson and Minerva Zimmerman.

Gratitude is also offered to people who assisted with information, proofreading, research and creative advice: Jessica Adams, Hera Crow, Alisa Fowler, Sara Gharbi-Reinking, Martin Gowdy, James Hem, Iska Johnson, Courtney Kint, Michael Kurt, Silvie Martinez, Bethany Moore, Heather Patterson, Bill & Arlene Philips, Heather Saal, Eric Smiley, Matt Steele, Jennifer Tanny, Joan Waldvogel, Lyle Walker and Chad van Winkle. None of this could have come about without the support of my friends, family and high school English teacher, Lee Anne Bowie.

Organizations to whom I am indebted include the Kettleson Memorial Library in Sitka for dry internet access and the Yakima Orchestra for schedule information. Extra thanks to Awadagin Pratt for his kindness to an unwashed commercial fisherman on the SE Alaskan panhandle.

This work was significantly composed while trolling and long-lining aboard *F/V Charity* and under the influence of Margaret Atwood, Emily Hahn, Maurice Bishop, Karen Russell, Hilaire Belloc, Tommy Douglas, Bohren & der Club of Gore, Janelle Monáe, rooibos tea, Raven's Brew Coffee, Rainier beer, black vanilla pipe tobacco and extreme sleep deprivation.

Dedicated to my little bee...

Table of Contents

Chapter 1: Prelude

"Something is beginning in order to end: adventure does not let itself be drawn out; it only makes sense when dead."

Jean-Paul Sartre. Nausea. 1938.

"I am not just one person...There are patterns of thoughts in me which I alternatively love and admire, others which enrage me and still others which I (at times) detest."

Albert J. Ellsworth. "Counseling: A Frame of Reference." Summer, 1963.

Portland, Oregon 2000. A cool afternoon in early December. The scuffed black boots of a young man pound down empty hallways of St. Vincent Hospital. Determined steps echo as he slows and pushes up the sleeve of an olive drab jacket to compare room numbers against scrawled permanent marker ink trailing down his pale left wrist. It still exudes a faint chemical odor which fades, replaced by the dull institutional smell of persistent cleansing. At the correct doorway, he pulls a thin curtain aside and peers within. Eyes and mouth open wide. He jerks his head back in alarm, but recovers, tears the cloth away and bursts inside.

Blood. Before the young man's gaze it pools on beige tiles, spots crumpled white bedclothes and daubs the figure of an elderly woman lying diagonally on her back in bed. A hand grips the aluminum rail and one bare foot presses flat against the crimson spattered floor as though in preparation to stand. She looks up through thick glasses underneath a matted grey wig. It threatens to topple off as her large round head swivels about. A flimsy blue gown gapes open and the other hand clutches a red soaked towel between her legs. She spots the visitor and lets it drop. A fresh wave of blood sluices down wobbling thighs and the man runs over, his face drained.

"What's happened? Can you talk? Are you alright?" he asks.

She moans and replies, a thick European accent distorting her words. The man bends closer over ashen cheeks. He strains to hear.

"I know I don't have much longer..."

Both eyelids drift shut. In panic, the man reaches over to an emergency call button mounted on the wall and presses it repeatedly. Nothing happens. With his fist now, he hammers, two, three, four times. The plastic knob mocks him, insensible. He runs into the hall and spots a distant nurse.

"Help!" he shouts. The uniformed woman looks at him and pauses. "Hey there, help!" he repeats, feeling oddly self-conscious. After a moment's contemplation, she begins slow measured paces in his direction. He retraces red smeared footprints and finds the old woman upright. Determination twists her broad face.

"No! No! No! Hold still. Lie down, you'll be ok," he reassures her. "There's help on the way." At this, a hand flaked in clotted blood wraps around his forearm.

"You must get me out of here. I swear I can't stay a minute longer." Her voice is low, lips close to his ear. "They put these things in me, I can't bear it. I tore them all out... it is an absolute vision of hell!"

At this, the man notices a small oozing wound inside her left wrist and several clear plastic tubes on the floor. They lead to an IV stand and other baffling devices. Voices abruptly sound nearby and a trio of nurses enters. Two attend their patient and the man moves to assist, but the third pulls him aside.

"Are you a relative?" she asks.

"Yes. Her grandson." He hopes stress makes this sound convincing. The nurse shrugs, her countenance implacable.

"We are keeping Dr. Ellsworth overnight. She can't leave like this. Look here what she's done to herself! A catheter tube must be deflated before it's removed from the urethra, but she ripped it out regardless. I don't want to sound callous, but your grandmother has been nothing but a terror for everyone. Please

2

keep her under control." The nurse's mouth arcs downward in disapproval.

"Like an animal," the old woman croaks, "treated this way by you beasts!"

Each stone-faced nurse pretends not to notice and they swiftly exit, a fresh bundle of towels left behind. The man wets one at a nearby sink and wipes crusted streaks from the prostrate woman's arms. She turns her head and fixes him with a sober expression.

"You must take me out of here immediately. I know soon I can regain my strength. Enough at least we can fly to Las Vegas. We will be married. You may keep living in my house and preserve the library and no one can stop you. All my books..." Her voice drifts off.

She blinks behind thick glasses that magnify her lazy right eye hugely out of proportion. Its gaze drifts over his shoulder, as if plotting a next move; her left bears straight ahead. The man presses wan lips together and swallows, his two eyes meet her one, yet are still outnumbered.

"We shall be wed," she continues calmly, "and then so I never come back to a place like this, I will commit suicide. I have the pills. It will be quick."

"Babette!" he cries out. Hot tears course down his cheeks.

Chapter 2

"We should indeed be fools to sacrifice ourselves to the conventional."

Benjamin Disraeli. Endymion. 1881.

It's early autumn 1998. I am twenty-one years old and teaching myself to ride a motorcycle. The General watches through his open window upstairs in a dilapidated boarding house we both call home, near Seattle's University District. A wispy-haired Vietnam vet, he calls out in frustration as I kill the engine yet again. The machine sputters and nearly topples over as acrid smoke trails from dual exhaust pipes. I coast to a halt in crisp leaves spangling brown and orange down the block.

The kickstand to my 1981 Honda Magna is broken, so it must be raised up on its center support when parked. I remove my helmet, freeing the short bleached-blonde Mohawk underneath, then step on a short metal peg below the frame, bear down and shift rearward. This rolls the whole back end but requires a certain amount of technique to completely lift. Nearly fifteen tries later, sweat pours down my forehead. Joggers and dog-walkers smile as they pass.

"You sure you're doing ok there?" the General yells down, bushy eyebrows raised.

"I'm fine." I reply, gritting my teeth.

After another ten minutes, I finally heave the motorcycle upright and retreat inside for a break. It's unknown how many people share this house. My quarters are an 8x8 foot space built by creative remodelers who partitioned the former main dining area into two bedrooms. From outside, one can see drywall plastered flush against the glass window. It splits our chambers like bifocal lenses. Some past tenant proclaimed "Julian loves Rachel" in large red letters spray-painted on the wall. The place may be a fire-trap but at least rent is cheap.

In search of lunch, I open the refrigerator. It doesn't smell too bad. Food preservation in any common areas is risky. Some tenants identify their jars and containers with names and the occasional admonition "Keep Out." Thick permanent marker on my plastic jug of milk declares "OX JIZZ" and so far people have left it alone.

"I dumpstered a whole box of popcorn last night!" the General hollers down from upstairs. "It's on the counter, help yourself."

"Thanks!" I shout back.

I elect saving the General's find for later and prepare a sandwich instead. Then, fortified with ham and pickles, I return to motorcycle practice. A mere two hours later, I zip confidently around the block and, as dusk sets in, make an initial foray onto the freeway. A short trip, just one ramp to the next, but speed fills me with exaltation. Air batters against the cloudy windscreen of my second-hand helmet with just a hint of chill. Despite the hazy view, all becomes clear. *This machine is my escape to a new life.*

On October 1st, I ride south across the Columbia River into Portland, Oregon. A bright day billows all around and wheels vibrate along the bridge. Two backpacks bound together serve as saddlebags, slung across the rear seat with my sleeping bag strapped on top. The v-twin engine roars and a brisk wind batters against me as it rushes down the gorge.

Within a few days I move into a boarding house on the outer east side of Portland. Its owner, a stringy man in his late fifties, lives upstairs and rents out three main floor rooms. Every common area, including the bathroom, is wired with speakers dialed into a '70s music station. At night he turns the volume down, but in nocturnal stillness, disco and funk classics scrape along, just below a whisper. One housemate, a tiny wizened man, suffers some terrible debilitating illness. His bent frame moves slowly, supported by a walker patched with duct tape.

The other lodger is a woman in her early forties named Mona, whose room faces mine. She is obese beyond morbidity, her belly swinging down and suspended between thick blotchy knees. Dark bangs from a sloppy home dye job frame pink cheeks that beam in pleasant welcome.

After several weeks I find work operating forklifts at an aluminum anodizing plant. The swing-shift schedule runs three-thirty until midnight and one Thursday, I trudge indoors even later than usual to find Mona in the kitchen. Thunderous pops emanate from the microwave. My leather jacket is wet and I sling it hard over a chair. Water runs down the sleeves. Mona chuckles as I scowl and adjust my lower back.

"Couldn't tell if that was my popcorn or your spine! Tough day at work? You look like someone died!"

"Got pulled over, just a couple blocks down the street. The cop impounded my bike." I sit down and swipe a hand across my helmet's wet visor.

"Don't do that, you're getting water all over the table!"

"Sorry." I move it onto the floor.

"What happened? You speedin'?"

"Hell no, not in this weather. I did stretch a yellow pretty good, just enough a cop noticed and followed me. Problem is, my signal lights are broken. I use hand motions, y'know? Well, that's only legal during daytime. So, I got pulled over for equipment failure."

Mona raises an eyebrow. "C'mon, nobody gets towed 'cos of that."

"Well, I don't carry insurance. Or have a motorcycle endorsement either."

"Oh, that's a shame." Mona frowns. "Don't get me started on smoky bears. Didya know I used to be a trucker? Until last August, that's when I got fired. My boss really had it in for me. Lucky unemployment lasts a while longer." She snorts, opening the microwave door. Steam rises and a buttery aroma fills the room. Mona pours the popcorn into a large plastic bowl and points generously. "Help yourself."

"Thanks." I take a handful. It's very salty.

"So, can you just pay a fee and get your bike back?"

I grimace. "Unlikely. I don't have the title for it either."

Mona slaps her forehead. "God, child, you are a mess!"

I sigh and look down. The helmet glistens up at me, water

drying in streaks across the glossy surface. My cargo pants are soaked as well and I wiggle damp toes inside heavy boots.

"Why do you cut your hair that way?" Mona asks. The Mohawk lays compressed sideways from sweat and helmet pressure.

"That's how I like it."

"Don't people look at you funny?"

"Sometimes. That's their problem."

Mona purses her lips. "It's sure different. Course, 'atcher age it's still ok to do wild stuff."

I laugh. "Yeah? How much time do I have?"

"Until you're twenty-five. That's a good cutoff point."

"Glad you'll leave me a few years' grace then."

Mona cracks open a can of root beer. "Don't mean to pry, but what are you doing in Portland?"

"Well, I spent all my life in Seattle. Seemed like a good time for something new. Maybe stay and work here a little while, then keep exploring. Perhaps head toward Chicago next."

Mona frowns. "If there's anything ten years truckin' taught me, it's avoid big cities. This town is plenty large, probably too big for my taste. Ha! That sounds like a crazy plan! You seem a decent kid though. Got yer nose in a book half the time I've noticed. Never been much for readin' myself."

"That's just how I grew up. My parents kept television pretty much off limits. Literature probably raised me as much as anything else."

"Well, if you're not going right to sleep and want a break from all those books, the Golden Girls are on in a few minutes. Wanna join me?"

"Sorry, what's that?"

Mona draws herself up in horror. "You've never seen the Golden Girls! Oh, this is a tragedy! What about M*A*S*H*? That's right afterward."

I shake my head.

"Well, there's plenty of popcorn if you want to fill some gaps in your life." She lowers her voice. "Since that cheap bastard we rent from won't let us share his house phone, I got my own line put in. Seen ya in the booth up the street a few times. Use mine and save a walk. Just ask, ok?"

I accept her offers. Because we're both nocturnal, Mona soon invites me over to watch TV nearly every night. We sit in the dark and share snacks before the 12-inch screen as I discover a world far removed from historical monographs and antiquated novels.

As expected, the police impound lot won't release my motorcycle with no title, but fortunately a backup option exists. Before leaving Seattle, I lent a 1983 Toyota Celica to my friend James. I call him up and explain my situation. He agrees to drive it down the next Saturday. On our appointed afternoon Mona's phone rings. She knocks at my door and passes her cordless receiver over. The voice is fuzzy but familiar.

"Hello?"

"Ross! It's James. I barely made it. Your radiator overheated and burst. I just got off the freeway. It's pretty bad, looks like the block is cracked. I'm in a phone booth at a gas station in the Hollywood District, just off Halsey Street."

I ride the bus out to meet him. Stocky, with short blond hair and a dolorous expression, James leans against the side of my Celica. We embrace and he passes over a heavy paper bag.

"What's this?"

"A six-pack of Afri, y'know, that weird German soda we drank in high school. Not much consolation since your car is shot."

"Oh thanks! I haven't had one in forever. No stores carry it down here."

James kicks his heels against the front tire. "Sorry... there was no warning, just steam everywhere."

I clap him on the shoulder. "Ahhhh, don't beat yourself up. Just glad you made it here safe. So, it's not cold, but we can share one of these if you like."

James nods. I am about to pop the Afri's cap when one of Portland's many art cars pulls up at red light at in front of us. This specimen is entirely covered in potted plants and gargoyles, from green fronded bumpers to leafy hood and roof. The driver, wearing large aviator sunglasses, cranks the stereo and dances in his seat. He bounces cheerfully with a yard-wide smile. I amble over and hand him my soda. The signal changes green and with a jaunty thumbs up, he roars away. I smile. Portland is not the worst place to be stranded.

On a chilly afternoon in late November, Mona and I make a supermarket trip in her old three-speed GM pickup. Its suspension groans and lists to one side. The steering wheel measures only nine inches in diameter, a custom addition so her massive girth can squeeze inside the cab. Still, with the bench seat slid completely back, it jams into her chest. She maneuvers using a shiny chrome steering knob gripped in her left fist, the arm bent double. It nearly touches her chin. Even in cold weather, exertion makes her sweat. Mona turns off the engine and looks over at me, face serious.

"I've been thinking, Ross; you and me, we spend a lot of time together and already share a bathroom and kitchen. Why don't the two of us just get a place of our own? The only difference would be less money."

I mull this over for a moment. "Yeah... seems like a good idea. Someplace closer to the city center would be preferable, since I'm on public transit now."

We give a month's notice and at the beginning of December, rent a two-bedroom apartment in northeast Portland, off 82nd and Glisan. Over time, I accumulate more possessions, brought back piece by piece from Seattle when friends visit. My turntable, several crates of records, 1985 Macintosh computer and boxes of clothes. Mona empties out a storage unit, filled before her trucking days, which contains enough furniture for our new home. She lends me an old couch just long enough to stretch out my bedroll on.

Life progresses into March. Mona survives on unemployment and I work at the aluminum plant, now a very long bus ride away. She attends a Foursquare church out in an eastern suburb and, with few other social outlets, I occasionally come along. We often cook food together and watch television late into the night, but sometimes her gaze lingers on me, hungry and unsatisfied. Once, as I dry off from a shower in the bathroom, my housemate walks past outside, scratching her fingernails slowly across the closed door. I shudder.

Mona keeps in contact with one of the other truckers at her old company, a Nicaraguan man named Manuel. We have him over for dinner several times and I find him quite pleasant, though Mona claims his motives are less than honorable.

"He's fine when you're around, Ross, but as soon as you leave the room, he doesn't want to do anything but get in my pants!"

"Well, Manuel's a good looking guy– why do you turn him down?"

Mona scowls. "I won't sleep with a Mexican."

I laugh. "Then no problem– he isn't Mexican!"

"Well, it's still adultery."

"Not unless he's married."

Her eyes narrow. "Whatever. I won't sleep with someone like him...though I might take a black man if he's clean. Anyway, it's still against my religion. There's just one person I'd make an exception for. Only one."

I avoid her gaze and hurriedly leave the room.

One day, a Portland Community College catalogue comes in the mail. I idly browse classes from creative writing to foreign languages, then scan over the history section. Northwestern History, US History and History of the Holocaust catch my eye. Credits are cheap and eager for distraction, I enroll in two winter quarter morning classes. The campus pulses with political energy and soon I'm pulled into local activism. There is always a focus group on sweatshop labor, march against police brutality or lecture about Israeli apartheid policies. You can hardly walk from class to the library without getting roped into a giant anti-capitalist puppet building project.

Chapter 3

"All history is a lie, and to know it so misrepresented it would be far better not to know it at all."

Vicente Blasco Ibanez. <u>The Shadow of the Cathedral</u>. 1919.

By the end of March 1999 I've saved enough money to quit the aluminum plant and concentrate more on school. My first course spring quarter is History of Western Civilization, with a professor named Dr. Ellsworth. The first day of class, our instructor enters about five minutes late. She carries an old fashioned leather briefcase and iron gray hair mushrooms above a cherubic pink face. Her shoulders are wide, draped with a garishly patterned red sweater. She sits before us, black stockinged legs spread wide apart beneath an ill-matched orange skirt. From the briefcase, Dr. Ellsworth extracts a thick stack of papers, thumping them onto her desk in an ominous pile.

"Please pass my syllabi out amongst yourselves." Thick glasses distort her features, and each word tumbles forth through a dense French accent.

Students hand the stapled papers down each row, groaning. I take one packet and leaf through it. Can this really be a 100 level class? Six double-sided pages! The last contains a two-column list of potential subjects for the midterm in-class essay:

No. 1: Discuss the policies of Metternicht .... No. 13: Analyze the position of Napoleon III toward Italy .... No. 22: What did the fall of Bismarck signify in the development of Germany? Make an estimate of his contributions to the country.

Dr. Ellsworth smiles at the audible dismay. Her teeth are grey and tightly packed together. "You may find my expectations as set forth here rather intimidating. Please know much of what you see is for the benefit of my superiors. I must maintain an appearance of high academic rigor and of course, ask you all to buy a very expensive textbook. But I say right now, if you haven't purchased the text yet, don't bother. My main assignments will be book reports on period novels. Textbooks present the past as seen by modern day historians. That is all very well, but to arrive at a clearer picture of bygone eras, I always prefer first hand sources, people who were there. So instead of listed requirements, you will complete book reports on novels by such authors as Leo Tolstoy, Jane Austen and Victor Hugo. There, don't you all feel better?"

I am intrigued, but many of my classmates appear puzzled, and those who have already purchased a 13th edition text mutter with annoyance. Dr. Ellsworth launches immediately into a lecture without notes, summoning endless streams of facts and often risqué historical anecdotes from memory. Costume jewelry on wrists and fingers flash beneath the fluorescent tubes and a large silver crucifix dangles on a chain around her neck. The spectacle is mesmerizing: We cannot look away as our professor describes with relish Catherine de' Medici's intrigues and the fate of Henry VIII's many wives.

Though a brilliant storyteller, Dr. Ellsworth struggles with more mundane activities. As I wait for my bus one day after class, a little blue Toyota pulls out of the parking lot and noses directly into traffic on Killingsworth Street. An oncoming delivery truck screeches to a halt. The car begins an agonizingly slow left turn and another vehicle brakes in the far lane. Burnt rubber fills my nose. Horns bellow and motorists yell as the Toyota inches along, still blocking both directions. It gradually accelerates up to speed and I spy Dr. Ellsworth behind the wheel. Her head shakes at such unseemly commotion.

Some weeks later we cross paths outside the school library.

"Justine?" she asks, bushy eyebrows raised. "You are the student who wrote a book report on the Marquis de Sade's Justine, correct?"

I nod. Dr. Ellsworth smiles.

"Oh, what a delight. But not for the faint of heart. I hesitate to openly recommend the Marquis, so it fills me with joy you picked his masterpiece. It has been many years since I read the book myself, but you helped me relive its sheer horror!"

"Thank you. There are several other authors I'm excited to

write on. Octave Mirbeau and J.K. Huysmans."

"Oh, Mirbeau and Huysmans! I adore those two! Now, what is your name, *excusez-moi?*"

"Ross."

"Ahh, yes. Wrahs." Her low voice transforms the R of my name into a soft W. "I would be honored," she says, "if you joined me for lunch."

"That would be... very nice," I agree. After the day's lecture, she drives us to Wong's Garden, a Chinese restaurant in the southeast Woodstock neighborhood while I clench my fists at every near-miss of parked car, approaching bicycle or nearby pedestrian. We sit in a booth and the waitress brings menus. She also sets down two glasses of water. My professor glares at the one before her, then snatches up a fork and lifts out an ice cube.

"Do you mind?" she asks.

I tilt my head. "What?"

Dr. Ellsworth reaches over, fork vibrating in unsteady hands, and tips the ice into my glass. After two more cubes, water splashes over the rim. I dab it up with a napkin.

She frowns. "My apologies for the mess. I despise this American obsession with frozen water. There, perhaps mine will become drinkable soon. So, Wrahs, have you enjoyed my class so far?"

I grin. "You scared everyone at first with that syllabus. Yeah, I like the way we use old novels to learn about different time periods. It's fun for someone like me who reads all the time anyway, but also draws in people ordinarily turned off by textbooks. The lectures are amazing too, you've really got the dirt on everybody!"

Dr. Ellsworth's lips stretch into a wan smile. "Ah yes, the foibles of historical characters. I do what I can to focus attention when young people are so easily distracted."

When the waitress returns, my professor requests a cup of tea. Rings sparkle through steam as her fingers hover over the wide cup. She bobs her large round head and beams. "Much better. That some people drink cold fluids is positively barbarous. Now, Wrahs, from your papers, I gather the impression you are somewhat of a political activist, is that correct?"

15

Her left eye skewers me directly, but the right drifts, hugely magnified by thick glasses. Its focus angles lazily past my shoulder.

I nod. "You could say that. I work with a few different groups right now. There's an anti-globalization rally downtown next weekend. Is that an event you might attend?"

My professor smiles indulgently. "You know, Wrahs, I admire your enthusiasm, I really do. It is wonderful you should be involved with such causes. But while I agree totally in what you are doing, being so public a rabble rouser is no way to ensure your own survival."

She savors her tea. "You may think me a hypocrite. But as surely as we sit here today, later this month I plan to lunch with friends who will tell me about the gathering you speak of and complain if police have not arrested enough troublemakers. 'Arrest them?' I will say. 'Where are the truncheons and fire hoses?' And we will conclude that young people have been coddled far too much and should attend church more." She toys with the silver crucifix.

"But of anyone, surely you don't believe in religion?" I ask. "Your lectures on the popes gave me nightmares and things only got worse once we moved onto the Reformation. It's mystifying to see you wear a cross."

"You are correct," Dr. Ellsworth responds, "I possess absolutely no faith, but, as you can observe, care a great deal about social standing. Affiliation with the Catholic church has also been ..." she pauses "in many ways very beneficial for me. But notwithstanding gratefulness, it would simply be torture to abandon the rituals or never hear mass. You must think me terribly duplicitous."

With a clatter of plates, our food arrives. We eat in silence until Dr. Ellsworth spoons up a final mouthful of soup and swallows noisily. She wipes her mouth with a napkin. "Well, young Wrahs, I have quite enjoyed your company. Perhaps we may spend time together again sometime soon."

Chapter 4

"I have already declared that without being pious, I have religion
all the same. Say and do what you like, religion is always
religion."

Octave Mirbeau. The Diary of a Chambermaid. 1900.

"That teacher of yours with the weird voice called again,"
Mona announces the following Saturday afternoon. She faces
away, stirring macaroni and cheese on the stove. The exhaust vent
sucks steam upward with a low rumble.

"It's her French accent." I explain.

"It just doesn't seem right," Mona sniffs. "I never heard of a
decent professor who took so much interest in their student."

I dial Dr. Ellsworth back.

"Hello?" she answers.

"Hi, this is Ross, from your Western Civ. class."

"Ah yes, the young man with such debaucherous taste in
literature. Tell me this. Do you have plans tomorrow?"

I think for a moment. "Not really."

"Excellent! Would you accompany me to Mt. Angel Abbey?
It is a Benedictine monastery south of Portland. Oh, such a
beautiful place. They give regular mass and the services are a true
joy. I promise you a wonderful time and lunch afterward. Say you
will come!"

"Well, ok." I write down her address and early Sunday
morning catch a bus westbound. After one transfer, the final stop
is at 39th and Woodstock, mere blocks from Reed College, a
private school with beautiful architecture and immaculately
landscaped grounds. Three blocks down Woodstock, I turn left into
the Eastmoreland neighborhood. Perfectly-painted Queen Anne,
Victorian and Colonial houses are set back from the street, wire
fences ring lush lawns or gardens just beginning their spring

bloom. Stately shade trees line the sidewalks. I lift my boots over pavement hillocks, bulging where roots almost break through. Every street tunnels under its own leafy green canopy.

After a few minutes, I reach Tolman Street and halt before a half-timbered Tudor revival structure. Much of its steep roof is covered with bulky solar panels. The house is nearly hidden behind large evergreen hedges forming a dense perimeter around the front yard. Four tall fruit trees, rhododendron bushes, and other plants complement a towering acacia. Two wooden columns flank the inset front porch. I follow a narrow concrete path to the door. Beside it lurks a small moss-encrusted gnome

Dr. Ellsworth responds promptly to my knock, dressed in a mustard yellow sweater and purple skirt. "Right on time, I am very impressed," she beams, and ushers me inside. A long staircase ascends to the left and past it I can see an elegantly furnished living room dimly visible in light filtering through tightly-drawn curtains. Oil paintings crowd every wall, clocks tick from several directions and over the front door, suspended by two hooks, hangs a corroded bolt-action rifle. My eyes rove wildly.

"Well, Wraths," Dr. Ellsworth says, "it is still early, perhaps you would enjoy a tour of my library before departing?"

We descend narrow stairs into the basement. A thick scent fills my nostrils, the unmistakable musty odor of books. Halfway down, a metal sign nailed to the angled ceiling reads: IMPAIRED CLEARANCE. Dr. Ellsworth switches on overhead lights, revealing a large cellar filled with cabinets, cobwebbed shelves and boxes. I follow her to a pair of iron-bound oak doors where she clicks open the massive padlock to release a metal crossbar. She lifts it out of the way and one side creaks open.

Behind this is a second room is even bigger than the first. Concrete gives way to rippling hardwoods puckered from long-ago water damage. A gas fireplace burns near the center of the room, and on either side stretches row upon row of shelves packed to capacity with books. Maps, pamphlets and bulging folders fill every other available space in massive quantities.

"Here we have the Northwest and Oregon section, with history, geography and geology," Dr. Ellsworth begins, gesturing, "and to the right is Canadian and Catholic Church history, most of these are French of course– the language of God, but many in English as well. I do my best to keep an open mind." The word English she pronounces with a long e, making her mouth twist.

We move past the fireplace and she navigates me from geology, anthropology, astronomy and ancient history through the Middle Ages.

"My section along here is mostly 19th and 20th century history" – she extends an arm, "then this last shelf to the far side of the room is all novels, some English, but the majority French and Spanish."

Directly in front of the fireplace reclines a plump red sofa and nearby are two curious benches. Dr. Ellsworth beckons me closer and, to my surprise, flips the back of one so it faces the opposite direction.

"These came from the original streetcar line in Portland," she informs me, eyes shining. "Back in the 1890s, operators would reach the end of a route and then turn them over so riders could sit the other way. These are off the old Tolman St. line which used to run in front of my house here. It was only years later Woodstock became the main arterial through this neighborhood. There! Look at all the information I give you for no extra cost!"

I gaze about in awe. Several half-open cupboards reveal more shelves groaning under vinyl LPs and hundreds of videotapes. A wind-up phonograph is nearly concealed by trunks and boxes. Dr. Ellsworth pauses her commentary and sits down on the sofa.

Despite evidence of past flooding, I detect no mold or rot. Warm air from the fireplace makes dust motes dance in light shafts from streaked casement windows. Delicately, I brush my fingertips over nineteen thick volumes of what looks like a very old series, each labeled by region. *Africa I-IV, South America I-II, Asia I-IV...* the list goes on. I pull one free and flip through its pages.

"Those are very interesting," Dr. Ellsworth observes. "A wonderful ethno-geographic encyclopedia called <u>The Earth and its Inhabitants</u> by Elisee Reclus. Do you know him? Reclus was a French geographer of the highest caliber, besides a notorious anarchist. He supported the Paris Commune in 1871 but survived its destruction and spent the next twenty years on this project. No one before succeeded so triumphantly at such a compilation.

Reclus covered the entire globe, not only physical features, but local cultures and peoples everywhere. Look at the illustrations and maps! What a masterpiece!"

She crosses the room and removes another book. A photograph flutters out and lands face down on the floor. My professor bends to pick it up. She grins mischievously, then folds the photo in half. It disappears into the front pocket of her yellow sweater.

"Be careful as you read these. I occasionally forget curiosities which are not suitable for the general public."

I travel from histories of the Huguenot and Fenian movements, to writing by Disraeli and von Clausewitz before an extensive World War II banquet unfolds before me. Joseph Goebbels' diaries, memoirs of George F. Kennan, General Kesselring's autobiography and a 1938 English edition of Adolf Hitler's _Mein Kampf_. Curiosity whetted, I delve further into this section which stretches on behind a large armchair.

Dr. Ellsworth clears her throat. "You know, Wrahs, I really must suggest we start our day trip."

Fortunately for my nerves, she allows me to drive and we head south on Interstate 5. About half an hour later I motor her Toyota up a moderately-sized hill with fourteen small chapels spaced thirty or so yards apart from bottom to summit. A bell tolls as I park.

"Hurry along without me," Dr. Ellsworth urges. "I am cold and must warm up in the office." She directs me toward the main chapel and makes for a smaller building off to one side.

I enter a simple but elegant structure through large doors. Painted biblical scenes festoon every wall and statues of saints retire in alcoves along the sanctuary. Arranged to form a horizontal cross, austere wooden pews fill the main chapel. I select a spot near the back. Only three others are ahead of me, older men with shiny pates or thinning white hair but as the bell's final ring echoes, two middle-aged women enter. They bow toward the altar and sit down.

Moments later, about a dozen black cassocked monks file in slowly from a side entrance. They take seats along the forward benches. A long silence ensues. Then, abruptly they stand, face us in two rows and begin to sing, alternating Latin with English. The notes rise and fall in graceful solemnity. After about twenty-five minutes they finish and shuffle quietly out of the sanctuary, bowing as each circles past. The left row is three monks longer than the right and these extras bend forward together in a solemn salute to emptiness before they exit.

I discover my professor fixated by a religious magazine with Pope John Paul II on its cover in the other building's lobby.

"That sanctuary is so drafty," she explains, tossing her head, "and I get abominable chills these days. But I hope this experience has done wonders for your spiritual well-being." She laughs. "We shall return and I will prepare a delicious lunch! You know, I am quite a well-regarded cook!"

After driving back to her house, she leads me into the sunlit kitchen. Orange enameled pots and pans hang from hooks around the room. 1950s red marbled Formica tops each counter and a small matching table fills the rear breakfast nook. This half of the room is decorated in wallpaper featuring tiny tattooed sailors, whimsical tall ships and water-spouting whales. It looks like decor for a child's bedroom. On one counter is a round wooden board and thick glass bell. Underneath lies something triangular, draped with black speckled skin. Dr. Ellsworth gestures at this. "Would you like some cheese?"

I wrinkle my nose. "No thanks, I don't eat cheese."

"Oh, what a tragedy. You could scarcely find better. It is aged to perfection. In France we kept our cheese until a special variety of little red worm dwelled there."

An enameled metal contraption sits beside the oven. It resembles an old fashioned refrigerator but narrower, with a recessed lid.

"What's that?" I ask.

"My calcinator!" Dr. Ellsworth declares proudly. "The most modern way to dispose of rubbish. Or it was fifty years ago. You open the top and incinerate anything burnable inside. Oh, that reminds me."

She removes the folded photograph from her pocket and with a wooden match ignites an edge. I catch a brief glimpse...*is it naked skin?* Her foot presses on a pedal at the bottom of the device and its lid flips open. Her fingers tremble as the paper bubbles and smokes in her hand. She drops it inside, steps away and the top snaps shut.

"Ashes collect below. It's a great convenience. But please sit ... down." She puts her palm against the wall to steady herself.

"I am sorry, Wrahs, but I really don't feel well and must rest. There is leftover chicken in the refrigerator you may eat but I'm afraid I can't join you. Thank you for a lovely afternoon. Please let yourself out when you have finished."

She turns and leaves. I hear leaden footsteps mount the staircase. Sunlight floods through tall windows and I gaze out into a small grassy backyard. Grapevines twist around a high wooden fence along one. Finches chirp and fluff brown feathers on the rim of a concrete birdbath. Across the face of a pedestal mounted sundial, Roman numerals await afternoon shadows. I rise and fix cold chicken on blue and white flowered tableware.

Once it is consumed, I wash my dish in the sink and set it to dry on a wire rack. The house is still, only clocks ticking from the other room disturb it. On my way out, I pause and examine a framed photograph by the entryway. It shows a cheerful Dr. Ellsworth, much younger, engulfed in a Christmas Santa costume. Her buoyant round-face makes me smile as well. I shut the front door firmly behind.

On Monday I arrive in Western Civilization before any other students. My professor sits up front, her countenance impassive. She beckons and I come forward.

"Wrahs," she asks plainly, "I would like you to come live with me."

"What? ..." I stumble, trying to think, "that's so kind, but ... I really can't just move out and abandon my roommate ..." As I speak, the echo of Mona's fingernails scraping across our bathroom door fills my ears. "Yes," I declare.

Chapter 5

"Not (quoth he) that I do mistrust her Virtue. . . . but I must freely
tell you, she is a Woman; there lies the Suspicion."

Francis Rabelais. Gargantua and Pantagruel. 1534.

My roommate sits at the kitchen table, half a summer sausage
on a dish before her.

I clear my throat. "Mona?"

She cuts off another slice and looks up, questioning. "Yeah?"

"This afternoon Dr. Ellsworth offered me a place to stay at
her house. I accepted."

"What?"

"I'm moving out. My rent share is paid through this month. I
told the landlady to keep my half of our deposit. That'll give you
more time to find someone else or get a smaller apartment."

Her lips twitch. "No! How can you do this to me?"

"I'm sorry. You know this can't continue as well as I do."

"What do you mean?"

"Good luck, Mona, I mean that."

"I don't believe in luck, I'm a Christian."

"Well ... I wish you good fortune then."

The next day, June 8, 1999, I catch a bus to Dr. Ellsworth's
house and inspect my new quarters. It is the basement pantry that
escaped notice earlier. We enter through a folding glass door she
grandly proclaims came from Portland's old streetcar line. I see a
long chamber dominated by an immense model train table. This
diorama fills almost half of it, wide gauge tracks set on a plywood
base raised up with sawhorses. Engines, boxcars and tankers from
the Canadian National ring a papier-mâché mountain and miniature
plastic forest. At the other end, deep shelves contain enough
canned food and preserves to last a family of ten through many
winters. Jars, bottles, and cases are tightly compressed on every

level. In the middle is a twin bed, dressed with crisp flannel sheets and down comforter.

My professor holds out a key ring and removes one. "Take the car, Wrahs. Can you transport everything with it?"

I accept it and nod. "No problem. There really isn't much."

Her Toyota's trunk and rear seats will provide more than enough space for my meager possessions. I drive back to the apartment where Mona sits in our living room, eyes red and silent gaze bitter. After I carry out the first couple boxes, she retreats to her bedroom. The door slams closed. Soon her television wails from within.

Back on Tolman Street, I park, lug a crate of records in both arms up to the front entryway, set it down and try the door. It's locked. I rap sharply. Nothing. I ring the doorbell and wait several minutes. *How odd.* Just an hour before my professor entrusted me with her vehicle but not house keys. I knock repeatedly, to no avail. A light breeze rustles rhododendron branches nearby. I swivel around in frustration and scan over what little can be seen outside the leafy veil that encircles her front garden.

A moment later the door creaks open. Turning back, I see it held ajar and in the gap stands Dr. Ellsworth. Stark naked. Soaking wet. Flesh mottled and gray. She blinks at me through thick spectacles. Neither of us says a word. Neither moves. A small puddle forms drip by drip around my professor's bare feet. The spell breaks as a strident female voice sounds from behind me.

"Get inside, Babette! Stop making a disgrace of yourself! Do you want the whole neighborhood to see?"

I look over my shoulder and see a roundly-built young woman advancing up the steps. Blonde hair cascades around her pale face. At this interruption Dr. Ellsworth draws back. Quickly, I grab my crate, duck down, and slip by her into the house, heading straight downstairs. I sit on the bed and listen as indistinct voices converse above. After several minutes they fade, but not until much later do I venture back to the main floor and continue unloading. This is no good. At least Mona never ambushed me without clothes. If Dr. Ellsworth plans a seduction, this will be one brief stay.

For now, though, I unpack. A wooden commode against one

wall is stacked high with gold rimmed china. I carefully clear the service and store it in the double cupboard below. This makes room for my old Mac and printer on top. I line record crates in a row beside the train table. There is enough space for several boxes of clothes as well to stretch opposite, leaving a narrow walkway between. Above the bed hangs a large wool tapestry of an Aztec eagle. I tack up several band posters beside it and pause. The room already feels comfortable. Soft light slips through dusty casement windows.

That evening my professor, now wrapped in a terrycloth bathrobe, calls me upstairs. Pieces of beef are lined on the cutting board and she slashes away, wrinkled hands flying as she chops carrots and onions. Canned vegetable broth stands on the counter.

"I am sorry if I gave you a start earlier." She chuckles. "I was taking a bath upstairs and all of a sudden heard your furious racket and became afraid you might leave so I ran to let you in without thought for anything else. Some people have suggested my modesty lacks on occasion. All outrageous lies of course."

Dr. Ellsworth tips the ingredients into an orange enameled pot and laughs. As it heats on the stovetop a wonderful aroma rises. My professor taps her wooden spoon against the rim. She sprinkles in some *fleur de sel* and inhales the steam extravagantly.

"That woman you saw earlier today is my granddaughter who came by to pick up a few last things. Until last week she lived upstairs. We sometimes had our little quarrels, but one day after a terrific row she said 'You are too much! I'll have you committed!' Well, I immediately called my attorney to discover if this could be possible and with absolute horror, found out it might, depending on how long a relation lived with me. That is why I made her leave."

Once dinner is cooked, we sit at the kitchen table, bowls of meaty stew before us. After two enthusiastic gulps she flings her spoon down with a clatter. Broth speckles the front of her robe.

"What I would like from you is help with the garden, housework and some other things which are now difficult for me. In return, you may stay the summer and decide what to do next with your life. This arrangement will be good for both of us, *oui*?"

"That sounds excellent," I agree.

"Some persons have criticized my driving. I'm sure you observed no such difficulties." She purses her lips.

I pass a skeptical glance.

Dr. Ellsworth exhales slowly. "Do not bother with an answer. I see it on your wretched face. True enough, last week I backed into my neighbor's truck across the street again. He really possesses no sense of humor about that monstrous thing. Perhaps on occasion you might drive me to appointments or school as well."

Over the next several weeks we develop a routine and I assist Dr. Ellsworth as much as she requires. Her most desperate need is a chauffeur and soon I motor her almost everywhere, school, doctor's office or the grocery store. High-strung and impatient, she abandons English fluency during intense moments. Out of necessity, I soon learn basic French directional instructions. Rings flash from the passenger seat as she points and cries out *a la gauche, trop tard,* and most commonly *vite vite!*

My professor often requires assistance with her wardrobe. I discover her inability to match articles of clothing is not carelessness but color blindness.

"I loathe that term," she barks. "Color blind. It's an accusation. As though there's something wrong with me! I see just fine, only not the same colors as everyone else. The French word is so much better. It's simply called *daltonisme,* after a scientist named Dalton who studied it."

Her mouth arcs downward. "However, as with many things, how I perceive the world is not consistent with majority viewpoints. On occasion people suggest colors I find entirely appropriate ... in fact clash. Perhaps you could take time and arrange the closet so I might dress myself with greater ease."

"Certainly," I agree. Her eccentricities amuse me more with every passing day.

Dr. Ellsworth's chambers are in the master bedroom upstairs, with blood red carpet and felt wallpaper striped in blue and green. She chatters away from an ornate chaise lounge while I organize her large closet, segregating easily confused colors on hangers into defined sections. There are many tops, from professional blouses to sweaters with garish patterns. The hues vary from black and navy blue to vibrant orange and hot pink. The skirts are more straightforward, almost all shades of black, blue or grey. Underneath lay piles of shoes, mostly flats or low heels. These I match together and line up. My professor inspects the new system and nods approvingly. "Perfect," she says.

I discover that her untidy mop of hair is a wig. Rather, a succession of wigs. Seven foam mannequin heads are glued to an upper closet shelf, each with consecutive days of the week scrawled along their bases. Blank eyes stare beneath rows of ragged gray bangs. Dr. Ellsworth views clothing as an inconvenience tolerated only in public, but however nude my professor stalks around the house, she is never without wavy curls atop her head. Sometimes after retiring for the evening, she calls me from the top of the stairs, and I see a completely bald skull silhouetted against light from her bedroom.

While friendly, Dr. Ellsworth keeps a modest distance physically, and my initial fear that she desires more intimacy evaporates. Our life pattern becomes comfortable. We eat together, often out at elegant restaurants, and she pays the bill. A large satellite dish in the backyard streams French news and other foreign networks. Everything possible she experiences in French, from Quebec broadcasts to the caller ID setting. A monthly newsletter from Reed College lists public events, plays and lectures, which we often attend. Her social life far eclipses my own and the telephone rings at all hours. The early morning or late night calls are usually from France. She laughs loudly and once breaks off as I pass nearby.

"My cousin in Port La Nouvelle just called me her little rat," she explains, the receiver covered with her palm, "it's a great compliment."

We view movies in her chambers upstairs, selecting from a vast VHS film library. Just off the master bedroom is a parlor with comfortable chairs, a couch and one wall completely papered in forest motif with leafy branches wall to wall. Her VCR and television sit beside an ornate easel. It holds the large print of a young blonde girl surrounded by flowers and greenery, chilly blue eyes staring under a wide-brimmed straw hat.

One evening Dr. Ellsworth shows me a BBC series adapted from Balzac's 19th century novel Cousin Bette. She sits on the edge of her seat and cries out with delight at every devious turn by which its title character orchestrates the destruction of a family who wronged her. At one point, Cousin Bette's victory seems complete. My professor scowls in sudden irritation, lunges forward and presses stop.

"There we are." she informs me, arms folded obstinately, "this is the end ... well, at least it should be."

I stare in surprise. She sighs. "All right. We will see it through to the true conclusion if you insist. But I warn you, these next minutes are unforgivable. I hope Balzac roasts in the deepest circle of hell for ruining such a perfect story."

We continue, and as predicted, Balzac betrays her heroine at the last minute.

"I wish I knew a way to permanently delete that," my professor grumbles. "See, you must understand women, Wrahs. We are not so physically strong as men, and therefore other means must be found for survival. An ideal female might not even stab her opponent, but should persuade someone else to use the knife. That is why I love these tales where women achieve their goals by any means. The war against our sex is total and it invades every area of our lives, even language!"

She ejects the videotape and feeds it into a rewind machine. The device cries in shrill dismay as it whirs.

"As far as gender bias goes, English is not so bad linguistically. The words however, are still deplorable. Start with what you study: history. Well, that's easy. The story of men and what they say happened. Then a pen– well that is literally a penis! An ink suffused penis which a man uses to record skewed versions of the past while his biological penis writes the future through women's bodies! Whereas the word vagina? That means nothing but a sheath for a sword! So I take great pleasure when Cousin Bette appears triumphant and it nearly kills me that she fails."

The machine squeals to a halt. My professor removes her tape and slides it into a case on the coffee table.

"If you will take the time, next I might show you a multipart series called The Praying Mantis. Oh, it is unparalleled torture. Two women concoct plot after plot against one another using every wile and trick they possess. They exploit the men in their lives with absolute malice. Afterwards you will never trust a female again."

I grin. "Past experience suggests I may still take the chance."

Dr. Ellsworth chuckles at this. "Then perhaps *Belle du Jour*. It is in French with no subtitles, but I would translate for you. You might find this slow, but the conclusion is worth it, such a tragic story. Or maybe instead 'The Last Seduction,' a film more current and in your own vile language even! That would be delightful. It depicts a woman who achieves her ends through chicanery on a level it makes my pulse explode! Oh, just thinking about these marvelous stories gives me shivers. There are so many more as well. I am certain we shall have a splendid time together!"

Over time I notice our daily mail contains many peculiar things. My professor subscribes to several periodicals, from the Canadian news weekly *MacLean's*, French *Le Monde Diplomatique* and cultural publications from Germany and Russia. I observe nearly half are addressed to Albert Ellsworth and the rest Elizabeth Ellsworth, Bobbie Ellsworth, or Babette Bonnefont.

"That was my husband, you see," she explains, with a dry laugh, when I inquire about Albert. "He died many years ago. Some people even suggest I had him murdered." At this she licks her lips in satisfaction.

"What would you like me to call you?"

"In France I was known as Babette, which translates to Elizabeth. But the use of several different names has often proved valuable for me. Are you aware when the French first heard English, they described it as a sound like the barking of dogs?" She grits her teeth. "And now I must speak it every day."

From that point I call her Babette.

Chapter 6

"...words, if they're used too much they wear out, lose their force, they switch from delights into lights and we're left dazzled, ready for the wool to be pulled over our eyes."

Max Aub. <u>Field of Honor</u>. 1943.

On the way home one sunny afternoon, a strange vibration fills the air. I stop, halfway from the bus stop after class and look around curiously. Dogs bark angrily and neighbors pause front yard conversations. I begin to walk again but now the sound is louder. It builds and builds as I near Tolman Street until no doubt exists. This cacophony emanates from Babette's house. It elevates in pitch until the crescendo resembles a boiler about to explode.

I break into a run, burst through the front door and seeing nothing, rush upstairs breathless. Babette rests in calm repose upon the sofa, her face a picture of absolute rapture. Trumpets, French horns and timpani drums blare at high volume from enormous speakers set against the wall. Red lights on the equalizer blink madly. She reclines, eyes closed, as though in a trance.

"Babette! Is something wrong?" I cry, grabbing her arm. She starts, frowns and turns down the volume with a remote control.

"I suppose it is a bit loud," she says, "thank you for your concern. I'd hate if my neighbors called the police."

"They were more likely to call the Air Force!" I exclaim. "It sounded like we were under attack!"

"Ah, what a sublime description! Do you know this? I adore Anton Bruckner's Symphony Number Four *Romantishe*. His third movement is simply divine. Doesn't it make your blood catch fire? This was the final piece played by the Berlin Philharmonic in 1945. You appreciate my music, don't you? Despite that horrid noise of yours I sometimes hear from the basement?"

This makes me smile. "I do actually. I've always enjoyed

classical music. What are these CDs on the coffee table? They look curious."

"Oh, reissues of wartime symphonies by Wilhelm Furtwaengler. What a fantastic conductor, he was one of the best! I always tuned in to hear German broadcasts back in those days. Of course I couldn't understand a word but the music was so magical. Here is one where the pianist Walter Gieseking performs Beethoven's Piano Concerto Number Five, oh, an absolute master also."

My professor queues up the CD and we sit back, buffeted by sound, though now at a more reasonable level.

"Listen!" she breaks in after several minutes. "You can hear anti-aircraft gunfire in the background. Look at the month in 1944 this was recorded. Do you realize by autumn that year every member of the orchestra must have known the end was near? The whole audience aware their fate would be upon them in an instant? But can you hear the passion in their performance? To have known such death and horror already amidst cities destroyed by bombs but still summon enough strength to play." Tears fill her eyes.

I am puzzled. *A Frenchwoman expressing sympathy for World War II era Germany?* Information about her past has escaped in bits and pieces, but when pressed on certain topics she changes the subject or simply ignores my questions. It becomes clear I must earn her confidence. This may take time.

As summer progresses, Babette and I discover more common interests. On evenings when she doesn't select a film for us to watch, we play Scrabble, which she enjoys as long as I do not win too often. We use a French edition of the game and while deciphering *lettre compte triple* or *mot compte double* doesn't take long, the letter bag is vowel heavy, making English words difficult.

With her fantastic memory, my professor usually wins, despite my challenges after I discover her sneaking in antiquated or foreign words. She possesses great advantage doing so because we use an immense 1878 Webster's unabridged dictionary for reference. It weighs more than nine pounds. On the few occasions where I manage two or more victories in a row, she sulks and refuses to play again for several days.

"It's because of my mind, you see," Babette explains one

night. "I have known so many elderly people who are completely brain dead. My greatest fear is becoming like them. So, whenever I see you have beaten me more than once, I think, maybe it's not an accident, perhaps my sanity is on the way out." She tears open a box of Manichevitz crackers and bites into one savagely. Crumbs drip from her lips.

I gesture at our tally sheet recording multiple games. "You don't have much to worry about there."

Her laugh is shallow. "You say that, but I have witnessed what happens over time. I am seventy-three years old. There is little I dread more than losing my intellect. Perhaps three quarters of people my age should be shot as no further use to society. I meet them and they talk about blood pressure or strokes or their idiot grandchildren. But I am nice so of course I listen and nod and say 'Oh, how perfectly awful' and the whole time I just want to tell them 'I hope your arteries explode!' but I stay quiet in keeping with what you know is my essentially patient nature."

Babette's encyclopedic knowledge in so many areas continues to impress me. One day the phone rings and I answer it. The businesslike caller identifies herself as a representative from the mayor's office and requests Dr. Ellsworth.

Babette takes it and smiles with pleasure. "Yes, of course I will be there ... thank you ... see you in the morning." She hangs up.

"Did she mean the mayor of Portland, Vera Katz?" I ask.

"Why certainly!" Babette replies. "I am one of the foremost experts on local geography. City officials often consult me about water issues and drainage problems. I strive for modesty, as you know, but it truly is a balm for the ego to be consulted by people who matter in society. I have always followed my desires ambitiously, but taken care they do not lead where my talents become unremarkable. People, especially my family in France, look at me and say, but you have a doctorate from the University of Bordeaux! Why do you teach at a community college in Oregon of all places? Well, much of the answer is I love life as a big fish in a small pond. An English expression, yes? But within my pond I can very much enjoy myself! Now, Wrahs, you are how old?"

"Twenty-two." I reply.

"Oh," she sniffs, "well, when I was your age I had already earned my master's degree."

Chagrined, I stare at the floor.

Chapter 7

"She believed in God; but she believed also a little in Voltaire."

Emile Gaboriau. <u>The Widow Lerouge</u>. 1873.

Religious philosophy crops up often in our conversations and Babette declares the Roman emperor Marcus Aurelius as her true messiah.

"Here was a man who said acquisition of fame and wealth during our lives is futile!" she exclaims. "We are born, we struggle for a time and then evaporate into dust! The moral path is live as best we can during those precious few moments and be kind to one another. And furthermore, he advised that, despite people who are vexing and troublesome, one should always recognize sparks of divinity in everyone. Jesus never said anything so beautiful!"

"You attend mass nearly every day. Could I come along sometime?" I ask.

My professor's face clouds.

"No! In fact, I would prefer you remained ignorant of which church ..." –she pauses– "or churches I attend at all."

This seems a final verdict, but her reticence is forgotten one Sunday morning.

"You know, Wrahs," she chuckles. "I adore the Catholics but sometimes can't resist teasing them. I belong to a church that is steeped in so much history but among people who are almost entirely ignorant of it. I heard mass just now at St. Agatha's and afterward mingled with the old biddies as I like to do. One wondered who St. Agatha was and I happily reminded her. 'Oh, that is the one martyred by having her tits cut off!' Well, she didn't appreciate my description at all, though I could perhaps have phrased myself better. But it's true, that's what happened! And now she is patron saint of breast cancer!

"Sometimes on travels I bring along images cut from

pornographic magazines or photographs of Hitler and carefully insert them into hymnals or prayer books. Caution is important obviously, but sometimes I can't resist causing trouble. There have been moments I found myself in a grand church all alone and managed to put a truly obscene picture in a Bible on the main pulpit. Oh, when I imagine how this will be discovered by some pious old goat in the midst of their religious platitudes it makes me giddy.

"But I have scored points with the church ladies recently, thanks to you," Babette continues, "I mentioned how I took into my home an underprivileged Presbyterian youth with a goal towards his spiritual development, the son of clergy even, oh, everyone loved to hear about my progress educating you on the one true Catholic faith."

"They aren't clergy!" I interject.

Babette winks. "But you said once your parents are quite involved with their church, as elders even. Well, it is similar. The essential point remains correct."

My professor maintains her relationship with religion the way some people keep mistresses. She considers it a matter of paramount priority that one place of worship never find out about the other. Besides St. Agatha's, she attends an Episcopalian church near our house, though only weekly. One afternoon I hear brakes squeal and out the front window see Babette trot up the walkway. Her car is parked at an awkward angle. She bursts in the front door, chest heaving.

"What's wrong?" I ask.

"Oh, Wrahs! It's those horrid Episcopalians! I agreed to give a lecture for them next week on the Church of England, but just now was mortified seeing my name on the front signboard! Dr. Ellsworth presents! This is a catastrophe! Excuse me." She rushes to the telephone and dials frantically.

"Yes," I hear her say, "I realize you wanted to advertise the event … oh, no, that's all right … it's only that I'm very modest, you understand, and don't like my name in large letters where everyone can see. You will remove it, won't you? I'm sorry for the bother… yes... thank you very much."

She hangs up, shaking her head. "You know, Wrahs, several

of my Catholic acquaintances live in this part of town and any one of them could have seen that – it's not funny!" She protests as I laugh. "You don't understand the trouble I must go to!"

"Do you really think it would matter? You're a well-known professor in town, both churches know that. You should be able to lecture on whatever you please. Are you afraid of being excommunicated or strung on the rack?"

Babette sighs. "I sometimes wonder if I would know what to do with my life if it wasn't so complicated." She picks up her trusty package of Manischewitz crackers and brandishes them like a club. "I am taking my Jewish cookies upstairs. To eat in good company. By myself."

My professor delivers her lecture at the Episcopalian church but afterward quits it entirely. This represents no declining interest in religion, for her preoccupation only intensifies. She spends even more time at St. Agatha's and at least daily has a mass or prayer group. Then one Saturday morning Babette requests I drive her to the airport for a brief day trip to British Columbia. When I pick her up that evening she reveals little about it, only smiling mysteriously the whole way home. Soon she makes plans to visit Canada again for a whole week.

"Now Wrahs, the timepieces are very important," my professor informs me as part of her pre-departure tutorial. She beckons me into the living room. "This grandfather clock next to the piano is easiest, so we will begin here. It is brand new, purchased at the Meier & Frank department store downtown in 1961. Once a week you pull both chains here, like so. The weight on your right controls time and the other hourly chimes. It doesn't matter when this is done, but I keep a routine of Sunday night."

She turns toward the entryway where a rectangular clock is mounted on the wall. Elegant woodwork surrounds its painted glass cover, and transparent areas expose the swinging pendulum.

"Now this is a little older, made in Quebec in 1845. It is quite beautiful, yes? But also more temperamental. Like myself! Open the door and through these small holes in the face you must wind seven and a half rotations with this small key every Sunday evening. Do not wind it during the times of a quarter before the hour until five minutes after the hour. Otherwise it can bind up.

Since your young memory is not so adept as mine perhaps you should write all this down."

I fetch a pad of paper and take dutiful notes. At last we come to a diminutive clock fastened high on the dining room wall. Its tick is deeper than the others and resonates differently.

"This piece is a Black Forest clock," Babette crows with pride, "from around 1760. The workings are entirely wooden, can't you tell by the way it sounds? With this one you should be extremely careful. Pull these chains and avoid the same times as with my Quebec clock but also from a quarter after the hour to half past. Do it every evening since this has only a twenty-four hour mechanism."

After a few additional words of advice, she is gone. I skim through *Maclean's*, one of her Canadian newsmagazines but can't concentrate. Faint grumbles sound above as an overhead pump circulates water through the solar panels. Asynchronous ticking from Babette's three clocks batter the silence. Frustrated, I turn on the kitchen radio– obligingly, Mozart pours out. There's only one channel available now; early in my residence, I switched it to hear news reports but never moved it back. Horrified, Babette cemented the dial in permanent position, slapping on thick globs of epoxy.

I venture upstairs and notice her bedroom door is open. Dense perfume drifts across the threshold. I have never stepped inside unsupervised, but this time I enter, past a wall-mounted holy water dispenser. The black metal bed is unmade and costume jewelry sprays across a dresser. Dust motes float in shafts of sunlight, illuminating an oversized toy tanker truck and model Stuka dive bomber. On her bedside table, a framed photograph depicts the much younger Dr. Ellsworth, whose broad features smile up at me. A thick wallet lies next to it. Sheaves of bills protrude. With careful footsteps I retreat. Checking downstairs, I find the main floor office door locked. The library is sealed off as well, metal crossbar padlocked in position.

Apparently I am still only selectively trusted.

When I pick up my professor after this second excursion, she radiates euphoria and can't resist tantalizing me once I carry her luggage inside.

"You see, Wrahs," Babette begins, her smile sly. "I have

decided to become a Benedictine nun!"

I keep a poker face.

"...and may soon join a convent outside Nanaimo, British Columbia. In the future I will spend a great deal of time there and would like you to watch the house when I am away."

I frown. "Doesn't becoming a nun require a vow of poverty? If you couldn't own property there wouldn't be much for me to house sit, would there?"

Babette turns away with a sniff. "We shall see about that. I forgot your skeptical nature which spreads little but gloom upon a month of sunny days. In fact, I now feel quite unwell and must retire. Perhaps tonight I may take revenge through Scrabble." She marches upstairs and soon Mendelssohn reverberates throughout the house.

I turn to go downstairs, but brush something cold and damp. I jump back. From the glass doorknob dangles a wet pair of light green panties. I shake my head. Babette always washes her undergarments by hand, then drapes them to dry on the first available protrusion.

In the basement, I pass two extra freezers and refrigerators packed with provisions. They throb a perpetual hum that lulls me to sleep each night. I place a Severed Heads single on my turntable. The needle bites down and electronic beats thump from speakers tucked between canned pickles and chutney tins. I lie down across my small bed and look up. Across the ceiling from a hammock of twine, hang bandanas and bootlaces that formerly adorned my hair. I recently gave up the Mohawk as too much trouble and now sport a Chelsea cut, shaved all around with bangs spiked forward.

I laugh. This is my life with an aspirant Benedictine nun, a nun very much prepared for the apocalypse.

Chapter 8

"Besides, what can you expect in a religion where criticism and inquiry are allowed, a religion devoid of discipline, into which everybody may enter as into a mill, and believe what he pleases!"

Alphonse Daudet. The Evangelist. 1883.

"The Catholics are right, you know," Babette asserts over breakfast one Saturday morning. We're at the Eastmooreland Golf Course Bar & Grill yet again; her favorite nearby eatery. The sunlit room is dotted with small round tables and a harried waitress sets down our food before rushing off.

"Protestants always want you to read the Bible and understand things that cannot be comprehended. They expect this of people with scant historical knowledge, no basis for comprehending ancient or Roman era scrolls certainly, and think sense will result from it. Christian theologians have disagreed for centuries on what scriptures mean, that's why you need priests and a pope to interpret them and reach uniform conclusions. Look at what good Bible literacy has done for Protestants. They all believe something different! Every person looks at the old texts and takes a completely different message. Then they go out and form another sect because, of course, God has shown them the way. The way and the truth and the life? People find whatever truth suits their ways and life in that book!"

"Hmmm." I mutter. "The truth is my waffle couldn't be more delicious. How is your pancake?"

Babette grimaces with annoyance. She slams her cup down so hard the coffee sloshes over and over-easy eggs tremble. I am transfixed by her determined eyes.

"What frustrates me is that Protestant churches make the mistake of saying you may criticize, you may ask questions. One time years ago I attended Bible studies where skepticism was encouraged. I held back until one woman spoke about what a wonderful moral guide the Bible is for children. At that I couldn't be contained. 'Have you even opened this book?' I asked her. 'How can you read these horrible Old Testament stories to young people where a god showers his favor on worshippers who commit the most obscene and murderous acts?' I then quoted examples for them of rapists, drunkards, murderers– all chosen above others simply for membership among the right tribe of savages. 'And then the New Testament,' I told them, 'where a very select few are rewarded with some heaven where their greatest joy will be watching eternal torments of friends and relatives in hell?' I tried to rein myself in, Wrahs, but the damage had been done. At least Catholics are straightforward. They feel, 'We don't care what you think the Bible says, keep it to yourself,' and I much prefer that."

"Really? Sometimes it seems that drives you absolutely mad." I retort.

Babette smiles. A chunk of pancake drops unnoticed from her fork. "True. Of course even at St. Agatha's it's hard to resist being a pest. There was a time when I found myself in conversation with some nuns at a picnic. One said she thought it was such a shame so many young people these days indulge in masturbation. 'What?' I asked. She repeated herself. 'No.' I replied. 'What is this, how do you say, master-abatement?' She didn't wish to explain further, but I made a wide-eyed picture of complete incomprehension! She then spelled it out in detail, and at that I drew back horrified, saying 'I had no idea people did these things, what an absolute shock!' Oh, she felt so terrible for having tainted my innocent mind!" My professor laughs, falling back against her chair.

A well-dressed couple at the next table glance over quickly, then look away. Babette's voice carries as usual. The man draws on a napkin to distract two small blonde children. The woman sniffs and scowls.

"I still don't understand why on earth you go to these churches when you despise them so," I say. My fork handle is sticky from maple syrup.

"I think this will be difficult for you, Wrahs. First of all, your being raised by wretched Presbyterians destroyed any sense of guilt that a proper education under the Catholic system would have developed and nourished. So you can't understand the compulsion to go someplace I abhor, feign religious devotion and mumble words of prayer I don't believe in. For me, masses are pure torture. But not attending would be a thousand times worse. You know, I cannot enter a church and hear sermons without my mind in turmoil at what a fool I am. The laughter of my hero Marcus Aurelius convicts me for my weakness that even after so many years, I cannot break free.

"As a woman, it is especially insulting. I follow a religion which declares my entire sex at fault for the original sin of mankind! And furthermore, you have ancient church fathers such as St. Augustine who hated females with an absolute passion and laid the foundation for centuries of terrible abuse. Women, you see, are so wicked and ungrateful! To produce life in imitation of God, but give birth between where they piss and shit! That is what he wrote! *Inter faeces et urinam nascimur*. It sounds a little less vulgar in Latin, naturally."

Babette forks up a final bite of her limp pancake and sips at what must now be quite tepid coffee. "As much as I tease the Catholic church," she continues, "I desire its survival, and this continued ban against priests taking wives will only make that more difficult. People possess desires, and suppression often results in rather unusual expressions. For instance, many years ago there was a priest at one of my schools in France who had a taste for young children. Not the most remarkable thing sadly, but this man's great peculiarity was he could only achieve sexual arousal from scripture read out loud. So, on occasions when he took me to an out-of-the-way dark place, I would bring my little prayer book. As you can imagine, it was quite difficult reading by candlelight as this sweaty old fellow pushed and rummaged behind me. Therefore, I soon memorized long passages for recitation and by that way brought him pleasure. Really, such experiences more than anything I credit in the development of my memory."

Babette sets down her empty cup and wipes crumbs from the side of her mouth. "Are you ready? Shall we go?"

I look down at my plate. One last waffle segment languishes in a puddle of congealed syrup. Sweetness clogs my throat when I try to swallow.

The skies are a glorious blue as we drive home, and beside the road, two joggers plod along, their white shoes drumming on the sidewalk. Babette glances over at them.

"They keep running, but they'll never get away!" she chortles, her grin wide.

Chapter 9

"Her malady is fear, which is the most common illness there is …
you would not believe how many customers it sends us."

Charles Paul de Kock. Little Lise. (early 1800s).

"I sometimes ask myself, Wrahs," Babette begins one day, eyeing a jumble of pill boxes, "if I really need these. Oh, doctors always say they are so important and write out prescription after prescription, but I wonder what would happen if I decided to flush the whole damned lot down the toilet. Do you know why I take them? Because deep down I am afraid they just might be right."

With a sigh, she lifts several multicolored capsules and swallows, chasing them with a gulp of mineral water.

Besides her physical health, from the multiple freezers and refrigerators, it becomes clear my professor suffers major food scarcity issues. On shopping trips, most any dry or canned goods on sale she sweeps into her cart with frantic abandon. After one such excursion, while putting groceries away, I can no longer find space in the kitchen cupboards.

"Babette!" I exclaim, "We had no need for pasta. Look here. Ten packages still unopened and you bought eight more. There just isn't room. And twelve new bottles of mineral water? Well, at least you drink that by the gallon. But more tomato sauce! Do you realize in the pantry downstairs I'm practically buried? This is ridiculous."

Babette yawns. "You must understand, Wrahs. Once people experiences true hunger, they will never trust a full larder again. I know it is difficult to imagine, but wartime deprivation stays with me as if 1944 were yesterday. Whenever I see a store shelf brimming with food, I am filled with terror that perhaps if we return tomorrow, it may all be gone."

"Makes sense," I agree, "there's nothing wrong with

reasonable supplies on hand, but we could do a much more efficient job. Here, let me take inventory for a start."

In my room I count the stacked bottles, jars, cans and boxes, writing quantities on a pad of paper. Just when I think an end of the tomato sauce has arrived, more surface. Reaching to the back of shelving units more than two feet deep I discover some cans have completely rusted out, their contents now fine odorless dust. I tie a bandana around my face and inhale through clouds of ancient particulate. There are curious old-fashioned soup labels, strange preserves from Spain and Hungary plus a multitude of unlabeled glass jars. Their contents swirl ominously when moved.

Once this project is completed, I find Babette upstairs in her study watching French-Canadian news. She lowers the volume as I enter.

"So, here is my report," I begin, "six jars of pickles, seven cans of sardines, sixteen cans of consommé beef, ten bottles of ketchup, sixteen bottles of barbecue sauce, thirteen bottles and one gallon jug of vinegar, twelve bottles of chutney, do you even like chutney? Four jars of wild thyme, two crates of Samos Greek dessert wine, which looks pretty delicious I have to say."

Babette's fingernails tap on her chair's wooden armrests. She frowns uncomfortably. I continue.

"Ten bottles of salad dressing, forty-eight, let me repeat that, forty-eight cans of tomato sauce. Do you realize I'm only counting ones that didn't have to be thrown out? Wait, there's more."

"Stop!" Babette sputters, "I don't want to know. You have made your point."

"And we can't forget," I add, "forty-four unlabeled canning jars with questionable contents. Do you have any idea what's in those? I would actually be afraid to open them."

My professor rolls her eyes. "Oh, yes. We used to can many things. I suppose it's all gone bad long ago. Perhaps you might dig a hole in the backyard and dispose of them that way. But please, be off. Such talk makes me feel quite unwell."

She turns the audio back up. I am dismissed.

From the garage I find a long-handled spade, then select a spot between the pansy patch and wine grape ladder. I start digging. The soil is soft and turns over easily. When my hole reaches more than two feet deep, I bring out the jars. Direct sunlight reveals their iridescence, with varied hues from brown to yellow and purple arrayed against freshly mown grass. With trepidation I select one and slowly unscrew the lid. It breaks free with only a soft pop. Apple! The odor comes thick and powerful, as if primeval winds disturb a thousand dead orchards. Shuddering, I pour this mixture into the pit.

Other jars contain bulbous objects floating in murky fluid; they could be scatological specimens from deep sea diving expeditions. Some release clouds of fruit vapor I can identify as pear, peach or cherry– but others are too decayed for classification. A foamy ichor fills my trench nearly halfway before I shovel earth back in. I imagine this backyard, years hence, ripening into a sinister bog where bubbles of fetid brew rise occasionally to the surface. Strange lights may flicker on warm summer nights from seeping gas and neighborhood children will shudder at the smell.

Chapter 10

"When we see the deadly and increasing repugnance excited in their posterity by these men of gigantic stature whom the glare of the thunderbolts too often shows besmeared with mud and livid with gore, – when we consider the bold logic of their characteristic doctrines, and how soon these were made the occasion or pretext for terror and counter-oppressions, – we cannot wonder that their crimes, their violent, iniquitous, inhuman measures should have left, if only upon the imagination of descendants, permanent, fatal, contagious marks, which reveal themselves now in exaggerated imitations of their theory, now in narrow and pusillanimous fears."

C.A. Sainte-Beuve. Portraits of Celebrated Women. 1868.

One summer evening, my professor and I sit together at the kitchen table, windows raised to invite a warm breeze. Another decisive Scrabble victory for Babette spreads across the board in front of us. She smiles and stretches.

"You are a little bit curious to learn more of my history, are you not, Wrahs?" Her eyes blink at me.

I nod and begin clearing letter tiles. "A little, yeah."

She leans back in her chair. "Be kind and fetch me some bubble water then. I will tell you a story."

I rise and crack open a fresh bottle of mineral water. It fizzes into a glass, which I place before her. She drinks and sets the vessel down carefully, as if it might shatter.

"I will never understand this American obsession with making every liquid they ingest as cold as the arctic. It can't be healthy. You have perhaps noticed the upstairs freezer does not contain a single ice tray? I threw them away long ago."

She shudders as though this memory pains her. "But enough of foolish American habits. You have lived with me long enough I feel comfortable sharing personal details with you. My story begins in 1928, when a teenage girl wandered into a hospital in Yakima, Washington. She gave birth to a child, quite prematurely you understand. The father's identity she didn't know or wouldn't say. Afterward, she showed almost no interest in the infant. And of course, this adorable child was me." Babette beams.

"Well, it happened a woman named Germaine worked at this hospital as a nurse. She came from a wealthy family called the Bonnefonts in southern France and had several years previously married an American man named Robert Brown. She fell in love with this tiny baby who nobody cared about. Once I grew healthy enough, Germaine snatched me from the bassinet, and they caught the first train out of town. We traveled by ship back to France, but there must have been some disagreement as Robert Brown disappeared from the picture soon afterward. Germaine raised me as her own, but of course, the police knew who to look for and there was an international warrant for her arrest.

"So, as a child, I remember many unexpected moves. We traveled most often by train at night and the clatter of rails always put me to sleep. Such a reassuring sound. My mother would be quite high-strung and nervous, but as soon as we left the station I could feel her relax. I have loved trains ever since. While young, I discovered model railroads and kept a collection until recently, but now my hands are too shaky for things with small parts."

Babette rises. "Come to the study, I have some photographs from those times."

I follow her and my professor rummages around the bottom drawer of her small writing desk. She removes a battered file folder and tips out several black and white photographs.

"Here is Germaine in 1920."

I take this brown-edged photo, holding it carefully, and fixate on the image. An oval-faced woman with dark hair tied back and elegantly arched eyebrows faces the camera, her expression pleasant, yet somehow calculating.

"She was beautiful."

My professor chuckles. "Even yet her charms can affect one. Now there was someone who knew methods of getting what she wanted from the world. Not one to cross, that is for sure. A woman who lived quite a mysterious life. My adopted mother grew up amidst complete luxury in southern France but somehow ended up with the British Army in 1919 as they crushed an Irish uprising. Here, this picture is from Mullingar, Ireland, which was a flashpoint of the rebellion."

The sepia print shows Germaine in military uniform, her bobbed hair peeking out from under a cap. She regards the camera seriously, a long cigarette holder cocked in one hand. Cursive script along the bottom reads: "In His Majesty's Service."

"How on earth?" I ask, incredulous.

Babette shakes her head. "My mother would never speak of such things. She treated her past as a locked chest. I was truly amazed to find any photographs among her possessions after she died in 1983. If these were preserved as clues or mere nostalgia, I will never know. At any rate, here is one of her several years later in America with Robert Brown and me."

In this picture Germaine smiles with unguarded joy. She stands beside a careworn man in a dark suit. He towers over her, at least two heads taller. Germaine holds a tiny baby wrapped in white, its face barely visible.

"Brown looks gigantic," I observe.

Babette nods. "I never knew the man but he was said to be well over six feet tall. My adopted mother clearly loved him but never spoke of what happened between them. Ah, here is the last one I will show you for now."

She passes me a photo of her mother with child clutched close. I blink in amazement. Though still an infant, this is clearly my professor. The round head and facial features are unmistakable, even seven decades later. Germaine gazes into this baby's face with pure joy. No picture of Madonna and Jesus could convey more adoration. I hand the picture back to Babette.

"The Bonnefonts, my adopted family, owned property all over, in Spain as well as France, so I soon spoke Spanish quite naturally. And they had political connections there, you know, of the very best sort, with General Franco."

Babette pauses. "Now there was a talented leader. He kept Spain out of the Second World War, played each side for every advantage and then remained in power for another thirty years!

Who would deny the greatness of such a man?" She waits, daring me to disagree.

"But George Orwell is your hero also!" I interject. In my professor's library, Orwell's books occupy a section of honor. "And he fought against Franco in the Spanish Civil War."

"This is true," Babette agrees, "yet even Orwell found qualities he could appreciate in the Nationalists. You may read about Catalonian anarchists and they seems quite admirable, but could they have defeated Franco on their own? Stalin's communists were the only force organized enough to do so and had they succeeded, I wonder what state we would find Spain in today."

I bite my lip silently.

"You see, my family understood how to recognize authority and stay on its good side. That is a lesson some of us haven't learned yet. Why, only a few weeks ago, you and some others were thrown out of the *Oregonian's* office downtown while distributing some of your anti-capitalist leaflets, correct?"

At this I grin and nod.

"Of course, you are absolutely correct to be angry!" she continues, "but being right is no guarantee of survival, and that is what counts. Do you know who my true hero is? It is Joseph Fouché of the French secret police. He served under Jacobin, Napoleonic and Bourbon regimes in the late eighteenth century. One might say, 'Arrest Catholic authorities' or next 'Defend the monarchy' but he did his duty, made sure not to become too compromised by any one side and do you know what, he survived them all and lived out his days in great comfort!" Babette's eyes flash.

"So, my mother did all she could to prevent discovery. Of course, the authorities expected a kidnapped girl. Well, clever woman she was, it made sense raising me so I might pass as either gender. She discovered that for a little extra money I could be enrolled in Catholic school as a male."

Babette leads me to the living room and gestures at a large oil canvas on the mantelpiece. It stretches four feet across. In the center stands a grandiose white stone mansion with an extravagant circular drive. The crescent staircase leads to its main entrance behind a large fountain surrounded by flowers. Seagulls circle above double chimneys. Toward the foreground, a round-faced child in an altar boy's gown peers through large spectacles. Further back, three adults cluster underneath a tall gas lamp post. One man in a white shirt stands next to a brunette woman and on her other side, an elderly gentleman wearing some kind of blue uniform strikes a dignified pose.

"Here is the Château du Lac, where we often lived. A beautiful old house, build around 1760, I believe. This is the Sigean region, quite close to the Mediterranean coast near Narbonne. As you can see, I enjoyed an entirely high class upbringing. But, even for a member of the bourgeoisie, I experienced quite an extraordinary childhood. As I said, we kept close to some of the best families in Spain and traveled there often, but later developed connections with many wealthy Russians exiles as well."

She sits on the couch but I can't take my eyes off the picture.

"This is you then?" I ask, pointing to the youth.

Babette nods. "I always participated so enthusiastically in the religious rituals. It's complete rubbish, of course, but the genius of a Catholic education is that it never goes away. I would sooner chop off my right hand than abandon mass. Protestants foolishly never mastered guilt, though it's such a powerful tool. You, with your deplorable Presbyterian upbringing couldn't possibly understand."

I shrug. "What about the Russians?"

"Yes, them," she continues. "Probably the most well-known was Prince Felix Yusupov. You know of him, who assassinated the monk Rasputin in 1916? He poisoned, shot and finally drowned the man. I remember sitting on Yusupov's lap, oh, he had terrible breath and smelled so strongly of cigars."

She gestures at the painting again. "He is there, in a white shirt near the bottom of the stairs. Now talk about someone who led an interesting life! As a young man Yusupov possessed incredible beauty and would dress in women's attire to attend elegant balls and parties. This was just great fun even back then, of course. You must understand, among the upper classes, a great deal of personal eccentricity is tolerated. Yusupov fled Russia after murdering Rasputin, but numerous powerful people supported this act and he brought along his family, plus much personal fortune.

Soon afterward came the Russian Revolution and many nobles who weren't executed managed to escape, a good number of whom settled in Southern France. Of these, beside Yusupov, you can see Prince Kochubey, a Ukrainian, and Countess de Lareinti-Tolosan.

"During this time I learned many lessons that stayed with me. You know, perhaps, how skeptical I can be? Well, my grandfather, who I never knew, was said to have been a real hero, a general in the Franco-Prussian War. We often visited the town where my grandmother lived and in the nearby square, a statue had been built to honor him. It depicted a stoic pose, one arm held out defiantly as if he cried 'They shall not pass!' Everyone in society showed my grandmother great deference because of her late husband and his bravery.

"Once I grew older, I became interested in history and curious about more details. It sounded so dramatic! However, researching my grandfather, I discovered he had indeed served as a general, but only in charge of rations and clothing supplies, a sort of grandiose quartermaster. Furthermore, he never came near a battle or ventured into the least danger. Such deception filled me with complete outrage!

"Then a woman came to one my grandmother's tea parties who hadn't heard of our family's illustrious past. Everyone fell all over themselves informing her about my grandfather, who every time sounded more impressive. At last they came to the statue and how it memorialized his most famous exploit, arm held up against the savage Huns, you know. I couldn't resist and shouted out 'Yes indeed, he was measuring a soldier for a new uniform!' Oh, that made my grandmother furious!" With some effort, Babette pushes herself up from the couch and heads for the stairs. I follow close behind.

In her bedroom, below the only window, is a large wooden trunk. Ornate yellow characters spell *M. BONNEFONT - OFFICIER*.

"My grandfather's military kit," she says. Her wrinkled hand trails across the faded letters. "Of course, few soldiers traveled in such style. Oh, but you may find these of interest."

From the middle drawer of her dresser, she pulls out a cloth bundle. My professor unwinds the fabric and removes dull brass binoculars. I examine them, then raise her venetian blind. The magnification is low, but even under dim evening light, our neighbors' flower beds focus into clear resolution. I give them back.

"What a treasure!"

"Besides his field glasses, there are two other relics."

I follow her into the hall and toward the guest room. This chamber is impossibly ornate and grand, with a large brass bed, gas chandelier converted to electricity and several beautifully upholstered low chairs. On one wall hangs a large Rubenesque nude and beside that, the portrait of a priest who grimaces as if dismayed by such fleshly display. An ornate full-length mirror on a stand reflects us from the opposite corner. My fingers brush against the wallpaper's narrow stripes of blue and green velvet.

"All furniture here is French Second Empire, from the time of Napoleon III. These chairs close to the floor make it easier for a woman bound up in her corset to breathe. This is a boudoir, it means a pouting room. Don't you wish you spoke French, the language of God?" She leans close and adopts a clandestine tone.

"Actually, Wrahs, were I dictator of the world, I would declare English abolished and sentence those who insisted on speaking it be shot. Do you know why? Because it makes French look bad. Truly! The uncomplicated grammar, the absence of gender and class distinctions. Your language is structured with a simplicity I reluctantly admire. Proper French isn't spoken anywhere now, even in France. It's too difficult, all the complicated forms and tenses." She raises her voice again. "So you see, that is why English must be destroyed!"

Babette turns and motions at a small octagonal frame on the wall. Inside, behind glass, hang three military medals against blue fabric. She points to the largest in the middle. I squint and read *Republique Francaise 1870* within a wreath of green oak leaves.

"That is my grandfather's Legion of Honor medal," she informs me, "and on the right is his *médaille militaire,* I suppose something like a good conduct badge. Now, to the left is my uncle's *croix de guerre*, from the First World War. He was captured within the first weeks and spent four years in Ingolstadt Fortress, a punishment camp for troublesome officers. But there's more. Come downstairs."

We descend and Babette points out the corroded rifle over her front door.

"This is a Model 98 Mauser rifle. The main infantry weapon of German soldiers in the First World War. Look at that bayonet! What a fearsome sight! See how the breech is shut? That small lever pushed far left means it is ready to fire. But it never will again. The barrel is completely choked with rust.

"As a young girl I once explored with my cousin in some forested part of France and we came upon this firearm in the underbrush. It must have moldered away almost twenty years by then. We dragged the rifle back with us, and it eventually ended up in some relative's basement. Ages ago they found the thing and I brought it back to America. Now, come along."

I follow her into the study, excited these household artifacts are at last making sense. She runs a finger along several oversized books on a shelf, each titled _Le Panorama de la Guerre_. I open one at random and am instantly impressed. My ignorance of French is not an issue– stark photographs, melancholy paintings and detailed engravings fill every page.

"This is a work of art!" I marvel.

"Yes," Babette replies, "and it's quite remarkable how they were put together. The publisher compiled war news and hired talented illustrators to put out monthly issues, about the size of a magazine. People would purchase them as they became available with the idea one could have it all bound up for free if you bought the whole set. Of course, no one suspected it would at last fill up seven volumes back in 1914!"

She pulls out the first book and extracts two black-and-white photos. The first is undated and shows a trim middle-aged man in military uniform, his dense mustache waxed and jaunty. By the second, marked 1916, grayed hairs escape from under his peaked cap. He now wears a thick wool greatcoat with stenciled white ID numbers. The black mustache is no longer upturned.

"This second picture my uncle sent of himself from the camp. Now, his wife, who possessed a vicious sense of humor, collected these serials avidly. After the armistice in 1918, she made them a coming home present, because didn't he want to catch up on all the war he missed while interred? She hounded him to read, so he started, but soon died from a heart attack, my aunt said, in bed with one volume open before him. She claimed to have marked the page, but I never found it."

Babette looks at a clock on the wall, mounted beside her giant topographical map of Canada.

"Of course the First World War is almost forgotten by Americans, which in many ways makes sense, as this country only entered during the final period and suffered hardly any casualties compared with other nations. But at the time it raised such public fervor! Do you realize here in Portland ordinary people found it intolerable living in neighborhoods with Germanic names? And since numerous early Oregon pioneers emigrated from German speaking parts of Europe, there were many. The old streets Bismarck, Frankfurt, Karl, even those named after famous poets like Schiller and Goethe, were all changed to more acceptable Anglophone terms.

"One exception was Liebe Street, you know, just a little north of us here. The City Council couldn't manage that, since it turned out old Mr. Liebe was still alive and a perfectly respectable member of society. The fact this word means 'love' must have made it somewhat easier for society to tolerate. I suppose I will never understand depths of human hatred, the compulsion to wipe away even place names that remind people of their enemy's culture.

"But now is it late and I must retire. If you like, I will tell you more of my days in France some other time."

Chapter 11

"... every cause that would live must accommodate itself cheerfully to the progress of its epoch and study how to serve itself by it. Every cause that is in antagonism with its age commits suicide."

Octave Feuillet. Monsieur de Camors. 1867.

My professor possesses a very fractious relationship with technology. While hardly an electronics expert, I assist with every appliance, from the satellite dish to microwave clock. Despite this, Babette remains fascinated by hi-tech devices. One day, I come home and find her in the kitchen, a wide rectangular box on the table.

"Can you imagine what this is, Wrahs?" She points, her smile wide.

I examine a label on the side. "Oh, you bought a DVD player?"

"Why yes! You know, just because I am old is no reason to ignore modern things. But you can make it work, Monsieur Wrahs, say yes please? I have waited hours, just trembling with anticipation!"

I shrug. "Sure. If you like I can do it right now."

Babette follows me upstairs. Her slippers slap against my heels. I open the box, then study her TV set.

"See here." I gesture at the device. "It's an older model so we need a different connection."

My professor moans in dismay.

I leaf through the manual. "Calm down. It says you can find an adapter at any electronic store. I'll just run down the street and pick one up."

She practically flings the car keys at me. It's a short trip to Radio Shack and soon enough I return, converter cable in hand.

Minutes later, all is properly connected and my professor purrs with delight as the red power lights blinks on.

"We must watch a truly special film now, Wrahs!" she exclaims.

"All right," I concur, "what DVDs did you buy?"

Babette stares blankly.

"You know, the discs to play in this ..."

Her lips droop, horrified. "What do you mean? No one said anything about special discs! This is terrible news!"

Babette sags morosely on the couch. My professor's enthusiasm is contagious, her dismay equally so. I frown.

"There are lots of things available on DVD now. I'm sure we could track down a film or two you'd like."

My professor sighs, then points to a yellow phonebook by her upstairs telephone.

"Could you look up Classical Millennium? I buy all my music there."

I flip through thin pages to the C section, then read her its number. She dials, fingers unsteady.

"Ah, hello, I am calling to see if you have any operas ... Of course ... But they must be on special disks, they are called dee vee dees ... Yes, you say? ... Oh, wonderful, we shall come directly over." She hangs up.

We drive north to Classical Millennium on Burnside Street, a small shop, crammed with music on every format imaginable. Against one wall is a shelf filled with operas on DVD. Babette scans along them excitedly.

"Oh, they have *Carmen,* what a delight. . . and then *Giselle,* just wonderful. . .of course *La Boheme,* I must bring that home as well and also *Adriana Lecouvreur.* That should be enough for now. I know you will love *Giselle,* a story where tortured spirits dance mortals to death, but *Carmen* is so tragic also. We must watch that first." She hands this small stack to me and I hold them by the check stand while she rummages for money in her purse. As we drive home, she gushes on and on about Carmen, the beautiful gypsy whose seductive wiles inspire heartbreak and murder.

Back upstairs I put this DVD into the player. We sit down together as it begins, but after fifteen minutes Babette rises. "I am sorry, all this excitement has completely tired me. I must lie down." She never mentions the machine again. It crouches resentfully beside the television, its unused surface gathering thicker and thicker coats of dust.

Babette's taste for new things is only blunted momentarily. One afternoon I come home after a stop by 2nd Avenue Records downtown. My professor looks up from a plate of goat cheese and blood sausage. She smiles, something dark caught in her teeth.

"Good afternoon, Wrahs. And what is that you have?"

"Oh, a few records. Some LPs and singles I just picked up."

"May I take a look?"

I shrug and slide my vinyl stack next to her lunch. She examines the first. "Cocteau Twins? Well, if that is any reference to the writer Jean Cocteau, it must be good! And this other one here, what imagery! Front Line Assembly? It looks like a man turning into an insect, how macabre! On the back is a list of songs, let me see. Oh, one is called 'Don't Trust Anyone,' well, that's good advice. Will you play this record for me?"

"Sure, but I don't think you'll like it."

Babette sniffs. "Just because you think you know what I like is no reason to withhold new experiences. Let me hear it at once!"

She abandons her food and marches upstairs. I follow, double LP in hand. Babette sits on the couch and I drop her turntable needle on track one of the first side. It begins slowly, with synthetic chatter that burbles but soon speeds up. Harsh break beats rush past us and bass vibrations shake the floor. Processed vocals growl behind barely recognizable guitar chords. My professor purses her lips together in concentration, eyes inscrutable. At last the song ends. With a curt nod, she stands up.

"Thank you, Wrahs. I must now finish my meal."

Chapter 12

"In the century in which we live there are so many modes of belief and of unbelief that future historians will have difficulty finding their way about."

Anatole France. The Revolt of the Angels. 1914.

Around late August my professor sits me down in her study.

"You see, Wrahs, I now only take students on local bus tours for the community college, none further than Seattle, as I tire easily, but years ago we would charter airplanes and visit distant · places like Beijing, Moscow and Cairo. The whole wide world! For me this was a fantastic opportunity to travel and lecture on subjects I love and be paid for doing so. But those days are long gone and I must be satisfied with the Pacific Northwest. This next school year I will continue my limited trips– the coast, Mt. St. Helens, southern Oregon and so forth. I would like you to accompany me and assist."

"Certainly," I agree.

"So," she continues, "one of my favorite tours is the central Oregon high desert. We take Highway 84 east along the Columbia River. You will see the most fantastic geology exposed by water through the gorge. We visit a delightful little town called Shaniko, which used to be a major sheep exporter, Fossil, where, as you might imagine, there have been many geological finds, and also Antelope. Do you know the significance of that place?"

I shake my head. "Not that I can think of."

Babette rolls her eyes. "Well, since you can't be bothered with your own regional history, I will tell you. During the early 1980s, an Eastern spiritual leader called Bhagwan Shree Rajneesh relocated his commune from India to a large ranch near that town." She pronounces Rajneesh thickly as Reich-Nicht.

"The Reich-Nicht Puram, as they called it, consisted of several thousand people. They worked the land, dammed a creek for irrigation and lived in small huts. It seemed a meager existence, but they emphasized spiritual affairs. The Reich-Nicht Puram attracted numerous Western converts, who in many cases came from affluent backgrounds and contributed their wealth communally.

"This appeared strange because the Bhagwan afforded himself great style with a fleet of Rolls-Royce automobiles. It sounds vile, but is this any different than the Christian tradition, where congregations may live amidst absolute poverty but worship in a beautiful church while tithing so grand cathedrals can be built?

"At any rate, while the Reich-Nicht Puram toiled away industriously, other central Oregonians were not pleased with such an unusual group in their midst. It became popular to criticize the Bhagwan for his excess and local people found it obscene some followers might bathe in the stream naked or what-not. I don't care for this religion personally, but the people seemed happy, though of course it was supposed they must have been brainwashed.

"I observe this because I contacted a woman named Sheela, who if you ask me was the real power there, and received permission to make their commune part of my high desert tour. We would bring in a bus full of forty students, view the area and see what we wanted. Everyone was quite friendly and this went one for several years but then after some property disputes, a commune building burned down mysteriously, as well as other incidents changed things. Well, the Reich-Nicht Puram reacted as any people do when under attack. They became defensive and much more closed in. Going through their security procedures no longer made sense with time requirements for the rest of my tour and I lost contact with them.

"Then in 1986 catastrophe struck. There seemed to be an internal struggle within the group leadership. Sheela fled to Europe and a great number of people became sick in the town of Antelope after eating at a restaurant owned by the Reich-Nicht Puram. The government swept in and uncovered a conspiracy to poison regional water systems as well as massive immigration fraud. With his commune destroyed, the Bhagwan traveled back to India where he died some years ago, though this sect still exists under the name Osho. Their land went up for auction and was purchased by a wealthy rancher from Montana. Then, not too long ago, I found out he had donated the property to a Christian youth organization called Young Life."

"Oh, I know about them!" I break in, "my parents worked for that group when I was young."

Babette nods. "I possess a connection there as well. My sister, though you perhaps did not know I have an American sister, is a Young Life minister."

I shake my head.

"Well," she continues, "Young Life renamed the Reich-Nicht Puram as Wild Horse Canyon and started a summer camp program which just ended its first season. They have invited a select group to view their transformation of this center for evil paganism by their much more socially acceptable religion. My sister put us on their list for next weekend. Would you please accompany me?"

"Yes!" I exclaim.

Babette smiles. "You know what a pagan is, don't you Wrahs?"

"What, literally?"

"Literally linguistically."

I think for a moment. "No."

Babette bobs her head. "It makes so much sense. What is one of the main characteristics of Christianity? That it took root as an urban religion. City dwellers no longer found spiritual resonance among gods based on agricultural patterns or natural cycles. Where is power located in an ancient metropolis? A king, a ruler, a strong man! So they looked for something else to translate their religiosity into, often a messiah figure. But out in rural areas, what are called in Latin the *pagus*, old beliefs tended to remain. Therefore, a pagan is someone from the boondocks! Very similar to the term heathen, which of course means people who live out on the barren heath. Look at all this knowledge I pass on for no extra charge!"

I offer a half-smile. "That does stand to reason."

Babette looks at me seriously.

"Reason. Such a new concept. Wrahs, when was the last time you read the Bible? Have you ever studied it?"

I reflect on this. "Not since childhood. Once I tried reading the whole thing straight through but paused to highlight sections that didn't make sense or conflicted with other parts. Soon half the book was marked up and though my parents helped explain, it just became harder to take the thing seriously. The further I progressed the more it fell apart. Sunday school just seemed so false, the way passages would be picked from one chapter or another to manufacture messages that meant something. Really, it often just made me feel ill."

Babette nods, her lips pursed. "That is not an untypical reaction. You had no intellectual background to understand the old texts and for elucidation, only people who accepted them as inspired supernaturally. I quite think you would benefit from a good academic look at the scriptures. Come along!"

She leads me downstairs to the library and scans along her ancient history shelf. "Now, one of the earliest modern biblical criticisms was by a man named Ernest Renan during the nineteenth-century. Ah, here we are! *Vie de Jesus*. But it is in French which might as well be Swahili for all the good it will do you. Albert Schweitzer also wrote some good texts on the subject, but who you will find most valuable is S.G.F. Brandon."

Babette pulls a volume down. "Brandon was an Anglican minister of the early twentieth century but as you will discover, quite an independent mind. You may find this a surprise, but in Europe where there is state-financed religion, church authorities are much freer to examine their faith. His books are a true joy. I recommend Jesus and the Zealots to start with." She holds it out to me.

I accept the book, flip through a few pages, then turn it over. The back carries a brief author's biography and I stare at Brandon's picture. He is a sober man with grey hair, dark bushy eyebrows, and wire-rimmed spectacles.

My professor squints and removes a couple more titles in the ancient history section. These she lays down on the floor. From behind, her shaking fingers remove two dark brown bottles without labels. A small number of pills rattle at the bottom.

"For many, religion provides succor in their final years. I carry no such illusions. These are my suicide drugs. I have seen enough old people languish away painfully to know it is not a fate for me. There is nothing I value more than independence. As soon as that vanishes, this is my escape."

I catch her eye. "That's a funny way for a junior Benedictine nun to talk. Does the Pope know about your stand on euthanasia?"

Babette waves a dismissive arm. "Hush Wrahs, really, you ask too many questions sometimes."

Chapter 13

"Mark my words, we're in for bad times if some man or god
doesn't have a heart and take pity on this place. I'll stake my luck
on it, the gods have got a finger in what's been happening here.
And do you know why? Because no one believes in the gods,
that's why."

Petronius Arbiter. The Satyricon. circa 100 CE.

The next Thursday we wake early and head east. Along the
Columbia gorge I crack a window as solar rays warm us. Trees and
boulders rush past outside our windows. I reach for my sunglasses
on the dashboard.

"What I hate is that we sanitize history so much," my
professor declares. "Look at Dr. John McLaughlin. We call him the
'Father of Oregon' and speak about his greatness, but here he was,
chief factor of the Hudson Bay Company in the Northwest and a
complete traitor not only to England but his employers. During
early parts of the nineteenth-century, American pioneers sought
Oregon farmland and the company forbade McLaughlin to help or
encourage them. However, he sensed a regional power shift and
assisted the settlers anyway, so as to bake his cake and eat it too.
This idiom is English, *oui*? Then, as soon as Great Britain
abandoned the area, he contacted American leaders and said 'Look
at me, I am such a Yanqi-Doodle-Dandi who always helped you.'
But you know, he got what he deserved because once Americans
controlled the region, they betrayed him in turn, confiscated almost
all his land and he died in absolute misery." She concludes with a
satisfied sniff.

We track the Columbia for almost two hours before turning
south. Soon the high desert stretches all around us and Babette
almost explodes with joy. She waves out the window at alluvial
deposits and explains conditions that favor sheep herds as opposed

to cattle ranches. Everything holds significance for her: the type of sand that blows across shiny blacktop, piled rocks supporting old fence posts, and hillsides desiccated by erosion

Around noon we reach our first destination, a small town called Shaniko. It consists of only a few scattered trailers around the small urban core. We park near a rather ornate two story brick building. Warm wind filters down the empty street under bright cloudless skies.

"It really is fascinating here, though almost a ghost town now. This is the Shaniko Hotel." she declares as we step inside the front door. "It still operates. We shall stay here tonight and leave for the camp tomorrow."

I gaze around a faded, but well-maintained interior. Framed black-and-white photos from Shaniko's glory days line the walls. Babette greets the sole occupant, an elderly receptionist with short gray curls.

"Dr. Ellsworth!" she cries, delighted. "This isn't your usual tour season. I'm so glad you came early! What's the occasion?"

My professor grins broadly. "Oh, you know, I love this part of Oregon, I really cannot stay away."

The woman reached out and clasps her hand. "Well, it's good you're here. I assume you and this gentleman are staying overnight. Do you have a room preference?"

"It's so hot!" Babette exclaims. "Which room has the largest tub I could fill with cool water and soak?"

The receptionist gives a small shrug. "Our bridal suite."

Babette smiles widens. "Then we will take it."

She scribbles on a registration form, then ascends the large staircase nearby while I collect our luggage.

"Oh Wrahs!" Babette calls out from the landing part way up, "I do hope you remembered to bring some condoms!" She breaks into a deep laugh. The receptionist snorts with mirth behind me.

I discover our bridal chamber is quite an elegant room, which fortunately contains an additional small cot besides the luxurious queen. I stake the former out while Babette draws water for her bath. That evening she retires early and I crack open <u>Jesus and the Zealots</u> by light of a small bedside lamp.

It captivates me at once. As I begin this serious study, the scriptures feel increasingly real. What before seemed so ethereal and vague now makes sense. S.G.F. Brandon's steely observations take me to a place of comprehension where the drama in ancient Judea can be understood just like any other historic events, with logical economic and political explanations. Every leaf I turn feels like stones lifted off my chest. Stones I hadn't even realized were there. I fall asleep at last, my face pasted across open pages as cool desert breeze wafts through open widows.

The next morning we rise early and eat breakfast in the small cafe downstairs. Babette's knife squeaks against her plate as she saws eggs and toast into bite-sized pieces. Sunlight plays along faded wallpaper.

"It may not look so impressive today, but this town used to be a great wool shipping center in the early 20th century. Eventually railroad lines changed regional trade routes enough that business dried up around 1911. Now, it was named after a German fellow named Scherneckau, one of the early pioneers. Of course people couldn't pronounce it properly so the place became called Shaniko. This man lived quite a life. He fought for the Union during the American Civil War, survived being wounded, moved west and at last settled here in Wasco County.

"Years later, as an old man, Scherneckau traveled back to Germany, but while visiting family, the First World War broke out. With a return ticket impossible, he stayed for the duration. Then in 1918, Scherneckau came home and discovered his land confiscated as a traitor! He finally managed to get his property returned, but treating an elderly person such ways for being caught on the wrong side of a war? It reminds me of the endless hunt for Nazis you read about almost every week in the paper!"

"Well," I respond, somewhat startled. "Surely there shouldn't be a statute of limitations on truly terrible acts, like war crimes."

"Of course," Babette agrees, "but what angers me is when I read about the arrest of, say, some poor old railroad worker in France who happened to sign a manifest back in 1942 for a transport of Jews who later met their death. We call it the banality of evil and condemn such a person to prison for the rest of their miserable life. But who is different? What did your grandparents' generation do when Japanese neighbors were thrown out of their houses, beaten in the streets and taken off to camps in the wilderness? Did they object? Did they visit and make sure everyone was being treated well? And are your grandparents not good and decent people?"

I nod. "They are."

Babette grits her teeth. "Precisely."

We finish our meal and walk across the street to a small second-hand store called "Jones Antiques & Things." The proprietor, a wiry old man, greets us with enthusiasm and shows off his collection of rusty farm equipment. I look over vintage sheep shearing tools while Babette skims titles on a rickety bookshelf. The man seems quite eager to talk, follows her around the store and asks questions about future tours. Babette frowns and then makes as if to leave.

"Hold on!" he cries out, "do you like blackberries?"

The man rushes into his back room and returns with a glass jar. "This jam I canned myself last season," he proclaims, all smiles.

Babette accepts the gift and slips it into her large handbag. She thanks him and turns away.

"What about zucchini?" the man presses. "Wait! Wait!" He scampers off again and comes back. His gnarled fingers clutch a paper bag full of green vegetables. "They're from my own garden!"

Babette takes them, thanks him again and we leave. It doesn't take very long to reach Antelope, a settlement only somewhat larger than Shaniko. We pass through and after a while spy posted markers for Wild Horse Canyon. We turn off the paved road and drive about eight miles along a bumpy dirt track with cheerful signs intermittently mounted along the way:

JUST ANOTHER MILE! . . . ALMOST THERE! . . . AROUND THE NEXT CORNER! . . . ONLY KIDDING!

Babette shakes her head. "I forgot how exuberant these Protestants can sometimes be."

"Will your sister be here as well?" I ask.

"Hrumph! No! I hope you will be locked in a closet any time

my relatives are nearby, French or American."

At last we reach the compound, several clustered buildings near the floor of a wide canyon that stretches between rocky hills. A sluggish stream trickles into the reservoir created by a dam which lingers in great disrepair. Thick green scum covers the stagnant water. On a hillside, numerous small wooden huts sag, some completely fallen over.

Babette points towards these shacks. "That is where the workers lived, they called themselves *sannyasins*, which means a wanderer who seeks the truth. I was curious to know what transpired since I last visited but it saddens me to see all neglected so. Still, *c'est la vie*, enough nostalgia. Let us discover who is in charge here."

Cars pull into the lot behind us. People exit and greet one another as they mill about. We enter the main structure and Babette questions an official-looking woman with the name "Margaret" pinned to her blouse. She directs us towards a man who smiles and gestures with a small group of others. I follow, luggage in tow.

"Excuse me!" Babette exclaims. She touches the man's elbow, then heartily shakes his hand. "I just wanted to offer my congratulations on everything you have accomplished here. It's so wonderful seeing Christians at work together creating new ministries from an absolute den of paganism!" Teeth flash as she turns to smile and wink at me.

"Also," she continues, and with a flourish pulls the blackberry jam from her purse, "I brought some preserves I canned last season to thank you personally. Do you like zucchini? I have some as well– grown in my own garden!"

I shake my head at her.

We leave the grateful man and are directed to our quarters. I find myself in a dormitory room with ten beds but only three other residents, all older fellows in their late forties or fifties. They studiously ignore me. Around lunchtime we meet up in the meal hall, a large room that easily handles the crowd of a couple hundred adults. While we eat, Young Life youth pastors discuss their first summer program in retrospect and explain our group will undergo a condensed version.

This means almost every minute fits into a regimented

itinerary of group song, Bible studies and other related activities they call clubs. Babette and I soon weary of this. The landscape around us is so beautiful it seems a sin to spend any more time indoors than necessary. We explore the nearby canyon and afterward soak in a large pool sunk into the valley floor that spreads out for miles along a desiccated topography of dried mud.

Early on our second afternoon, we sit beside the dam. This area is vacant, but muffled praise songs emanate from a nearby building. I rub sunscreen on my face and forearms. Babette yawns, her round face dappled in light beneath a wide-brimmed straw hat. She waves her hand toward the jubilant sound.

"People are so desperate for meaning in their lives. The Reich-Nicht Puram came here searching of it and now these poor souls do as well. Some people remain within the bounds of one particular religion and others ... the journey leads from faith to faith their whole lives. *Sannyasins* all, though by different names."

"I've certainly known people like that." I reply.

Babette nods. "It is sadly common. For me, the seeds of doubt were sown at an early age. Religious rituals felt so empty yet I flung myself into them regardless. When I grew older everything fell into place. There really is no escape. The ways out are all cruel mirages on the walls of a room without doors or windows."

"Sounds a little bleak to put things that way."

"If I could recommend one book, it would be Nausea by Jean-Paul Sartre. That will make you redefine bleak. But it is wonderful! Sartre explains perfectly what happens when we seek ultimate truths. His protagonist is a historical researcher who seeks to understand the past and write a biography. Of course it is futile! He fixates on the hopelessness of this task which soon drives him mad. It becomes clear reality is just a word we use to ignore the void that stretches beneath our feet. Oh, not a book for the weak-willed, but it might help you understand this tragic farce we call existence."

At this I smirk. "If it's all just a farce, I don't know why I should bother reading S.G.F. Brandon. It may be useless to seek truth, but we still search for something in the study of history. Imagine you were in the Garden of Eden and God forbade you to eat from the Tree of Knowledge. What would you do?"

Babette laughs. "I would consume the whole orchard's worth! Just because life is an absurd game doesn't mean you should refuse to play. But consciousness of this, for me at least, has served as a balm. You must draw your own conclusions."

Later in the day, my professor and I walk down to the pool and cool off under blue cloudless heavens. Its concrete edge extends only a couple of inches above the canyon floor. Floating on my back, I grip the side and look across this vast expanse from the perspective of an insect. Blue skies stretch forever overhead and the pool caresses me with its warm fluid embrace. I let go, spiraling in this azure-tinted womb until a cheery voice breaks my trance.

"Excuse me! There's a praise club in ten minutes."

I raise my head and see a pair of legs. They are hairy, belonging to a red-headed young man in sandals and khaki shorts. He grins down at me.

"Thank you." I return his smile.

"Club is like a puzzle, you see," the fellow continues, "you have to get all the pieces together before it makes sense."

Babette clears her throat. "Is this...khlub mandatory?"

The man frowns. "No. Look, I'm sorry, but if you won't attend, I don't think you should be allowed to stay in the pool."

I glance over at Babette. She stands at waist depth, wig slightly askew and floral print swimsuit glistening. With no more debate we climb out. Under desert heat, I forgo drying off and simply pull on a t-shirt while Babette wraps a towel around her stout middle and walks towards the compound. As I lace up my boots, the man sighs.

"Look, I guess if you're really not going to club, you can get back in the water."

I pick up my books. "No, that's all right. I have my own Bible study."

Not far away, I find a picnic bench under some shade and resume work. This research doesn't go quickly. S.G.F. Brandon intended his book for a highly academic audience and at several points breaks into French, German, Latin or Greek with little provided by way of translation. I take studious notes, frequently looking up references in my Bible. Time passes and before long people amble past as club lets out.

I look up, rub my stiff neck, then notice two girls strolling nearby. Distracted, I stretch and pretend to read again. They enter my peripheral vision and stop, whispering to each other. One gestures in my direction. Both wear bright sundresses and are perhaps in their early twenties. Pale hands cover strawberry lips as they speak with low tones. After a momentary discussion, both approach me.

"Excuse me," one begins. She is taller and more tan. The other giggles. I close S.G.F. Brandon and give them my full attention.

"We just want you to know," the second picks up, "that we really appreciate what you're doing."

"We're so impressed, and moved honestly, by the great things you're trying to accomplish," the first chimes in, fingers clasped together. A tiny crucifix dangles around her slender golden neck.

My forehead furrows. "Great things?"

"Oh!" comes the second, "we mean your work converting the heathens in Africa! It sounds so wonderful, but must be dangerous too!" She twists her flip-flops in loose sand.

"And then coming back here to continue your studies in seminary school," the first continues, "but is your mission work finished or will you return overseas after graduation?" Smiles run wide across both freckled cheeks.

I frown again. "Wait … tell me, where did you hear this?"

"From your grandmother, of course!" the first proclaims, "she told us all about you. She's so proud of what you've done and we just wanted to congratulate you as well."

"No!" I break in, "that's not true at all! I'm not a missionary and I'm not in seminary ... in fact she's not my grandmother either!" The girls stare back and forth, at each other, then me, eyes wide. "She's my history professor." I continue. "We're just good friends ... It's a long story."

"Oh," says the shorter one, her cheeks now rosy, "I'm sorry, we made a mistake."

"Quite," observes her lovely companion slowly. She eyes my religious books and notes strewn across the picnic table. "We must have the wrong person."

They retreat and I continue reading, my own face now flushed. Twenty minutes later, Babette approaches, a leer from ear to ear. She sits across from me but I refuse eye contact. At this a low chuckle builds up in her throat.

"You know, Wrahs," she begins, as laughter now fully erupts, "after what you told those two young girls, they became so confused! They didn't know what to make of you. But I cleared everything up. All that time away from civilization in dark African jungles turned your head a little. You simply need more time to acclimate and regain your social graces. And of course I explained you were embarrassed for people to know you came here on vacation with a close relative. You realize how young men can be, I told them. Oh, they were quite sympathetic." She cackles with mirth.

"Babette," I cut in, "you've already gotten a bad name for yourself with club attendance. There's plenty of information I'm pretty sure you'd like kept private around here. You're quite a heretical wolf among sheep in this fold."

"Aha!" she cries with delight, "now you are threatening me! That is no way for a grandson to behave!"

The rest of our trip passes with no more rumors spread about my alleged theological career and we drive home Sunday afternoon. En route, Babette directs me to pull over for lunch in Fossil. We find a small cafe with outside seating and order food off greasy laminated menus. I shade my eyes and squint down the tidy main street.

"This is such a charming town," my professor declares. "It was named because of rich fossil beds nearby. The John Day formation is splendid. It dates from the late Oligocene and early Miocene epochs, that is to say ..." She looks uncomfortable and scratches her neck. "... over thirty million years ago."

"Are you all right?" I ask.

"I'm fine," she replies, "but a bee stung me yesterday, there, below my ear."

I look and see two tiny pinpricks, spaced about an inch apart, surrounded by slight swelling. "Looks like it got you twice. Must have been a wasp."

After eating hot sandwiches, we get back into the car and continue toward home. The yellow hills and dusty expanses of central Oregon pass outside the windows. Babette stares ahead, her expression pensive.

"So much time," she says at last, "so much time for every little piece of sediment. Each solitary fragment finds its own place, then waits and builds upon others. All the centuries and pressure required to create it all. And then you think, these formations have lasted thousands of years. I know I feel as though 1942 passed by just yesterday, but for them, it was yesterday. It happened not even a minute ago." She sighs.

"If you desire happiness, Wrahs, study geology. History, which you foolishly pursue, will only lead to trouble. Astronomy is good too, but my advice is, stick with sediment. It is non-political and an absolute joy. With my own views, I never teach a history class beyond 1939. I refuse, and declare anything more recent is not history, but current events. Of course, that is not true. The times of Catherine de' Medici and Napoleon are also current events. The Crusades and Protestant Reformation are current events. It is all turbulent and controversial even if few recognize it now. Look at S.G.F. Brandon, who you now read. The world he analyzed so brilliantly is gone two thousand years, but still people argue."

I nod. Sweat trickles down my collar. Babette flings up her hand.

"I wonder truly how much you understand. But now I am tired. I must rest for a while." She closes her eyes. Soon light snores whisper through parted lips. The road straightens and we pass across a wide, flat expanse covered with brown sagebrush under brilliant blue skies. In my rearview mirror, the hills fade smaller and smaller.

Chapter 14

"I asked him whether he had been a member of the arrow-cross
[Hungarian Fascist] party.
'Of course I was,' He replied
'And what makes you a social democrat today?'
'The same thing. One must make a living.'
'And did you believe the Nazis?'
Exactly as I believe the social democrats today and the
Bolsheviks tomorrow!' He replied, smiling at me."

George Faludy. My Happy Days in Hell. 1962.

"I really possess no appetite this evening," my professor
admits, "but please fry up a pork chop from the refrigerator. There
is pasta also, which you could boil as if it were a Protestant."

I laugh. "Thank you, how vivid."

We returned from our trip to eastern Oregon several hours
before and my hunger is now quite sharp. I cook the meat in a cast
iron pan with slices of onion, heating a pot of noodles on the next
burner. Once everything is ready, I sit down at the kitchen table
and begin to eat. Babette watches from across the red Formica.

"If you wish, I will continue my story for you," she offers.

I bob my head. "Please do."

She clears her throat. "You see, all of this turmoil in my
childhood ended around 1939 as World War II began. Everyone's
last concern was a kidnapped American from over a decade before.
The next few years, Wrahs, were truly the best times of my life.
And in many ways, you know, I haven't stopped living in them."

She sips at her usual tepid mineral water from a tall glass.

"It seems whenever people speak of a rival to France in
history, it must be Germany. But of course Germany is a very
modern creation which did not even exist long before the 20th
Century. France's enemy has always been England. I remember

patriotic radio broadcasts I tuned into as a child; they signed off the air every night with the words: 'England, like Carthage, must perish!'

"So when British forces retreated from continental Europe, we saw how they abandoned France before fighting even ended. It seemed a complete betrayal! And then Marshal Pétain, the old hero of World War I became president and worked out such a generous peace with the Germans. Do you realize his negotiations left most of the country unoccupied including the strategic southern coast? Well, for a defeated nation, it was better than anyone could have expected! He declared us neutral, but what happened next? In 1940 English forces attacked and sank the French navy in their North African port of Oran! An absolute slaughter!"

Babette's eyes shine with anger. I remain silent.

"So, as a prominent patriotic family, we naturally developed close connections with Pétain's government in Vichy. Like thousands of other Frenchmen, several relatives of mine enlisted in the *Waffen SS* which was the German foreign legion. One uncle and two cousins. They wanted to fight for France and for Europe! We never even saw our first foreign soldiers until years later, and they weren't even German. They were East Indians, either recruited from troops abandoned by the English early in the war or volunteers who traveled from there directly to fight Britain under a brave leader named Subhas Chandra Bose. To free their own country! Well, nobody held a grudge against them. They seemed quite nice, except for not speaking a word of French."

I shake my head. "Really? Indians fought alongside Germany in Europe during the war? I never heard of such a thing!"

"Oh, Wrahs," my professor smiles, "there is so much you don't know. But there is also much I don't know! The more I learn the more ignorant I feel. But simply look at our perspectives. Great Britain rules South Asia, an entire sub-continent for nearly two hundred years with a complete iron fist and absolute cruelty. We shall probably never know how many millions of deaths resulted from their policies and no one cares! Those who suffered were only brown-skinned people in a distant land. Is Queen Victoria's name forever tainted? Are people who hang her picture on their wall regarded with suspicion? Of course not. We draw distinctions. An

Anglophile may easily say they appreciate English culture and not immediately expect to defend, say, the Amritsar Massacre or Indian genocidal famines. But Germany invades some nearby countries, harshly persecutes other Europeans and we see them as evil incarnate. Imagine what happens when people display Hitler's picture!"

Babette pauses and smirks.

"Of course, years ago I did keep an old portrait of Hitler on the mantelpiece, so my example is not entirely academic."

I choke. "How did that go over with dinner guests?"

"Not so well I admit. You may notice it is gone. I donated it to a historical society years ago. With any other personages, you can make the argument one's adoration honors their great qualities but disregards the rest. For instance, I observe you sewed a patch of Mao Zedong on one of your jackets, but do not therefore suggest you view the Cultural Revolution in a positive light."

At this my back straightens. "No, not at all. I appreciate Mao as a great liberator of Asia. His policies killed millions, I know, but it is for breaking the foreign chokehold on China that I admire him."

Babette jerks her head. "Exactly. And I have a similar view of Hitler. He will one day be recalled much as any of history's conquerors are, from Genghis Khan to Hannibal Barca. All leaders with bloody pasts but who can be recognized for their great qualities."

"I have found your thoughts on World War II quite unusual," I say, "but it does seem our perspectives are fundamentally racist. The examples of Nazi cruelty towards Jews and other Europeans become emphasized in a way that obscures what colonial powers did to subject peoples around the world."

Babette flings up her hands. "It drives me mad. Especially in academia where I have spent my life. Just look at the history department course catalogue. You can always find a class solely on the Jewish Holocaust, but try to learn about the fate of American Indians! Some professor might mention them in passing or offer an occasional cultural course. Imagine that! Instead of facing uncomfortable parts of their own history, Americans focus on misdeeds that took place half a world away."

"That's terrible!"

Babette sighs. "I have become distracted from my story. At any rate, when I met real German soldiers, they were not monsters. I would encounter them often at mass. Such polite young men! I could certainly understand why my relatives fought with them. And they also died with them. My uncle and one cousin were killed shortly after the Normandy invasion in 1944. The last cousin retreated and we later heard news of his death near Berlin."

My professor sniffs and nibbles at a Manischevitz cracker.

"So, in 1944 and '45, France descended into fierce civil war with large number of people killed. German sympathizers, as well as unpopular individuals, were murdered en masse. Our grand house from the painting? Burned to a shell. Now, anti-German fighters in France were quite small in number. But amazingly, by the end of the war it seemed everyone was a secret resistance member! For most of my relatives, it was too late to change sides. Among descendants of the survivors I represent ..." she pauses, "... an embarrassing link with the past and it is much better I remain far enough away not to cause trouble."

She takes another drink and sets the glass down hard.

"Even when I visit, social engagements can be difficult. There was one time years ago we visited a town where I sometimes stayed back in those days. My relatives knew the mayor, a local man around my age. We went sightseeing with him and a group of people that included American tourists. Now, in this place there formerly existed a small chapel from the Middle Ages. During an Allied air raid near the end of the war, some incendiary bombs fell nearby and it burned up. Compared to other tragedies at the time this seemed of little consequence, but we walked by the old site and the mayor told everyone how charming it had been. One American asked what happened and he replied 'Oh, the awful Germans burned it, you know.' The tourists all nodded sympathetically. Well, I was outraged! I said 'No they didn't! I was there! It was your own damn airplanes!' As you can imagine, they didn't like hearing that at all."

"What happened then?" I ask, "At the end of the war?"

"So," Babette continues, "with my family either murdered or scattered, I could not remain anonymous anymore. The new authorities soon discovered my identity and shipped me back to the United States. At seventeen, under the law I belonged to my birth mother who still lived in Yakima. I sailed back across the ocean with only what possessions fit in my trunk. Remember, this was a journey into the land of the enemy which of course filled me with absolute fright. Then, adding insult, when I passed through customs in New York, officials confiscated my portrait of Hitler! It made me furious, but what could I do?" She snorts sharply.

"I stepped off a train in central Washington to meet this person who people said was my real mother. For me it seemed as foreign as a trip off the planet. The woman who gave birth to me was still only in her mid-thirties. Years before, she'd married a man called Ellsworth and bore two children with him, my half-sisters. I never liked him, but from then on had to use his terrible name.

In France, my family were the Bonnefonts. A *font* is like a fountain, where fresh water springs from, and in southern France groundwater often tastes brackish and salty. *Bonne* means good of course, so my aristocratic relatives descended from people who controlled the 'Good Water.' Do you know how Ellsworth translates? It's English, purely insulting just on that note, and the ell was a medieval unit of currency. The smallest unit of currency! All of a sudden my very name declared I was worthless! And it is what I have kept until this very day." She halts, face petulant.

I think for a moment. "So, you didn't take your husband Albert's name? That must have been quite unusual for the times. When was that anyway?"

Babette shifts in her chair. The legs squeak against linoleum.

"Really, Wrahs, you ask questions in very bad taste. To continue, Yakima felt intolerable. I just wanted to escape and after several months simply bolted. The first night I spent in a field, then caught the first train out of town which carried me as far as Portland. I slept on the streets and survived through prostitution while my English improved from sheer necessity. Then I discovered a Catholic charity, it still exists, now called the Blanchet House downtown. They recognized potential in me and arranged educational scholarships. Out of gratefulness I donate them money every year. I studied very hard and graduated from Portland University in 1949.

"Before earning master's and doctorate degrees, I worked many jobs, once more or less as a spy for the Department of Interior. My ability to pass for a man or a woman allowed more than usual access and I traveled through rural towns in Idaho searching out people who cheated on farm subsidies. I would ingratiate myself with local pastors and church leaders, because who knows a community better? After gaining their confidence, I revealed the nature of my work, but then it became quite curious. They happily turned in corrupt members of their congregation, who I found were often quite stingy contributors to the collection plate. The moral is: stay on your parson's good side and tithe regularly!"

"But what about Germaine?" I ask "Did your mother survive?"

"Ah," Babette muses, "now there was a woman, my mother. To answer your question, yes, she survived, though after the war as our family disintegrated, I lost her. But what she managed still impresses me. In 1947 she portrayed herself as a veteran of the glorious French resistance and some Jewish aid agency subsidized her voyage to America. We were then reunited in Portland while I was still a student. She soon moved to Nanaimo, British Columbia and became the governess to children of a wealthy family. Years later, I remember once she actually lectured at a church, something or other about the horrors of Hitler and how she bravely fought Fascism. I sat in the back, barely able to keep a straight face. Afterward she pulled me aside and said 'If you speak a word, I'll cut your throat!' Oh, I couldn't believe her audacity!

"But this sort of thing was not so uncommon really. For instance, if you read the autobiography of our Russian friend Felix Yusupov, he is remarkably silent on activities during the war. But of course Yusupov hated the Communists who slaughtered his relatives and association with my family certainly indicated where his sympathies lay. Who can blame him, really. That's how most people survive. They support prevailing powers but realign when the status quo shifts. It is only human."

I shake my head. "That's true ... but still awful. How can you admire George Orwell and others who took stands against authority?"

My professor smiles, her lips thin. "It is true, Orwell's works are genius, though I myself am a coward. But a coward who survived! I may have unorthodox ideas or heroes who are not popular in this time and place, but I make certain these passions do not lead near danger. Some people are less cautious." She squints at me.

I shrug. "It's true, being an activist can be hazardous. I'm careful and stay safe though."

Babette rolls her eyes. "To be safe is keep your head down. It seems like a game now, but I have seen what happens when the hammer descends. Ah, I am distracted. Poor Pétain who served France his whole life was actually kidnapped by the Germans and taken away when they retreated. After the war, he made his way back through Switzerland, where he could have stayed immune from prosecution, but instead returned where duty led him. Pétain was put on trial as a Nazi puppet and thrown in prison at ninety years old, where he died soon afterward." Babette grinds her teeth together with barely contained fury.

"At any rate, my education continued, finally with a doctorate at the University of Bordeaux. A well-known French historian named Henri Guillemin took me as his lover and quite furthered my career. You know, in general, I find sexual relations with males abominable, though often useful. My advice is, if you must have sex with men, do it in the style of dogs– that way you don't have to see their ugly faces.

"So, after university I began the career I love, teaching history and French and Spanish ... later geology, astronomy and geography, first at Portland State, then for a short time at Reed, just across the street here. Eventually I was among the first group of teachers hired when Portland Community College opened in 1964. And I have stayed there ever since."

She tips her glass dry and sets it down firmly. "But, *c'est la vie*, that is enough for tonight. At least you learned something worthwhile. I will see you tomorrow."

Babette scratches absentmindedly at her neck. The two punctures have swelled somewhat. She shrugs, smiles and leaves the kitchen. I remain seated, half my plate of food cold and uneaten.

Chapter 15

"... I went to hear the Seattle Symphony … I couldn't help wondering why it was that we could all meet and be lifted up by the music while had it been a picture exhibit we'd have had no shared sympathy at all. Has music something art lacks? Is the eye more earthly than the ear?"

Emily Carr. February 4th 1930.

"Would you like me to buy you a new motorcycle?" Babette asks.

I bite my lip and glance outside through the open kitchen window. Late summer breezes waft around us, heavy with the aroma of freshly cut grass. Dark shadows cut sharply across the sundial.

"That's very generous, but the bus gets me around ok these days."

My professor blinks. "Well, please understand, it means much having live-in help."

I nod. "That's understood, but I really can't ask for more. It would be hard attending school full time and also earn rent elsewhere. Your pantry and food are enough."

Babette smiles. "Then we are useful for one another. A symbiosis. However, this coming autumn I shall require more of you. The college tours resume in September and become more difficult each year. Sadly, my health isn't what it was."

"Can't you retire? After working so long for the college they must have some kind of pension ..."

Her eyes flash fire. "No! Students are my life. Should I stay at home all day before the television like other brain-dead seniors my age? Never! While blood still flows through my veins, I shall play the game. Existence as a spectator is unacceptable!"

In September, when neighborhood leaves turn orange and carpet Eastmooreland yards, I sign up for a full load of classes that include my professor's next-level history course. Nearly every Saturday morning, one of her tours leaves from the great sloped parking lot at Portland Community College's Sylvania campus in a forty-seat bus. The students hand cash to me as they board, and Babette sits behind the stairwell, marking each one off her master list. She lectures through an intercom and occasionally passes it off to informed drivers or sometimes me if I know any history around certain areas.

"Tours completely exhaust me," she comments after the first several, "but you see, they are the only way I keep working. The college would love to cancel all my classes and hire some young teacher at a third the salary but they make great profit from these weekend trips. I arrange the bus, make all other accommodations, collect rental fees and so forth. Students must write a brief paper afterward for which they receive one credit. The school's only cost is my few hours' wages but they make back whatever college credit is now times forty. Once my supervisor suggested I make a tape recording of these lectures! Can you imagine that? And make it easier for them to replace me! Of course I said absolutely not!"

On a Sunday evening in early October, my professor winds the clocks before bed. I watch her pull the chains, then push each pendulum until it ticks away again. She smiles with satisfaction, then turns.

"So, Wrahs, next weekend I would appreciate if you accompanied me on an overnight trip to Yakima. I always buy season tickets for the symphony."

"There's a symphony in Yakima?" I ask. "Will we have to sit on bales of hay?" The central Washington city brings to mind apple orchards, but not black tie events.

"No!" Babette sniffs, indignant. "They have one of the best orchestras in the country and their symphony hall is world class. My French cousins scoffed as well before I took them years ago, but you will see."

She rubs her neck with agitation. The twin punctures now erupt from her skin like angry volcanos.

"Are you ok?" I ask. "Those don't look good."

Babette sighs. "My doctor says these lesions have become cancerous. I made an appointment for them to be removed soon."

"Wasp stings turning into tumors? How odd. Your doctor said that?"

Her eyes narrow. "As soon as you finish medical school, rest assured I will happily consult you about personal health matters."

Early the next Saturday, we drive east through a rainstorm that pounds along the Columbia. Water streaks down the windows, though Babette still attempts identifying physical geography where the river exposes layered sediment. My professor mutters irritably, but as we approach the turnoff for Highway 97 that leads north into Washington, she cheers.

"Oh, we must break in Biggs Junction for lunch; they know me there and never charge for my meal when I bring tours through."

We pull into the parking lot of a small truck stop, hurry inside and are seated in the diner. Babette takes off her thick glasses and wipes away water droplets with a napkin. A middle aged waitress with brown curly hair sets down mugs of coffee at a nearby table and turns in our direction.

"Dr. Ellsworth!" she cries out. "Just one student today? What, do you give private tours now?"

My professor smiles as this woman leans across the table and squeezes her shoulder.

"Oh, no. We are just on the way to Yakima this afternoon. But I will stop by with a full group next week and then again in November."

Another woman comes out of the kitchen to hug her and inquire about upcoming trips. Babette grins and basks under their attention.

"I can't tell you how much I enjoy these young ladies," she confides, after they take our orders for sandwiches. "Since I am not close with my family, it is important maintaining connections with people through other ways."

"Your relatives in France adore you." I point out.

Babette waves a careless arm in dismissal. "The French cousins call often enough, it is true, and we enjoy our occasional visits, but that is not authentic human contact. My real family are my students. You know, I really think I would die without them. I have no worse fear than being dismissed from the community college. It may seem ridiculous at your age, but imagine your entire peer group is only interested in their declining health or ridiculous television programs. You are fortunate to possess such a caring family. Do you realize your parents call at 9PM sharp every Sunday night?"

I laugh. "Yes. They've phoned every week at that time since I moved out when I was eighteen. We could wind the clocks by it."

"Well," she replies, "they seem very fond you. And I can understand why. It has only been a few months we have lived together, but I must say... you wear very well."

"Thank you," I smile and look down. Overhead, the rain beats down with a muted rumble, audible over clattering dishes and country music on the jukebox.

"So," Babette continues, with a curt nod, "once we cross the Columbia Bridge into Washington, we will pass near a full scale recreation of Stonehenge as it would have appeared when new. The structure was built by a wealthy man named Sam Hill in 1918 as a memorial to US soldiers who died in World War I. A very odd place. There isn't time today, but we should visit during my high desert tour this autumn.

"Hill was a Quaker and it may seem odd a religious American man would take pains emulating a monument sacred for ancient pagans in England. Well, he believed Stonehenge existed as a site of pre-historical savagery and human sacrifice. There is no evidence such things ever occurred; it was an astronomical observatory and religious center as I understand. At any rate Hill, quite horrified by assembly line slaughter in Europe, thought he could warn humanity against their warlike inclinations through resurrection of an alleged barbaric temple. I appreciate his motives, though the results are questionable. Images of a man being tortured to death in every cathedral never kept Europeans from slaughtering each other with great enthusiasm so it is unclear what effect a much more opaque symbol in the middle of nowhere would have on Americans. Still, it adds local color."

After lunch, we continue toward Yakima, arrive by mid-afternoon, and check into a Howard Johnson Hotel. I carry our luggage inside to a comfortable ground floor room with two beds. Through a sliding glass door, puddles of water in the large courtyard reflect dark clouds. A medium-sized pool is already covered over for winter.

"I always stay here because we are so near the hot tub." Babette points outside where a boxy shape emits small jets of steam only twenty yards away.

"Nice. Too bad I didn't know or I'd have brought my swimsuit."

My professor shrugs. "No matter. Very few guests stay here during the cold seasons. We should use it directly and then prepare for dinner and tonight's events. The chill is terrible outside, would you go prepare that boiling machine?"

I strip down to boxer shorts and traverse the frigid concrete barefoot, a thin hotel towel over my shoulder. The cover comes off with a quiet pop of suction and chlorine vapor rises. I shiver and yelp as my toes dip into an icy puddle. The digital temperature gauge reads 101 degrees. Carefully ascending slick wooden steps, I splash both feet into the water. Millimeter by millimeter I sink down, until only my head protrudes.

Through a veil of hot mist, the sliding door opens and Babette boldly steps out. She wears only pink panties and her wig. A terrycloth towel is draped over one arm. My professor reaches the tub and without hesitation, slips beneath the surface. Her thick glasses immediately fog over. I smell pungent lavender skin cream.

"Is this as hot as it will rise?" she questions me.

"I'm not sure. My fingernails have almost scalded away."

Babette snorts. "It's scarcely above body temperature! Some happy day I will get one of these put in the backyard." She pushes buttons and underwater jets kick in. Liquid heat flows around my ankles. I frown at her exposed neck. The twin lesions swell and glisten.

"Now," she continues, as bubbles explode between her full bosom, "tonight we are in for sheer delights. Young people from the Seattle Opera will perform a variety of splendid pieces. Selections from Strauss, Mozart and Wagner, plus a few others. You know, there is actually quite a rivalry between the two cities. Some time ago the Seattle Symphony came as guests but had the audacity to bring their own chairs! Many in the community took that as quite a snub!

"So, before the show there is a discussion period I always attend. You will hear all kinds of worthwhile information about the upcoming concert and get a chance to rub elbows with people who really matter in Yakima. It is a small town, but the wealthy here have created something truly special for themselves. The Capitol Theatre! A world-class concert hall in the middle of Washington! It is only a few blocks away, we can easily walk, oh, soon you will see! Say you are excited!"

"I am excited!" My face breaks into a smile. Her enthusiasm can't be denied.

After dinner in the hotel restaurant we dress for the evening. I button up a black mechanic shirt over army surplus pants in grey camouflage. Babette chooses a green skirt and heavy purple sweater after heavily applying Cabochard perfume. She wraps a long red scarf around her scented neck.

"Are my colors appropriate?" she asks

"They're good. Am I presentable for a night on the town?"

"You'll do."

Outside our hotel, a crowd of well-dressed Hispanic young people mill about. Babette grabs the elbow of a man on the periphery and questions him in fluent Spanish. He smiles and answers her questions. Misty breath hangs in the air. I rub chilled fingers together. At last my professor breaks off their conversation and we continue down the sidewalk.

"The reason we have a marvelous symphony here is of course the agricultural system which allows member of the richest class to subsidize their passions. Such beauty always bears human costs. In this case it is migrant workers who come and labor for comparatively little in return. But so it goes. Look at the magnificent palace of Versailles! Thousands of people died in its construction, though you will see scant mention of them there. Centuries later, the grand buildings stand as monuments to long gone royalty but really they are colossal tombs, even if no one recognizes it. Stop a moment, let me gather strength."

I pause as my professor leans against a brick building. She takes deep breaths and after a moment shudders.

"Are you better? Shall we continue?"

Babette sighs. "Yes. My energy disappeared with no warning at all. But we must go on. Help me a little, please?"

Holding onto my arm, she leans on me for another half block before we turn down a dark alley. Nondescript concrete edifices rise all around and we pass rows of locked dumpsters. She motions at an institutional metal door in the wall. I pull it open. Bright light spills through, harsh enough to make me blink. I am tugged into a warm crush of crystal and red carpeting. Women in long elegant dresses move by. A cluster of people glance our way as cold wind from our entrance blows past. The door clicks shut.

"This is a little shortcut," Babette explains, "Come, I will show you the main chamber."

We cross the expansive room and arrive at another door. This leads through a small hallway and suddenly we emerge. I halt in amazement. The ceiling stretches far above us in elegant arcs of pink and white. Gold filigree accents every angle. It glows with illumination from recessed lights. Deep crimson curtains drape the walls around a sea of red upholstery. The atmosphere billows with strings and woodwinds as orchestra members tune their instruments. I turn around and around, the grandeur a whirl on every side.

"It's just wonderful!"

Babette smiles. "So you see, sometimes I can be worth listening to. Now, we will sit down this right row about halfway to the front and several seats in from the aisle. I tell you; over years I have tried every section and discovered the best acoustics. But let us go downstairs and see if the pre-show lecture is ready."

We wend our way down to a lower level room where about fifteen dapper elderly people recline in chairs before an empty podium. Many turn and nod at my professor. She directs me to sit, then makes rounds among these attendees, arms wide in gestures as they talk and anticipate the evenings performance. Her bulky figure bounds gleefully. She is unrecognizable as the woman I half carried from our hotel. After several minutes Babette returns and collapses into the chair beside me.

"You know, Wrahs, I have said before it is preferable to live as a big fish in a small pond, but really, Yakima is my second pond.

Lately it is more difficult, but I try to stay connected with people who matter in Washington. Those people I talked with just now come from the real agricultural gentry out here. They were quite pleased I brought you, as I told them my grandson clearly needed to absorb high culture." Gray teeth gape in an impish grin. I glower back.

"Besides the classical music community I am also a member of the Yakima Historical Society. Perhaps we will visit their museum here some other time ... but wait ... the conductor is here, he will talk in a moment about the program." Her mouth snap shut.

After the conductor's lecture, we return upstairs and find our seats. Babette takes one on my left. Before long the concert starts and as predicted, it is splendid. Babette sits on the edge of her chair, fidgeting with excitement during Strauss' *Die Fledermaus Overture* and leans back in bliss when the Seattle opera sings selections from Rossini's Cinderella. She trembles with joy during the prelude to Wagner's *Die Meistersinger von Nürnberg* and then relaxes, closing her eyes during a quintet from Mozart's *Die Zaberflöte*. Her hands clap in exultation when the final notes slowly fade away.

Afterward we walk back to the hotel. Babette still glows under a rapturous spell.

"I tell you, Wrahs, I could die in agony tonight and still consider this evening an absolute success. To experience such delight we are truly the luckiest of people. Nothing could have made this time more perfect."

With a satisfied sigh, she purses her lips and we stroll together in silence.

Upon our return from Yakima the next afternoon, I head downstairs and flip my wall calendar ahead several days. Soon it will be November, 1999. Something doesn't seem right and I turn back to June. Indeed, my pantry residence has only lasted six months but already feels like years. I make notes with a permanent marker on several upcoming dates. November 5th, Babette has a medical appointment about the strange welts on her neck, then just a week later will need a ride to the airport for another mysterious Canadian convent trip. I switch on the old Macintosh computer, begin an essay for school and then make a brief diary entry. Outside the folding streetcar door, multiple refrigerators hum without letup.

On the designated day, I drive my professor to her doctor's office for surgery and, hours later, bring her home. White gauze stretches beneath her wig and the neckline of a blue sweater. She is groggy from medication, weary-limbed and unsteady. I try to help her upstairs but she pushes me away. "No, no," Babette mutters, hands clutching the metal banister. "I must do this myself ... even if death is my only reward." Step by step, she wrenches herself upwards as I watch anxiously from the bottom. At last she reaches the landing and totters through her doorway. Bedsprings squeak as she finally settles. Soon deep snores resonate from above.

The next morning I rise early to shower and eat before a 9AM academic writing class. In search of breakfast, I stumble upstairs, eyes still half crusted shut. Babette is already awake, sitting before the kitchen table. Impatient fingers pick at the bandages around her neck. A bowl of oatmeal lies abandoned, almost congealed in blue and white china.

I yawn, then squint at her clawed hands. "Babette! Stop! Are you sure those should be come off?"

"Don't ask so many questions," she snaps. "I keep scissors in the drawer there, this gauze is absolute torture. They turned me into a mummy. Come now, *vite vite*! That is French– it means take your time!"

I fumble amidst thumbtacks, screwdrivers and balled-up rubber bands before finding a pair of blue-handled shears. Tentatively, I begin cutting through the layers, but wince at tape that stretches across an incision from earlobe to shoulder. Her mottled skin is sticky. I wipe my knuckles, gummy from adhesive and antiseptic.

"A bit of this may have to stay. I'm pretty sure the doctors put it there for a reason."

"I don't care," she orders. "Tear it all away."

"All right. Brace yourself." I take a firm grip on the tape and yank hard. The material rips free, exposing a deep wound sealed with shiny staples. Bare flesh gleams– puckered and raw. With a satisfied nod, Babette returns to her breakfast.

Chapter 16

"To sum it up in one phrase, if [men] fail to smother genius in the mud, they fall on their knees and worship it."

Honore de Balzac. <u>Father Goriot</u>. 1835.

"That was the best I have ever seen." My professor's arms fly up for emphasis "It was completely tragical!"

"Yes," I agree, "quite good." Final credits of Alfred Hitchcock's "Dial M for Murder" rise on the television screen before us. Babette sits next to me on the upstairs couch and underneath thick spectacles, her magnified eyes shine. I focus on the incision that runs down her neck. Only two weeks old and with staples removed just days before, it leaves barely a trace.

"No!" she exclaims, "it wasn't 'quite good,' it was an absolute vision of hell! We cannot experience such an event and think our lives will merely continue as though nothing happened! That would be inhuman!" With a start she leaps to her feet. "We must celebrate, but where can we go? There must be someplace to celebrate this late...even if only for dessert!" She stamps black stockinged feet on the carpet.

I glance at the wall clock. "11:30PM already. Not much is still open except Denny's."

Babette exhales with a long hiss. She stares at me disapprovingly and shakes her head slowly. "Oh dear, Wrahs. I sometimes forget how very middle class you are."

She directs me to an upscale restaurant called Fiddleheads nearby on Milwaukie Street that stays open until 1:00 AM. We order chocolate chip ice cream and black forest cake in the elegant dining room. Babette sits across from me at a small round table, hands still trembling with delight.

"What a film! Hitchcock is an absolute master. There can be no comparison. I love these stories where people scheme against one another with perfect malice. You know, there is nothing more malignant than our human capacity for cruelty."

I spoon up a bite of ice cream and smile. "It was splendidly done. The Praying Mantis was my favorite until now, but Hitchcock has it beat!"

Babette nibbles at her cake. "Oh, and there are still so many more. I do love sharing my taste in cinema with someone appreciative. It is a true joy to spread the art of chicanery and deception."

I laugh. The restaurant is vacant but for us and one waiter who languidly wipes tables. Suddenly, my professor slams her fork down.

"Do you know what is wrong with people?" She looks at me sharply. "They have no passion for life. I might as well be surrounded by upright cadavers. The plague exists in church, at school, almost everywhere. It affects my friends and colleagues, many students ..." Here she nods to me in in deference, "and it's an absolute catastrophe! People never show enthusiasm. True, much we encounter in life is uninspired, but that should make us all the more appreciative when true genius is experienced. People love diminishing greatness. They will say, Wagner didn't like Jews so we shouldn't appreciate his symphonies, or Leni Riefenstahl filmed a Nazi rally so her movies cannot be admired."

"Well," I put in, "it's difficult to separate the personal from the creative. We can't help seeing art differently depending on who made it and what they believed. There was an exercise from one of my writing textbooks last week where one page reproduced a painting with no explanation. I turned it over and found the same image but a caption now stated 'van Gogh's final work before his suicide.' You couldn't view it the same way anymore."

Babette cocks her head. "That is quite true. But more importantly, I hope you can appreciate art without knowing its creator or particular curiosities that surround it."

I frown. "It seems we can't ignore the context behind any piece of work. Just like products for sale. I prefer ones made in a union shop. Consumer choices all carry ethical repercussions even when items hold identical value. For me, those considerations come into play whether the subject is food, paintings or music."

My professor nods. "I appreciate your perspective, but when I hear a beautiful symphony, it doesn't matter if it was written by Anton Bruckner or Gustav Mahler. If it is performed well, I don't care if the first violinist kicked their dog or held some unpopular political views. The experience of genius makes all else irrelevant. It cannot be described, but only understood when you are in its presence as we were tonight. I don't know about Hitchcock personally and I don't want to. It is enough we enjoy our time together when brief glimpses illustrate what people are capable of at their best."

I fork up a last piece of cake and push back the plate. The sweet taste of chocolate fills my mouth.

"Well, whoever made this dessert fits that category in my book. No matter where it comes from, genius inspires everyone toward greater achievements. I just try my best, that's all someone like me can do."

Babette pounds her fist. "Balzac wrote of genius, but you do not know because you refuse to read him! How people tear down talent among them because it exposes their own mediocrity, but later worship it blindly when the human will triumphs. You must read Balzac, it torments me his books sit unread."

I shake my head. "There is so much in your library. But never fear, Balzac is on my list. As soon as I finish Camus. You threatened tortures of the Inquisition if I didn't read The Stranger."

My professor smiles. "So delighted. Tell me your thoughts afterward."

The waiter coughs and stacks chairs against a far wall. I gesture toward the door.

"They're about to shut down. We should probably leave."

Babette pushes aside her crumb speckled plate. "My energy does feel diminished. Perhaps we may conclude this evening with few regrets."

Chapter 17

"Then Master Francis juggled jugs,
The one set near the other one;
And when the tapster, filling mugs,
Looked otherwise while this was done,
He asked 'What wine is this, my son?'"

Attributed to Francois Villon. "The Method of Getting Wine"
1400s.

On a late Friday afternoon in mid-November, Babette excitedly bustles around the kitchen and skims over her many cookbooks. They boast recipes for cuisine from almost every culture; Basque and Burmese to Italian and East Indian.

"You know Wrahs, this house used to be quite well known for fabulous dinner parties. I would print up a menu, cook fantastic meals and invite every friend and colleague. It takes so much energy, with my health, those days are long gone, yet smaller events can still be worthwhile. Tonight I have invited several students over for supper. There are standout individuals in every class and I often develop friendships with them. Pursuing personal relations of that nature is not entirely ethical, but at my age I don't care. I make the college too much money for them to dismiss me over trivial matters. Oh, look here!"

From a cupboard my professor removes two Tupperware containers. They rattle in her hands. She sets them down and pushes one toward me. I open the lid and see clusters of small conical shells.

"These are snail shells. Now, everyone knows the French adore escargot, but few Americans have eaten it or even know what it looks like. So, years ago, I would go into the yard and collect small garden slugs. I kept them in a plastic container for several days and made sure they consumed only store bought lettuce. This allowed time to expel pesticides they might have consumed in the wild. Then, once my beauties grew plump and fat, I would place them on a cookie sheet and bake them in the oven. Afterward I seasoned them and placed these shells on their backs before serving. Oh, my guests were always very impressed and said they never knew escargot tasted so exquisite!"

I chuckle. Faux escargot; just what to expect from Babette.

On the counter is a large beef roast. My professor takes olive oil and rubs the meat with both hands, her whole body in motion. After some minutes conducting this massage, she sprinkles salt, pepper and garlic powder over the top, then dumps the roast into a large orange enameled pot with carrots, turnips, slices of onion, some tomato puree and cooking wine. She slides it into the oven to simmer. I peel a dozen small potatoes, roll them in oil and add seasoning salt. The convection oven will make these tidbits a nice crispy side dish. For dessert I mix up a batch of apple scones from scratch. They take only twenty minutes to bake so I slip the dough on a cookie sheet into the refrigerator for later. Until then, many chores remain.

Several hours later, the main floor is vacuumed, floors mopped and bathroom cleaned. I have our table set and am selecting serviettes when Babette pulls me into the kitchen.

"You are aware of my devious nature by now. Look at this." She reaches into a low cupboard and pulls out an empty wine bottle. It looks incredibly old, the ornate label scripted with faded French characters.

"This is preserved from an evening long ago, before you were born certainly. However it has served usefully many times since. Fetch me a funnel, *vite vite!*"

I find a copper funnel and hold it while Babette pours red wine out of a gallon jug down the bottles neck.

"You know, Wrahs. So much that we appreciate in life is complete illusion. If we knew the truth of reality, our lives would become visions of hell! The mind can be so easily influenced by what it perceives rather than physical experience. Our guests tonight will believe they enjoy a rare vintage. But it will taste so much sweeter to me as well! Oh, but I hear a knock, it must be them now. Quick, go answer!"

I approach to the front door and swing it open. Before me, in a black hoodie with silk maroon scarf wrapped up to her chin against November chill, stands Dora, a slim attractive girl from my academic writing class. She stares at me oddly. I hesitate, but recover.

"Come inside and warm up. I didn't know you take Dr. Ellsworth's classes. You're our first."

She peers around. "Don't you mean second?"

"Oh no. I live here with the professor. It's ... a long story."

Dora shuts the door and smooths short brunette locks. Her pretty face is tan underneath wire-framed spectacles. I open my mouth to speak again but Babette bursts out of the kitchen.

"Dora! You absolute dear! I am so glad you made it. Let Wrahs take your coat and stay awhile. Would you like a tour of the house? I'll show you my library if you like. Come this way!"

Dora hands me her thin hoodie, smiles demurely and follows our professor. A trace of sandalwood marks her passing. I'm still standing, garment in hand, when the doorbell rings and another student arrives. This one is Angela, a chubby blonde in her early thirties from my current Babette class. I show her the living room, then scamper to check on dinner. The air swims with delicious odors. My potatoes are golden brown already and the roast steams away. From a drawer I select pink and white serviettes, but the doorbell rings again. This time I recognize Faisal, a student from Pakistan who must be well over six feet tall. He towers beside Harmony, a shorter girl with long dark hair who sits behind me in class. I invite them inside, just as Babette returns with Dora in tow and gushes over her new guests. She seats everyone around the dining room table while I bring out hot dishes of food, her face beaming with pleasure.

"I will not say grace tonight, but only note I am so glad you all have come. It is a true joy spending time with my favorite students outside of class. And no better way than a wonderful repast together. Wait, there's more!"

My professor leaps up and almost knocks her chair over. She darts away, then returns, the ancient bottle hoisted like a trophy.

"Now, here is something special I have saved. But you must, to use the American expression, hold your horses –this is old

French wine! It should breathe a moment."

A murmur of appreciation buzzes around the table.

"Oh, Monsieur Wrahs ... would you be a gentleman and pour?"

I do so, my lips tight. Once every glass is full and Babette deems the libation adequately ventilated, she stands again, crystal goblet high. "To dear friends– that is all of you, my students, who really are my family." She takes a drink and we all follow suit.

Angela, seated across from me, rapturously closes her eyes. "Oh, this is exquisite! Thank you so much for sharing such a fine wine with us!" Everyone else voices agreement.

My professor lifts her empty left hand with generous acknowledgment. To me she gives a sly wink. I shake my head. Dora is seated on my left and I pass her salad in a gold-rimmed bowl after helping myself. Faisal skewers several potatoes, then gestures at Napoleon III's goateed bust on the china cabinet. "Who is that man?" he asks, English lightly accented.

Babette sets down her fork and pauses, chewing. Once the mouthful of beef is swallowed, she radiates delight and launches into a lecture that runs from Napoleon I to Napoleon III and Waterloo to the Battle of Sedan. The guests focus on her, plates loaded with food as our professor revels in every detail. I glance over at Dora. She sits, mesmerized, then notices my attention and smiles.

The table conversation next switches to college gossip. Harmony mentions a particular instructor on campus. She tips back her wine and blushes. "Oh, whenever we talk, it always seems he might be flirting with me!"

Babette grins. "Yes, he is rather notorious among my colleagues. There were rumors of an affair with a student years ago that caused some domestic troubles. I understand his wife could be quite small minded about such things."

Everyone laughs. By now most of the food is consumed. I begin stacking tableware covered with meat juice and salad debris. My professor hands me her plate. "Does anyone have room for desert? Wrahs baked a batch of apple scones which I am sure are delicious. They are done by now, *oui*?"

I nod and retreat to the kitchen. Dora follows, a couple dishes in hand. "You needn't do that," I say, and take them from her. "Go sit, you're our guest."

"I'd like to help. So, tell me, is Dr. Ellsworth a relative? I'm very curious."

"No, we're not related. But please, enjoy yourself, I've got cleanup under control. If you like though, we can talk later. Do you have plans this evening? It's still early."

"No," she says.

I scrape congealed fat and fruit rinds into the garbage. "There's a new gothic night called Sanctuary at Moody's downtown, which has a pretty decent dance floor. They play good deathrock and stuff. Would you be into that?"

Her eyes meet mine. "Yeah, sounds fun. Been awhile since I made it out dancing."

"Right on. Actually, you could bring desert out for me." I hand her a clean plate and fill it with scones, still steaming from the oven.

She returns to the table where guests laugh as Babette recounts an anti-Russian joke from 1950s Poland. I've heard that one at least twice, but still smile. Once the dishes are dry and put away, I leave a couple pots soaking and pour a final glass of wine. Its taste is unremarkable. Our guests savored richness on a label. As for Babette, thrills of deception fill her glass.

By 9:30 Angela, Faisal and Harmony have left but Dora and my professor still sit, deep in conversation. With a damp sponge, I wipe down the table and grab soiled serviettes to throw down the laundry chute.

"Oh, Wrahs," Babette intones sonorously as she rises. "You don't mind giving this girl a ride home, do you? The keys are by my purse in the study. I am exhausted after so much excitement. Thank you for help with everything. Dora, you are an absolute jewel–I greatly enjoyed your company tonight. Until next time, I bid you adieu."

As my professor makes for the staircase, she lowers her voice near my ear.

"Quite an Aphrodite, is she not?"

She ascends with slow footsteps.

I glance at Dora. "My chores are pretty much done. I'll just change clothes and we can head out."

Downstairs in the pantry, I find a reasonably clean wifebeater undershirt and pull on camouflage pants with black braces. I stuff these into combat boots, then select a gray mechanic shirt and black hoodie to complete my outfit. Back in the living room I discover Dora before Babette's glorious painting of the Château du Lac. She turns as I approach.

"What is this, a castle?"

"Oh, more of a mansion really. I hardly know where to begin. Before we go, could you tell if my braces are even?"

I unbutton my shirt and hold it open. Dora draws near and runs delicate fingers down each strap. Soft breath pushes against my cheek. She adjusts one side slightly, then steps back.

"Perfect. Mind stopping at my place so I can change as well?"

"Sure. Where around do you live?"

"Just north of Southeast 11th and Division."

"Do you want to just walk from there? It's a short distance and the night is clear."

"That would be nice. Let's do it."

We drive until Dora points out a parking spot under thick trees on a residential street. I follow her upstairs to a sandalwood-scented studio in a rundown boarding house. While she changes, I scan along books on a small shelf. The single room is small, but cozy, with soft lighting and wall draperies. Clean dishes line up in a drying rack and Dora's bed is made with plaid sheets. When the bathroom door opens, it reveals her lithe figure wrapped in a tight black dress above scuffed Doc Martens.

"What's that you've got there?" she asks.

"Oh," I shut a thin hardback and place it on her nightstand. "I was reading your book of lyrics by The Cure. It's funny to see just now. Their song 'Killing an Arab' is based on The Stranger by Albert Camus. He's one of Babette's favorites and she insisted I read it. Perhaps someday I'll play that one for her"

Dora grins. "You should! Well, I'm ready, shall we go? There's so much I want to know about Dr. Ellsworth. So, you call her Babette?"

On the walk downtown I tell her everything, from Babette's

nude doorway greeting, to our various trips together, and the story of her childhood in France. I'm so distracted we almost walk past Moody's. Deep bass vibrates the pavement outside and a sidewalk sign with large Gothic style lettering reads: SANCTUARY. A doorman checks our IDs and we enter a large elegant room. The ambiance is dim and small intimate tables surround a wide hardwood dance floor. It's not quite 11 so much seating remains unoccupied. Portland goths rarely dress as well as those I remember from Seattle and most here prefer faded band shirts under patched hoodies with combat or lineman's boots. Still, several in attendance wear extravagant make-up, corsets, vintage suits and other finery. We pick up cocktails at the bar and select a table far enough from the DJ booth to hear each other talk. Dora's petite face leans close, her features illuminated by candles in a red glass bowl between us.

"Keep going," she urges, "tell me more!"

I begin another story but the music changes. My foot taps uncontrollably. "We can talk more later– no one ever plays Dance or Die, I gotta do this one."

The dance floor has plenty of room and I stomp away with wild abandon. It's a fast song and my euphoria is so great it takes a few moments before I notice Dora near me. Despite heavy boots, she is silken poetry, bending and floating, driftwood on a dark ocean. Her eyes are closed, lips parted, and she moves as if rushing beats are light eddies in the current of a stream she's known forever.

I can't take my eyes off her.

Several tracks later we take a break and sit down. I tip back my drink and melted ice cube slush slams reality back. Dora beams, errant locks of hair stuck to her forehead.

"Watch my purse a moment, ok?" She stands up and heads towards the women's room.

A dapper-suited man sitting alone at the next table eyes her passing, then salutes me. He stands and approaches.

"Excuse me. But I just have to ask, is that your girlfriend?" He smiles, a handsome fellow, his mien sincere.

I swallow hard. "Well, yes."

His eyebrows arch. "Just curious. She is amazing. But you

already know that. You are very lucky."

He walks away toward the bar. I sigh. Babette would enjoy even such a small deception but my stomach knots with anxiety. Soon Dora returns and we continue our discussion but the lie hangs heavily around my shoulders. Tales of Babette's antics that sprang so fluidly before now clot with deceit in my throat. Later we dance again and after final drinks, exit into the night. It's well past 1:00AM.

I walk closer beside her this time and our sleeves brush together in darkness. We cross over the Willamette River, still deep in conversation. Underneath the Hawthorne Bridge, slow water reflects yellow moonlight. The air around us is cool and crisp.

"Sorry to talk your ears off," I apologize. "I know I'm not the only one in this town having adventures. So, you're from New Jersey, then?"

"Yeah, I came out a couple years ago. My mother moved here as well, in fact we work at the same bar."

"That's gotta be awkward!"

"At times yes. She needs a lot of attention and I'm trying to be a good daughter but it's tough. That's one reason I enjoy school. It's a good excuse to have my own time. Plus, I've been working weekends out at an organic farm. That's what I love most right now. The smell of the fields after it rains, a first cup of coffee early in the morning and then how my muscles ache by evening, but I don't care– God, it's a whole different life."

We pass beneath a streetlamp and Dora's face shines with joy in the sodium glow. My heart surges. I want to take her into my arms, but hesitate. She is so perfect, touching her would almost be a profane act. Our boots clatter along the bridge and further into southeast Portland. At Dora's apartment we pause. Babette's car is parked nearby. I fumble in my pocket for keys.

"Do you want to come in for some tea and warm up?" she asks. "Your stories haven't bored me yet."

"Absolutely!"

We go inside and Dora sets a pot of water boiling. After our tea has steeped, she sits on the edge of her bed and sips daintily. I recline against puffy tasseled cushions on the floor and tell of Babette's mysterious Canadian convent, the old Rajneeshpuram compound, and Yakima symphony. Dora's brown eyes fixate me through steam above her cup's rim. At last the wall clock ticks past two-thirty in the morning. Reluctantly, I get to my feet.

"I really should go."

Dora stretches. "Yeah, it is pretty late, but thanks, this has been ... a really special night." Her voice trembles slightly. "If you like, I'll walk you out."

We trudge over wet grass. It sparkles under a streetlight that flickers across soft black hollows up and down the block. At Babette's car Dora stands very near. She looks down, tender features almost obscured in shadow. For a moment it seems she might turn away and I reach out; her hip presses against my palm and the next second I pull her to me.

"A guy back at the club asked if you were my girlfriend– I told him yes," I confess in her ear.

She laughs. "I'm glad. You know, it was pretty much over once you let me touch your suspenders."

Our lips meet in kiss after kiss. Her firm shoulder muscles relax as we hold together, sandalwood fills my nostrils and bliss engulfs us under dark hanging leaves. I am immediately in love.

Chapter 18

"'Tis but the love of a young girl, monseigneur, a fierce fire, which soon burns itself out."

Charles Paul de Kock. The Barber of Paris. 1826.

"That look you have. It is so unattractive to a woman." Babette shakes her head.

"What?" I stand in the kitchen, telephone before me. Outside the windows, evening has fallen and cold wind rustles leaves against the glass.

"Your expression. Like a whelp removed from its mother's tit. You just now spoke with young Dora, am I correct?"

"No ... well, you're mostly right. I did leave a message for her just now. That girl is hard to pin down. She bartends most evenings and works weekends out in the country. Then if it's not homework, her mother needs something done. Seems like she doesn't have much time for me. Maybe I should call again."

Just hearing this spoken out loud makes me sigh. Over the last three weeks, Dora and I have spent only two nights together, escaping the winter chill under warm blankets in her small room. Aside from those fleeting hours of delight, we sometimes kiss after academic writing for brief moments until she rushes off to another class. Her attentions that first thrilled me to the bone now feel almost indifferent.

Babette inhales deeply. "Do you know nothing of Aphrodite?"

I think for a moment. "Wasn't she the Greek goddess of love created from sea foam?"

My professor raises an eyebrow. "That is a good start. But remember, love is complicated, especially when it involves females. Aphrodite descended from the much older Babylonian goddess Ishtar, a deity of sex, and fertility. Connected, of course, with growing cycles! Therefore, I find it poignant you mention Dora's interest in agriculture. Ah, desperately capricious, Ishtar could not be satisfied by any one man. You must read my books on goddess cults, Wrahs, if you truly want to understand women. Beauty and destruction are qualities never far removed."

I frown. "Thanks."

"Aha," Babette shrugs, "well, you will find your own way in these matters of the heart. Advice given would be, as we French say, like seizing the moon with one's teeth. Young Wrahs, I know you are not a simp!"

"A what?"

"A simpleton. At any rate, what are your plans for Thanksgiving next week?"

"Oh, I'll probably catch a bus up to Seattle. My family always throws a big get-together. Let's see, it's on Thursday so I'll be gone the whole weekend, then come back in time for class Monday."

"Yes, I suspected as much. My own relatives are not such convivial company and you know how I hate solitude, so I arranged for a colleague from school to come stay a few days. Her name is Naomi Fields, she works in the college cafeteria."

"Oh, good, I'd hate thinking of you with just French news for company. Does your friend play Scrabble?"

Babette shakes her head. "Not so much. Still, we enjoy viewing films together. Anyway, I am off to bed. But first I will answer your other question. It is no! You should absolutely not call Dora any more tonight. You will weary that girl and no one appreciates a romantic partner who is wearisome."

She turns and walks away. I bite my lip. Once her footsteps have faded upstairs I look down at the telephone. Faint strains of Tchaikovsky filter through from above. With heavy heart, I pick up the receiver and dial.

The Sunday evening after Thanksgiving break, I catch a Greyhound back from Seattle. It pulls into Portland's downtown station around 10PM. I stuff my ticket between pages of Blasco Ibanez's The Shadow of the Cathederal for a bookmark and nudge the traveler beside me, a snoring man with sour breath and arms covered in dragon tattoos. He jolts awake, gives me a slit-eyed glance, then grabs his duffle bag from an overhead bin and wobbles toward the exit. I follow.

The #19 line runs down 5th Avenue, just south of Burnside, so I sling my backpack over stiff shoulders and walk through light rain for several blocks before finding a covered stop. It seems an eternity but is probably only twenty minutes before a bus chugs along. I flash my pass and take a seat just behind the rear exit. Two halts later an older couple boards the bus. They sit right behind me. The man's white hair billows under a dark beret with some kind of silver medallion pinned to it. His partner is a black woman with long grey dreadlocks that curl around her shoulders. She snuggles against him. I stare out the window and catch a reflection of their embrace.

"I feel like being decadent tonight," the man murmurs, his voice husky.

The woman laughs and I smile. We roll along together in winter darkness. Eventually the welcome lights of Reed College shine along Woodstock. I throw the driver a left-handed salute and hop down the rear steps at my stop. Chilly wind gusts around me on the three-block trek to Tolman Street. It's late, but lights still burn downstairs. I enter the kitchen and drop my backpack, then start in surprise. A strange woman sits at the kitchen table.

"Oh, you must be Ross," she says. "Sorry, didn't mean to alarm you." She sets down a Hollywood gossip magazine. "Bobbie said you'd probably come back tonight."

"Yeah, that's me. And you're her friend from school?"

"I'm Naomi, yes."

I find a glass from the cupboard and fill it with water. Naomi watches me take a long drink. I turn and regard her. She is plump, perhaps in her mid-thirties, with a halo of fine red hair.

"So you looked after Babette this weekend then?" I set the glass down.

Naomi coughs. "Well, that was the original plan, but things have changed. Apparently I'm moving in."

"Oh? Where is she keeping you?"

"Her guest room upstairs. You know, with all the fancy furniture."

"Right, the French 2nd Empire stuff."

"Yes. I've lived there before. More than once actually. It's complicated. Bobbie kicked me out a couple times and once I left myself. This may not be a good idea, but I really need somewhere to stay. She'll pay my school expenses if I keep her company so trying again makes sense."

"Right on, sounds like a good deal."

Naomi eyes me carefully. "I hope so."

"You say Bobbie I notice."

"Oh, everyone who works at the college calls her Bobette or Bobbie. It's how we were introduced years ago."

I stretch. "Well, for me it's time for sleep. Nice to meet you, I expect we'll see a lot of each other."

Over the next few weeks our household acquires a new dynamic. My professor dotes on Naomi and even buys her a used Buick in decent condition. Babette takes us to restaurants and we view movies from her immense collection together in the evenings. The increased attention makes her greatly affable; he breaks into contagious smiles or laughter more than usual. Still, my heart sinks after every unsatisfying encounter with Dora or unanswered telephone call.

One afternoon I come upstairs just as Naomi heaves a large parcel through the front door.

"What have you there?" I ask.

"Oh, Bobbie bought me a computer. I'm going to connect the Internet to it. You should have seen her face when I told her. In fact today the technology department set her up with a school e-mail address. She's right behind me, you'll hear yourself."

Footsteps clump up the front steps and Babette bursts inside, eyes wide.

"Wrahs!" she exclaims, "come immediately and see!" Her shaky hand clutches a white rectangular card. She hands it over. "These are fresh off the press!"

"Dr. Elizabeth Ellsworth, Ph.D." I read. "Oh, and here it is. Your new e-mail at pcc.edu! Pretty slick!"

"There!" Babette beams. "You cannot say I refuse to keep up with current things! Everyone says this is the most modern form of communication!"

Naomi laughs. "Yes, ma'am."

I place the machine on a desk in an alcove across from Naomi's bedroom. Once the dialup service is activated, we teach Babette how her inbox operates. At this we fail. Over and over again. Even following step-by-step instructions written in block letters, my professor never accesses the account without help. After several days of anguished cries in French from upstairs, I simply print out e-mails she receives and deliver them by hand. Later she dictates replies, as my quick fingers type out each sentence

"I really don't see what all the fuss is about," Babette complains after a week of this, "half the electronic letters you give me are just inspirational proverbs from one of the church biddies. She must do nothing all day but compile those insipid litanies! Can't you stop her somehow?"

"Welcome to the Internet." I reply.

Chapter 19

"Mercy, who could have expected it? He was so pleasing as a girl; however I believe he will be still better as a boy."

Charles Paul de Kock. The Barber of Paris. 1826.

"After everything I've done for you!" Babette cries with fury. Her voice bellows from upstairs. It's mid-evening in December and I stand before the kitchen sink scrubbing a fry pan. As I hang it to dry, more shouts breaks out, but individual words don't break through. I shudder, but not from chill. After several minutes a door slams. Soon Naomi quietly pads downstairs. She stands in the doorway, face long.

"Screwdriver?" she asks.

"Sure," I say.

She takes a bottle of vodka from the liquor cupboard and makes two highballs. I rinse grease off my hands, wipe them dry and accept a glass. We sit down at the small table.

"Is Babette ok? I've never heard her yell like that?"

"Oh, she's gone to bed with a headache."

Strong alcohol dilates my nostrils before I even drink. "Wish you two got along better."

Naomi grimaces. "It's the same old thing. I knew she wouldn't change. If I make occasional plans for an evening with friends, Bobbie acts like she's being abandoned on a desert island. So, enjoy your independence. While it lasts."

"I think our relationship is different. I've always been careful to keep things balanced between us."

Naomi cradles her cheek in one palm and stares darkly across at me. "I hope you can. God, that woman..." She runs clawed fingers through fine red hair with the other hand, then takes a deep swallow.

I stare past her at tattooed sailors on the wallpaper and take a breath. "So, do you believe the whole kidnapped story?"

Naomi shakes her head. "Sometimes I don't know what to believe. Our friend definitely has a bizarre past but it may not be the one she tells. You're the historian in training, how do you verify a kidnapping from the 1920s?"

"I'd probably dig through newspaper archives in Yakima. *FRENCH NURSE FELON AT LARGE!* That's a regional story at least, maybe papers here and in Seattle would have something from back then. It's quite a puzzle. Never expected I'd be involved in a story this unusual."

Naomi chuckles. "Well, we're probably both in over our heads."

"There's so much I'm curious about. So, when you lived here before, was her husband Albert still alive? It must have been recent, since his name is on all the bills, but she rarely mentions him..."

Naomi nearly chokes on her screwdriver. She blinks hard, then pauses as though deliberating. "Ross, I ... uh ... well, I guess I'll just say it." Her breath intakes sharply. "Bobbie is Albert. She—well, he had sex change surgery in 1994."

The red Formica patterned tabletop swims before my vision. I try to think of a response, but no words come. I simply stare at Naomi.

"You had no idea?" she asks.

"Well, sure, at first in class we all wondered, but after everything I've seen here ... I mean, she runs around naked all the time!"

Naomi brings a hand up to her forehead. "Oh please! Ross? You've seen her without a wig. Ladies don't go bald that way. And you know how deep her voice is. Plus, come on, no real woman her age has tits that perky."

At this I sit up straight. "Well, senior citizens never flash me, so I wouldn't know. Anyway, there are old pictures too, why, that one in the living room ... she must be thirty or so!"

"Yeah, exactly. While the surgery is relatively recent, Albert dressed as a woman much of his life in private. Seriously Ross, how could you not notice? Nothing she does is remotely feminine. Look at her eat! Like a construction worker! True, her neck is thick enough to hide the Adam's apple, but her legs– does she ever cross them?"

"Lord, no. But ... why do you think she didn't say anything? She told me so many things! We're friends! I've lived with her over half a year now!"

Naomi sighs. "She's afraid you might move out. You have to understand, Albert didn't come from a time when people accepted such things. He didn't give a lot of people the chance either. I know quite a few colleagues who were close friends for years but he cut them off immediately after the operation."

"I can't believe Babette would think I'd leave her for that."

"Seriously Ross, who knows why that woman does anything. I adore her, and it's clear you do as well, but she very much looks out for her own interests, despite being so generous with us."

My mind reflects and I laugh. "Oh, God, she really did murder Albert!" Now almost hysterical, I pound a fist on the table. "No really, I questioned her a long time ago, because of the mail. Babette said some people suspected she killed him."

Now Naomi joins me with cackles. "Yeah well, she did, right? Bobbie must have loved passing that one off on you."

A last swallow of the highball burns down my throat. "I've got early class tomorrow and should be in bed. Really though, I'm glad you told me. I won't say anything, but if Babette mentions this, please assure her I don't care who she used to be."

"Goodnight then," Naomi says, watching my face.

"Good night."

I head downstairs, undress and lie down on my small bed but disorientation surrounds me between cool sheets. Confused thoughts swirl through my brain until at last they fuse darkly together and disappear in sleep.

The next day, after our Academic Writing class, Dora meets me for a few minutes outside the library. Two military recruiters are setting up a table near the entrance and several student activists circulate nearby.

"I just found out the most unexpected thing," I tell her, "Babette! She's trans! Male to female. I had no idea!"

Dora shoots me a sidelong glance. "Well, yeah. It makes all the sense in the world to me."

"I guess I'm the last to know. Go figure, me on the inside and all. So, do you think you'll have a little time for me this week?" I reach my arm around her waist. She draws close and plants delicate lips against my cheek.

"I don't know. In all honesty, probably not. I've got school and work, plus my lease is up at the end of the month. I'm moving into a house with my friend Chris. Also my mother's having troubles and I need to be a good daughter right now. It's all so much at once, I'm sorry."

"Yeah, me too," I murmur. "So, you're moving? Can I help? Clearly, my gender intuition needs work, but I can lift heavy things and massage sore muscles if needed..."

"No, it's ..." she looks away and draws back slightly.

I drop my hand from her hip. "Look ... Do you really want this relationship with me? It's one thing having a busy life, I get it; but you've flaked out on me so many times. I haven't spent a night at your place in weeks. We grab fifteen minutes after class like this or nothing. I just need to know what's – well, what we're doing here. You know I ... that I've fallen in love with you."

At this Dora looks away, gaze distant. Three students now loudly debate the recruiters and a small crowd gathers. She allows a thin smile, then meets my eyes.

"Ross, I do want this with you. You just need patience. But I have another class shortly. Talk to you soon."

Dora gives me sweet, brief kiss and exits the building. Through plate glass windows I can see her slender form move across the campus. I sigh, and join the crowd where several activists recognize me and beckon.

But time with Dora doesn't come easily. After winter break, our schedules diverge even further. We make plans and she frequently breaks them at the last minute. I dial her number evening after evening, to no avail. Babette observes my anxious state and shakes her head in despair.

Finally, weeks later on a Friday in mid-January, Dora answers her phone.

"We need a solution," I declare immediately. "This just doesn't work."

Her voice is sad. "I know."

"Can we get together soon? Sometime definite?"

"Yes. How about tomorrow afternoon downtown on the big stone staircase at 4th and Washington. About 2:00PM, say?"

"I'll be there, but I'm afraid you won't."

"Ross, there's no way I can express how sorry I am. But I'll come this time, I promise."

I hang up, my nerves strangely calm at last. The next day I catch a bus to our meeting spot and recline on the marble steps under a light drizzle. Tiny specks of water dust E.O. James's <u>The Cult of the Mother Goddess</u> and I turn pages halfheartedly, eyes raised every couple paragraphs. At last Dora scurries across the street and sits beside me. A raised hood obscures her face. She says nothing, but draws the hood back and soft features crumple into tears.

"This is hard. I should have told you before but things have been crazy. Ok, so … deep breath … I … shit … I got drunk and fucked my roommate Chris last month. That's it. I am so sorry, Ross. I was an idiot."

At this I laugh. I squint my eyes and look into Dora's face. Despite thick clouds above, all seems newly illuminated. Suddenly she appears haggard and worn, not the tender vixen who danced like a sprite and kissed me in a magical hollow under tree boughs. Crystalline drops fall and drip off her chin. I do not touch her.

"I want to still see you," she says.

My voice comes low and hoarse. "I don't think that's a good idea."

I stand and walk away. Not once do I turn or slow my pace.

Soon the #19 bus chugs homeward. Silhouettes step on and off, moving through an icy mist. Chatter surrounds me in languages that seem scarcely human. My numb cheek presses against the window as unchecked tears begin to flow, mirroring raindrops on the cold glass outside.

Chapter 20

"It is a true saying that there is no more beautiful sight than a frigate in full sail, a galloping horse or a woman dancing."

Honore de Balzac. Father Goriot. 1898.

One Saturday night in late-January, I head out to the Tonic Lounge, a bar up on NE Sandy Boulevard. Sanctuary, my favorite weekly dance night, moved there recently and I haven't inspected the new venue yet. The bus rolls along and I squint through window condensation to discern street signs. Finally a small building with neon beer advertisements glowing blue and red appears. I step off the bus and approach up a slight incline. Inside the door, a large bald man examines my ID.

The dance floor is a mere ten by ten square of wood paneling before the tiny DJ booth. Two determined goths stomp across it as muted beats rattle undersized speakers and about fifteen others congregate along the bar or in booths. A fog machine sputters nearby and the ragged eucalyptus odor fills my nose. I buy a tequila sunrise and glance around. Additional ambiance is supplied by video-poker machines, pull tabs and a worn out dartboard. The handsome man who asked about Dora sits toward the back in a booth with several friends.

I savor my drink and lean against the bar, absorbing tart alcohol. My head bobs as the DJ cuts into a Fields of the Nephilim track. The dance floor is now vacant so I set my glass on an empty table and step out. It's a mistake. The floor is not only tiny but sticky from spilled beer. My boots cling to the checkered veneer and won't allow any range of motion. It's like dancing on used bubble gum. Frustrated, I give up and look for my cocktail. A tall portly man, with dark mascara eyes and an old-fashioned dress stands near the table, blocking it.

"Excuse me," I say. He obliges and moves sideways.

I tip back my drink and stare morosely around the room. The man bends close.

"Terrible set this evening. I can't believe they have the audacity to call this a gothic night."

I shrug. "Could be better, no question. The dance floor is what most discourages me. You either need a mop bucket or wading boots out there."

The man laughs. "It's awful every way. I'm from L.A., well New York originally. There's a huge scene in Los Angeles, everything is so much better. Portlanders hardly bother to dress up at all!"

"True. I'm guilty on that count myself." I admit.

"It's a charming city nonetheless." He smiles widely. Long dark hair is pulled back into a bun pierced with pink chopsticks. "I'm Salazar Manilla. You can call me Sal."

"Nice to meet you; I'm Ross."

"Oh, Ross, Ross...not the anti-Ross."

"What?"

"Ah, never mind. Someone who isn't you at any rate. So, what are you doing in Portland?"

"Funny you should ask. I moved here a year ago from Seattle and now live in the pantry of my history professor who's a septuagenarian French transsexual Nazi-sympathizing nun."

Sal frowns slightly. "That must be odd."

"Yes. Sorry, it's kind of a mouthful to drop on you like that. The full story would take about ten hours."

"Well, I plan on being awake for at least another ten hours so you can fill me in." Sal's friendly grin is ringed with black lipstick.

"Sure, all right, if you really want to listen. Oh, except my expiration date approaches fairly soon. The last bus home leaves around 12:30."

Sal waves a resigned arm. "Stay and hang out with me instead. I never expect other people to drive anymore. In L.A. people will lose their apartment and live out of a car before taking public transit. Here it's socially encouraged ... and bicycles are as common as herpes. I'll give you a ride later, but gotta get my roommate back to our apartment eventually. Her name's Zoya. The only black person here. Oh there she is. I'll introduce you later."

He points at a girl laced into a metallic silver corset who now dominates the minuscule dance floor. She stomps across it, high-heeled boots a blur and long dreadlocks whirling. Muscular arms flex and fan before her face, purple lips twisted with concentration. She finally slows as the DJ mixes to a new track with deep bass lines and several more goths join in, dark sylphs on the perimeter of a hurricane.

"That one can dance," I observe. Sal nods.

"You'll like her. She's from L.A. as well. We moved up here together a few months ago. The scene here could use some work but has great potential." He smacks his lips and calculating eyes sweep the room. "Anyway, thank fucking god for Sex Gang Children. It's about time they played some decent deathrock. We'll talk later, I'm all over this one."

With an excited bounce, Sal enters the fray. If most Portland goths base their club style around frenzied stomping, which Dora floated above in ethereal detachment, the Los Angelinos blend elements together. They reach skyward and sway back and forth in rhythm with each other, then swoop low into a new stance. Other dancers step back to give them room. I observe from the side and nurse my drink.

As the club winds down around 2AM, Sal finds me again.

"Are you ready?" he asks.

"Yeah." Though the hour is late, my mind tingles with anticipated adventure.

We cruise by the bar where his roommate pours herself water from an ice-filled pitcher. Closer now, I smell menthol residue and see tiny rhinestones sparkle on the frame of her cat's eye glasses. Under black light, sweat glistens on her brown skin with a silvery sheen. She tilts the glass and swallows a mouthful of water. Ice-cubes crunch between her teeth.

"Zoya, this is Ross. He's with us."

I give Zoya a polite nod. She scarcely glances my direction and sets the empty glass down.

"All right then, let's get the fuck out." Her voice is low and throaty.

We head out to the street and approach a green two-door Honda Civic. The rear bumper seems attached only with electrical tape. Picnic tableware is glued on every surface, from door panels to the roof. Plastic forks arranged on the hood spell out FILTH in large capital letters. I peer inside and discover this description is accurate. The seating area is filled with clothes, dirty blankets and other assorted garbage. Fast food containers, Mountain Dew bottles and torn magazines are mixed in, forming a solid mound.

Zoya wrinkles her nose.

"Shotgun." She opens the passenger door and folds the seat down for me.

"Will I even fit in there?"

"Oh, no problem," Sal calls from the other side. "We can pack three or four people in back. More if it was cleaned out, but well, who wants to do that?"

"Not me." I crawl into the cavern and crush several paper coffee cups. My boots tear a porn centerfold.

"There's no point looking for a seatbelt," Sal observes, "but you'll be safest in a crash. It's like a womb, only with more risk of hepatitis."

"Great," I mutter, as my legs flex into a more comfortable position. There is a strong odor of mold but with Zoya's windows rolled down to let her cigarette smoke escape, it's tolerable. We head west toward downtown on Sandy Boulevard.

"Hey!" Sal shouts after several blocks. "We're right by Everyday Music. Let's hit their dumpster."

He pulls over and parks beside a record store, its windows dark and silent. We climb out and approach a large trash container at the side of the building. Sal flips open the lid. Illumination from nearby streetlights allows a dim view inside. The dumpster is filled with detritus, from unjacketed records to old 78s and cassette tapes. I lean inside and can just reach the top layer. Working together, Sal and I extract a pile of media. We dump armloads on the sidewalk. There is scratched vinyl from every genre, broken cassettes that stream lengths of tangled magnetic tape and even a few old eight tracks. Some pressings are warped from heat exposure, now frozen in rippled waves. Zoya stands by, lips pursed. She pulls out a new pack of Capri 120s and lights one.

"It's mostly crap, of course," Sal observes, "but I've come across some good stuff here. People think I'm just a guttergoth but if anything I'm really more of a jazzpunk. An Anita O'Day LP turned up here last week. Are you into jazz? She was one of the best mid-century jazz singers– a complete heroin junkie as well. I'll play it for you back at our place if you like. Hey Zoya, didn't you find a Duran Duran single or something?"

His roommate flicks ash from her skinny cigarette in scorn.

"It's David Sylvian and he was in Japan, not fucking Duran Duran. Uhhhhhhh Sallie! I'm getting cold!" She stamps her boots in annoyance.

"All right, all right. We're almost done." Sal scans the remainders in front of us. "Everyone in L.A. calls me Sallie. Well, there's nothing I want here tonight except some plastic record covers. For the sake of my domestic bliss, let's toss everything else back in the bin and take off."

Once the sidewalk is cleared, we stuff ourselves in the car and drive through downtown. Sal parks before a large apartment complex across from the Civic Stadium. We exit and stand before the massive multi-story structure. Across the street, an old home bum rattles his shopping cart to a stop and stares at us.

"Wow, you guys live at the Civic?" I ask.

"Yeah," Sal replies, "have you been here before?"

"No, but this place is pretty notorious around town."

We cross the intersection at 18th and Morrison where there is an entrance. "Well then." Sal smiles. He unlocks the door and holds it open in welcome. "It's all you've heard and more. We call our apartment The House of Many Pleasures."

Stench envelops us with a cloud so thick my eyes sting. Vomit, greasy food and soiled diapers. A placard taped on the lobby wall screams:

PLEAZE BE WARNED ALL SUSPISHUS PERSONS HAVE
BEEN REPORTED TOO THE POLISE
–THE MANAGMENT.

We walk down hallways carpeted in stained beige and lift our boots over the legs of a man braced against the wall, eyes glazed above a hollow smile. His pants are ripped into strips below the knees. Sal opens a door on the first floor. The room is dominated by an immense mattress raised up on plastic milk crates. Those are in fact the main furnishing element, as other crates form chairs, shelves and record storage units. Zoya pushes past us. She disappears into another room.

"It's sure a house of many crates at least," I observe.

Sal laughs. "Right, Zoya and I cleaned out the southwest industrial area after we moved here. No businesses leave theirs out in the open anymore. But it's such good stuff! I even created a whole guest bedroom under my bed! There's a TV and radio down there too, all the amenities!"

"That's pretty good," I agree. My eyes are still roving. The room is a pop culture explosion. Each wall is covered with posters depicting everything from punk rock icons to scenes from Star Trek and The Golden Girls. A smell of mold pervades despite the large fan churning in a cracked window. Sal thumbs through his record collection. It fills up two walls worth of plastic bins.

"Anita, Anita, ah, here we are. I don't know if you appreciate jazz." He places the record very carefully onto his dusty turntable and drops the needle. "But you should. I play the piano myself, you know, though my fingers are terribly rusty these days. Anyway, this one is more big band style. Besides Anita O'Day you can hear Gene Krupa on it. He was a fantastic old time jazz drummer. Here we go!" He turns up the volume. Through large wooden speakers on the floor, I hear trumpets and a crackly dance beat.

Just then Zoya steps out, her voice plaintive.

"Sal-leeeeeeee! My turntable is broken. Can you fix it?"

Sal throws up his hands. "You got it for cheap enough, find another one!"

Zoya crosses annoyed arms and grimaces. My eyes catch hers.

"Maybe I can help. I've worked on mine before."

She cocks her head and retreats, but this time leaves the door open.

Sal raises a long penciled eyebrow. "Well! An invitation from the inland empire Zoya-Bird to visit its nest!"

I approach her room and look inside. The space is small and also contains a bed lifted on crates, though not as high as Sal's. It does in fact resemble a nest, topped in bedding and multicolored clothes that swirl together in avian splendor. Zoya perches on the edge, dagger-heeled boots kicking gently off the side. She gestures where her turntable sits atop a dresser beside jumbled records and hair accessories.

I inspect it and lift the center platter. Underneath, the drive belt has come off. I remove it, test the band for elasticity, then slip it back together.

"This'll work now," I tell her, "but your belt should be replaced soon. It's just old and stretched out. Unless there's constant tension this'll keep happening."

"Thanks." Zoya meets my eyes again. "For one of Sal's gentleman callers you're actually useful."

I frown. "Gentleman callers?"

She grins. "You also have more teeth than he prefers, but hey, tastes can change."

Sal pokes his head in. "You repair it?"

"More or less," I reply.

"Well, let's get a move on."

I turn to look at Zoya but she ignores me, absorbed in *Exotic*, a local sex industry magazine.

Sal leads me back out into the hallway. We exit out a different door onto Burnside. Here the sloped concrete brings several apartment windows down below head level. A cardboard sign over one reads: YOUR DEALER HAS MOVED - LEAVE ME THE HELL ALONE.

"Are you hungry?" Sal asks.

"Yeah."

"Ok. Let's grab a bite at the Roxy, maybe play a game of Scrabble?"

"Oh you play Scrabble? That fits with my odd home life in a way."

"Yes, please tell me."

We drive back toward central downtown and park in front of a small restaurant. Several gutterpunks lurk in front. They nod at Sal as the two of us brush past. Inside, a giant neon ringed crucifix fills the back wall. Post-bar-closing revelers have thinned out but enough token drunks remain to agitate the wait staff. Cigarette smoke competes with fry grease, both thick in the air. After selecting a booth, Sal breaks out his board and we pick tiles. I smile in happiness at my draw. S, E, K, E, I, W and R. A perfect mix.

"Babette and I play with a French game," I explain. "It's such a treat using one designed for my language."

Sal laughs. "I can imagine!"

I continue the story of my adventures, interrupted briefly by the arrival of a ham sandwich. Despite several good word combinations, Sal beats me by forty points. He waves a hand airily.

"Don't feel bad. I meet with the local Scrabble club regularly. It's highly rated and very competitive. Only New York has stronger players."

My fingers are still greasy from French fries and I wipe them on a paper napkin.

"No problem. I'm pretty accustomed to losing this game."

Sal folds the board in half. "So, tell me more about these tours your professor leads. I quite enjoy Northwest history."

"Oh, they were quite a big deal years ago. International and everything, but now only local since Babette's health isn't great. One of her most recent took us out east, we went by the Stonehenge re-creation for our first stop, then a little town called Shaniko ..."

At this Sal slams down his hand. A couple loose tiles fly off onto the floor.

"Well, that's wonderful! It fits with a plan I've concocted lately. So, here's my scheme. You remember Leona Helmsley? The New York real estate billionaire– queen of mean– only little people pay taxes? Well anyway, she had notoriously high standards and if Leona Helmsley was gothic, she would never put up with the mediocre nights that curse this town. Therefore, next Friday shall be the first incarnation of Club Helmsley. I'll bring L.A. style and music but keep the Portland flavor."

"Excellent!" I exclaim. "Do you have a venue in mind?"

"Stonehenge."

"That's ambitious! Do you think we can get away with it? Oh, that place has got to be so amazing at night!"

"Well, what's the worst they can do, kick us out? Perhaps, but we'll have fun until then. Remember, this is the middle of nowhere. A bunch of subculture kids just dancing aren't likely to be arrested. If cops show up they'll make leave but that's all."

"What are we doing for music?"

"Good question," Sal replies, "I'll create a set list beforehand and dub the tracks onto a series of tapes that we'll play on my ghetto blaster. Not club quality sound, but when the dance floor is a pagan cathedral suspended above the Columbia Gorge, who cares?"

The following Friday evening, I catch a bus to Pioneer Square in the center of downtown Portland. Commuters wait for light rail trains under clear skies while a small crowd of gutter punks and street kids loiter nearby. Sal stands out from both groups, fully made up and corseted, in a dark green dress and wide black hat. A small cadre of people cluster around him. I recognize Zoya, who looks adorable in a black dress shirt and tight pants with knee-high lineman's boots. She ignores me. Sal introduces the rest. There is Dawn, a chubby blonde girl wearing Day-Glo colors, Austin, with purple hair that nearly covers his prominent chin, Isis, a black girl with short processed locks dyed rust red and an elegantly dressed couple in Victorian attire.

"Ok, it looks like everyone's here," Sal announces, "There are enough of us we'll need two vehicles so the rest of you follow behind. I'm parked just across the street. Zoya, Dawn, Isis and Ross, come ride with me."

I follow this group to his car and clamber on top of folded pizza boxes in the rear. Zoya claims shotgun and the other two scramble after me. Pressed against the far left side, communication is futile, especially once Sal begins playing a mix tape with endless versions of the jazz standard "Summertime" at high volume. Our convoy travels east on Highway 84 for almost two hours until lights from habitation become scarce. At last we cross the Columbia River Bridge at Biggs Junction, wind upward, and turn down toward the monument. Giant stones loom out of darkness in a circular pattern, gray shapes rising before the black gorge below. Sal pulls to a stop and the other car parks beside us.

I squeeze myself out after the three girls and stretch. It's a still night but only moderately cold. Moonlight glimmers through patchy clouds and reflects up from the river, casting ghostly bands of chrome. As we approach Stonehenge on foot, our group scatters amidst support stones and freestanding pillars. Shapes rush past me in the darkness. Someone stands on the central altar, arms outspread and laughter joyous.

Sal places his boom box on a raised concrete platform. He presses play and the bass line to a Sisters of Mercy track begins. People spread out and move in time with the sonorous tones. Boots crunch on gravel under our feet. Soon faster music reverberates from stone to stone with beats that echo down the river valley. A cloudy sky fragments in rents and tears above us as we romp between the obelisks. Stonehenge is alive, transformed into a giant discotheque for our delights as we leap and skip and sway and whirl. No feet stop moving until the tape runs out. Sal quickly turns it over.

After slightly more than an hour, a strange vehicle enters the parking lot. It cruises slowly toward us and we pause to stare. The car halts a careful distance behind our small caravan, profile hidden from view. Abruptly, a searchlight switches on, playing over the vertical stones. Night evaporates into stark white glare and deep shadow. Sal silences the music and we shrink back, making ourselves as small as possible. Then a siren emits two short whoops.

"Well, this lasted a good stretch," Sal interjects, "no regrets if we call it good for the evening." He lifts his ghetto blaster and Austin helps him pick up scattered cassette tapes.

We abandon Club Helmsley and return to our vehicles. The police car sits silently, windows impassive. A wind has picked up and now that my limbs no longer move, chilly air claws at exposed skin with icy talons. I shiver and climb into the confines of Sal's car, Dawn, Isis and Zoya close behind. We circles around and cross the bridge toward home, yet the stark white searchlight still illuminates Stonehenge far behind us.

Chapter 21

"People said she was a hermaphrodite, and that as the active and passive principles were united within her in a condition of stable equilibrium, she was an example of a perfect being ..."

Anatole France. The Revolt of the Angels. 1914.

"Oh, Wrahs," Babette announces one Monday after school, "I purchased a hot tub today." She beams from her office armchair in front of the television. It emits a stream of satellite news in French.

I set down my satchel and squint at newscasters pointing to Centigrade numbers pasted throughout a map of eastern Canada.

"Nice! You've wanted that for a while."

"True, but there remains one small detail. The dealer can install this machine, but we must build a foundation. I told them you would construct such a thing, *oui*?"

I stretch. "Probably. Doesn't seem like too hard a project. I'll need dimensions and stuff. What day does it arrive?"

"They said Wednesday afternoon."

"Oh." Outside the window, a steady sheet of April rain spatters the glass with Wagnerian percussion.

I call the spa company and obtain foundation details before Babette sends me to Home Depot with her credit card. Soon I labor away in the backyard under heavy torrents that turn cleared ground into swampland. One lilac bush, three small azalea shrubs and several clusters of lamb's ears must be sacrificed. Once a ten foot square is leveled, I lay down flagstones. This secluded corner of the yard, between Japanese maples and grapevine tendrils, will become an exquisite relaxation place, but right now such reveries are numbed by cold water leaking inside my rain slicker. With numb fingers, I pour more sand to elevate several low points and sneeze. Wiping my nose with a jacket sleeve only drags grit across my face. Once evening comes, I rinse off mud-caked boots with the garden hose. Just untying knots in soaked bootlaces make every fingernail ache.

Inside at last, I strip off drenched outer layers. Underneath a damp woolen cap, my Chelsea bangs compress flat across my forehead. Babette waits in the kitchen, a cup of tea held out.

"Thanks." I take the steaming cup and sit down heavily.

My professor looks out the window. "That looks like a splendid start. I'm so grateful you began immediately under such terrible conditions."

I grin. "It's ok. Once I warm these sore muscles in the hot tub, all will be forgiven. There isn't much left. I can finish tomorrow."

As scheduled, on Wednesday morning a truck arrives with several men who install the hot tub on my foundation. While they work, Babette sends me off to buy chlorine and other water treatment chemicals. By the time I return, everything is prepared. A garden hose takes well over an hour to fill it and my professor peeks out the window every few minutes, inspecting the water level. She is almost beside herself with excitement by early evening when the temperature at last reaches 100 degrees. We exit into the back yard, I in my bathing trunks and Babette completely nude.

The location is perfect, a high fence on one side and tree boughs overhanging all around. Low sunlight filters through clouds, misty and grey. My bare toes curl against tendrils of long wet grass. Birds dip their beaks in the concrete bath and chirp from perches on the grapevine trellis.

I remove the cover and climb in. Babette clambers along behind. We switch on the jets and she emits a satisfied sigh. Her bosom bobs slightly under pressure from the foamy current. I slide both feet along the bottom, then let my toes rise amidst bubbles at the far end. Behind my professor, the east wall looms, our warm cocoon ensconced within its deep shadow.

"Why are those bricks so dark?" I inquire. "Some look almost scorched."

Babette removes her fogged-over glasses and sets them on the fiberglass edge.

"That is because they were. You see, this house was built in the 1920s by a master architect using masonry recycled from an old foundry. Many of these bricks formed the forge's interior. They were still structurally sound and made quite a decorative pattern laid out in such a manner. Another interesting element you can see, as a cellar resident, the way everything is supported by quite massive I-beams, not typical residential construction materials then or now."

"How long have you lived here exactly?"

She smiles lazily and a streak of perspiration drips from under her wig. "Since 1971."

"I'd expected longer."

My professor laughs. "If you are curious how this came about, I will tell you. First I must travel back a ways. After graduating college in 1949, I returned to Europe and earned a doctorate at the University of Bordeaux. Those years were quite enjoyable. I traveled extensively in Eastern Germany, even finding work with the Communist government. This might seem strange, given my sympathies for, shall we say, the old regime, but I really enjoyed their social experiment. I met so many earnest, good-hearted people.*

Anyhow, afterward, I came back to Portland and soon took a wife named Helen. You understand, gender has always been rather fluid for me, as I was in fact born a hermaphrodite, with sex organs for both genders. It is true, my breasts were surgically implanted some years ago, but this vagina has always been mine. I possessed a penis also, but some pitiful thing, not suited for sexual purposes.

"Helen was an understanding creature and the two of us adopted three girls. We lived in southwest Portland for many years and life continued as it does. Then one day in the mid '60s, a woman named Billie Shoemaker signed up for one of my classes at the community college.

"Now, this lady was born Francis Bertram Hine in 1925 to a very religious Connecticut family. They nicknamed her Billie from childhood onward. Her father served as an officer with the British army during World War I in France, Italy and Egypt. Soon afterward, he immigrated to the United States and became a Canon, eventually an Archdeacon of the Episcopalian church. Now, what Billie lacked in conventional beauty, she more than made up through a dynamic personality. Her passions ran strong and attracted many people. In 1946 she married a man named Raymond. They moved across the country to Portland and had a child together. This relationship was evidently not all she hoped for because after five years, Billie divorced and immediately married a much older local judge named Raymond Shoemaker. Now, this Raymond turned out more her style.

"Shoemaker grew up in Montana, worked on the railroads and later as a gold miner. He learned fluent Spanish which became quite useful after joining the National Guard which sent him into Mexico after Pancho Villa in 1914 during the Mexican Revolution. Now, Shoemaker was what people in the early 20th century called a freethinker. He opposed racial discrimination, supported abortion rights and felt very skeptical toward religion. Are you familiar with Emanuel Haldeman-Julius?"

"No, I don't believe so. Do you mind if I switch these bubbles off?"

Babette shakes her head. I cut the jets and stillness fills our corner of the yard. Thick steam rises off the water. Through it, my professor appears ghostly, caught in a warped prism.

"Well, for a leftist rabble rouser, much education remains before you. Haldeman-Julius published the Little Blue Book series which inspired an entire generation of American contrarians. I will show you some from the judge's collection later.

"After the First World War, Shoemaker made his living in Portland as an attorney. He did well enough, but during the Great Depression, people often couldn't settle bills with cash. Many clients paid him in property or bartered other goods and services for legal work. Long term, these arrangements worked out very well. He acquired this grand home for a fantastic deal and other land that only increased in value.

"Anyway, Billie taught high school as a physical education instructor as well as Spanish and eventually earned a Master's degree in French language. This desire for learning led her to Portland Community College where our paths crossed. We immediately fell in love. My wife was suspicious, though I tried allaying her suspicions. At last one day I came home from school and found all my things boxed up in the front yard. Helen had decided she was through with me. I stood there, surrounded by my worldly possessions, when Billie pulled up with a van. We loaded my belongings, drove back to her house on Tolman Street and I have lived here ever since."

"How did the Judge feel about that?" I ask. "Or was he still alive?"

"Oh, quite alive," Babette smiles. "That same day Shoemaker took me into his office privately. He explained his wife loved me and as a willful individual, would certainly leave him if forbidden to see me. The fellow was in his late seventies and recently retired from the bench. He feared solitude and proposed a solution. I could reside in his house and we would all make the best of things."

My professor scratches a shoulder and her right breast wobbles.

"Truly, I say the next several years were absolutely wonderful. All three of us lived and traveled together with great affection. This lasted until 1977, when Judge Shoemaker collapsed dead from a heart attack on the front steps.

"Afterward, Billie and I continued our lives and traveled extensively around the world on my tours. I had never conceived a more joyful existence, but it ended in 1990 when Billie contracted cancer. We married shortly before her death a short time later. This left me with the judge's house but his same predicament, as I also fear loneliness. Since that time I have striven to find companions I enjoy and who put up with my eccentricities in return. There, I answered your question. For the last thirty years I have lived here and pursued my passions as best I can. So you see, I led an interesting life, no matter what you say!"

I grin. "That's no exaggeration. But my fingers are nearly prunes. I think I'm done with this soak."

Back indoors, I dry off in the basement, then dress and head upstairs to find Babette with a stack of booklets on the kitchen table.

"Ah," she greets me, her loosely tied bathrobe swinging open. "Here are some of Haldeman-Julius's many publications. Look what a variety! Everything from 'Proverbs of Hindustan' to 'Popular Shakespearian Quotations.' But this publisher did not shrink from inflammatory subjects! Look at two here, 'The Lies of Religious Literature' and 'The Ghastly Purpose of the Parables.' Remember, both these are from the 1920s! Hardly a tolerant time for such criticism.

"Now, you can see Shoemaker read avidly, inscribed his name with dates and often took notes inside. Quite fascinating stuff and heady social material, especially then. Oh, look here at 'A Book of Familiar Quotations.' In the back Shoemaker added some of his own. He wrote 'a man who rolls the mantle of prejudice about him and refuses to consider any measure on its merit is fit only to starve. He is an encumbrance on the earth and should give way to others.' Well, I can't agree more! But come, Billie kept an album you will enjoy."

She leads me to the study and pulls a large binder from the end of one bookshelf. It is stuffed with newspaper clippings and photographs glued on black construction paper. Babette thumbs along and holds pages out for me to see.

"Billie compiled this scrapbook over many years. Look here, one newspaper article goes back to 1940 where her father, then Reverend Hine, is quoted decrying atheism as the real cause of war in Europe, then years later in 1954 Judge Shoemaker wrote an op-ed for the *Oregonian* criticizing Senator McCarthy and excesses of his anti-Communism crusade. Not a popular position during the Red Scare and risky as a public figure. That same year, Hine visited Portland, he was quite a religious celebrity, the media paid plenty of attention as you can see. Can you imagine what dinner conversations those two men must have had? A famed Archdeacon and a notorious atheist Judge? Nearly the same age, but one married to the other's daughter? But from what I understand, they actually cultivated quite a warm friendship!"

Babette flips through a couple more leaves.

"Here came a minor scandal for the Judge in 1956. The police caught a seventeen year with beer. Shoemaker ruled he should be freed since this juvenile was not a known troublemaker, married and had a job. It embarrassed him two weeks later, when the same young man returned, charged with auto theft."

"What is that?" I exclaim, and point at a black and white picture glued above one article. It depicts the living room, though differently decorated. A small fair-haired girl sits at the piano and smiles. Next to her looms a circus clown in white makeup. His wide grin leers.

"Oh, yes," Babette muses. "You know the famous early television show Howdy Doody? Well, one of the stars in that program was a clown called Clarabell, played by the actor Ed Alberian who Billie attended college with in Pennsylvania. He visited the Shoemakers in 1956 and put on a special show for neighborhood children. That is her daughter next to him.

"Anyhow, 1957 was a big year. Here Judge Shoemaker worked closely with a group who opposed the death penalty and then that summer came another newspaper op-ed where he condemned racism and the Little Rock Nine school integration controversy in Arkansas. I know it doesn't seem like much, but you have to remember in those days, such views were not well received, even here.

"The Northwest was never a friendly place for non-whites once Europeans gained a firm foothold. People think of this as a progressive part of the country, and perhaps today that is somewhat true. We remember Oregon was admitted into the union as a free state with no slavery, but forget the local constitution also banned black Americans from residence within it. At least in the South, a freed slave was not illegal for mere existence by color of their skin!

"Here is the final series of clippings. It seems in 1959 Shoemaker felt Portland police officers exhibited over enthusiasm issuing traffic citations. He wouldn't enforce many of them, so the sheriff boycotted his court and even took offenders outside the city limits to find more sympathetic judges. Quite a situation, that one. You can see it caused quite a dust up. There are several articles here. In this one deputies are quoted saying he doesn't treat them respectfully enough in court and sometimes makes them feel like they're the ones on trial! He responds by claiming his job is to stand between citizens and authorities who would rather run this country like a police state! Such speech from a judge in those times!"

I clap my hands together. "What an amazing man! To think he got away with it back then, oh, I wish I could have met him!"

Babette laughs. "I'm sure he would have appreciated your politics. But now we jump quite far ahead as Shoemaker retired soon afterward and his life became much more sedate. This next article is from a newspaper in Glasgow, Montana which reported on our last trip during the autumn of 1974. We traveled through the countryside where Judge Shoemaker spent his childhood, a wonderful way to say goodbye to the world as it turned out, don't you think? Here, it says "'Judge Ray D. Shoemaker 80, of Portland, Ore., was a visitor in Glasgow over the weekend. He was accompanied by his wife and Dr. Albert Ellsworth, a professor.'"** I wonder what they thought of us, all traveling together, such an odd picture." She chuckles, a little sadly.

"Well, those days are long gone. Soon I shall be as well. I think I will go to bed and lie down. That boiling machine outside is wonderful but truly evaporated all my energy. Where is that girl Naomi anyhow?"

"I think out for a visit with friends this afternoon. No doubt she'll return before long."

Babette grimaces. "Then, I bid you adieu for the moment." Her footsteps trudge upstairs.

I sit the kitchen and mull over snack options. There is a bowl of fruit on the counter and I have selected an apple when Naomi walks in the front door.

"Hello!" I salute her, "you missed our inauguration of the Jacuzzi!"

She shrugs. "Ah, well, I'm sure I'll try it soon enough."

"Did you have fun?" I ask.

Naomi nods. "Yeah, it was nice to get out of the house and have a cold drink. I think one more lukewarm cocktail will kill me. How's our old lady?"

My teeth penetrate the green skin and I chew for a moment. "Talkative. Gave me the story of how she moved here. Noticed you were gone, though."

"I'll get a lecture on my ungratefulness tomorrow. Or tonight if Bobbie stays up."

"Lame. So, I'm curious about some things. When you told me Babette lived as a man before her sex change, did you mean completely male? Babette more or less admitted it all tonight, but claimed she was born a hermaphrodite, you know, with both genitals. She couldn't reproduce sexually... "

"My God, Ross," Naomi cuts me off, "you should never take our friend so seriously. I can't speak to the originality of Bobbie's privates, thank heavens, but this one thing we will verify. Adopted ... what nerve!"

She marches into the dining room and sorts through a small pile of mail. "Let's see, she showed it yesterday. Should still be here. Medical, electricity, water ... aha!"

Naomi removes an envelope, already sliced open from Babette's efficient knife strokes. She tips out a color photograph and hands it over. I examine the picture. It is a woman and child, the youth perhaps seven years old. They are clearly kin and the common ancestor is without doubt Babette. I draw in my breath at the resemblance.

"That's Bobbie's daughter in New York," Naomi informs me, "and the kid is her grandson. So you see, as much as she might now deny her penis ever worked, those genes got passed on somehow. I've seen pictures of her other two daughters and there's no doubt with them either."

"Hmmm." I muse. "So, about the rest of what I heard tonight. Babette showed me a bunch of information about Judge Shoemaker but not much on his wife Billie. Did you know her?"

"No, I never met her but many old colleagues I've known were quite close with both of them. Albert abandoned his wife Helen for her and moved here in the early 1970s. Bobbie makes it sound very innocent, the way she abandoned her family, but it seems her life was never happier. That's obvious in their pictures."

"Oh, so she showed you some of Billie?"

"Sure, hell, they were in love, as much as Bobbie is capable of it. She still keeps a photo on her nightstand– you've seen it."

"Oh, my God! Yes, but I thought it was Albert in drag long ago. That's Billie?"

Naomi snorts. "Yeah, pretty creepy, huh? I know there's another one around somewhere."

She opens the china hutch and removes a decorative plate from underneath several others. Its edge is surrounded with ornate Chinese characters and small images depicting rickshaws and pagodas. Lacquered into the center is a photograph of two portly older people bundled up in warm jackets, their hands clasped together. Albert stands at one side with a black beret and orange scarf. Billie snuggles beside him, her face framed with greying bangs. Their pale moon faces smile up at us.

"So similar." I remark. "They could be siblings."

Naomi nods. "Like I said, pretty weird. Nothing feminine about Albert and the same could be said of Billie. The story goes they switched gender roles at home and when traveling. Since Albert probably never shared that part of himself with anyone, it must have been quite a relief.

"Now, from what I've heard, Billie was quite a character. While Bobbie, as we know, is quite willful, Billie apparently kept Albert very much under her thumb. He performed all the housework, lived as her servant and loved it. She won't admit this, but I find it significant they only married just before Billie's death. Of course, the judge passed away years before, why wait so long? Well, I suspect it was their power dynamic. Billie held the upper hand completely that way. In the end she relented– or the cancer made her relent, so Albert inherited Shoemaker's money and property, otherwise he could never have afforded the sex change operation on just a professor's salary."

She sets the plate back and shuts the cupboard. "You won't find pictures of Albert around much except with Billie. There's nothing Bobbie hates more than being reminded she was a man."

I glance toward the stairs, nervous for a moment Babette might overhear. "It must have been horrible, trapped in your own body like that. I just can't imagine."

Naomi exhales wearily. "I must admit my sympathy is waning. I woke around 2 last night and found the bedroom door open. Bobbie waited at the foot of my bed, staring at me. Oh, the most frightful sensation, gives me chills just remembering. I kept still, feigned sleep and eventually she left. That woman is on much better behavior when you're around. Without wanting to sound like her, I do wish you stayed home more. When we watch films now, she sits on the couch with me and cozies up close. Next she puts her hand on my knee, slowly moves it up further and further and then, yikes, I have to scoot away."

I wince. "Sorry, I didn't realize that. I've been making friends and my social life is a bit more active these days."

"Well, enjoy your freedom– while it lasts. Also, don't let Bobbie talk down to you. Sure, she probably had two Master's degrees by your age but everything came easy for her. The Catholic Church awarded scholarships so her education was paid off, then once she left her family, Albert lived here rent free. Most of her money came from the Judge through Billie, it's not like she earned it. I'm just saying, don't compare yourself."

I nod. "Yeah, thanks for the perspective. But if I'll earn even a Bachelor's degree, there's a paper on Vichy France I gotta work on."

Naomi slits her eyes and stares at the liquor cabinet. "Good luck with that. I'm going to fortify myself and then take my medicine upstairs."

In the basement, I leaf through texts for my research project but muffled shouts from upstairs are hard to ignore. At last, a thunderous Anton Bruckner symphony blots out their argument. When the music concludes, over an hour later, I hear nothing more.

The next day I come home from a full day of classes and discover my professor in the kitchen. She sits tensely. Bright eyes glitter behind her glasses.

"You may notice Naomi is no longer here," she begins. "I asked her to leave last night and this afternoon she packed her things."

"Oh no!" I exclaim.

Babette sniffs. "It became clear she held other priorities than our friendship. After everything I did for her. But *c'est la vie*, it will not help if I dwell on such ungratefulness. But I am so glad you are here, it is time we discussed your future."

I take a seat across from her at the Formica table. "How do you mean?"

My professor takes a drink of mineral water. Her wet lips smack together. "Soon this quarter will conclude. Do you anticipate continuing your studies in the autumn? With enough community college credits, you might soon transfer to Portland State University. Is higher education truly your goal?"

I meet her gaze. "The answer is yes, if you still want me here. I know it means a lot having help around the house. It's also a good deal for me to work as little as I do and concentrate on homework.

That's a situation I couldn't manage so well anywhere else."

Babette smiles. "Delighted. Then I extend an invitation to continue living here as long as you stay in school. Summer will come soon and I have wonderful trips planned, oh, there is Eastern Oregon again, the coast, Vancouver Island, also a small place north of Victoria I adore, called Cowichan Bay. If you accompany me, we shall have a delightful time!"

"Absolutely!" I agree.

Chapter 22

"If thought of love deter you so,
Because of tricks in those you name,
You rail unjustly since you know
That these are women of ill fame."

Francois Villon. "Ballade of the Fair Adventuress to the
Daughters of Joy" 1461.

In late September, after a long summer traveling with Babette, I meet the goddess of destruction. My first course at Cascade campus is creative writing. I enter the partially filled classroom and select a chair from around thirty arranged in a circle. The professor, a middle-aged man with grey hair, writes on the chalkboard.

Raymond Carver
Joyce Carol Oates
Amy Tan
Andre Dubus
Kate Braverman

All chatter halts and a deep silence falls. American short story authors don't usually inspire such reverence. I glance to my right and notice three men sitting bolt upright, lips parted and eyes wide. "Holy shit," says one quietly. "Goddamn," echoes another in response, his tone hushed.

Their attention fixes on a woman in the doorway. She stands tall in stiletto heels, dark braids wrapped up in red and yellow satin. Her skirt is short and above it, a tight white blouse barely contains the immense bosom within. A contemplative expression drifts across her creamy brown face. She can't be older than twenty-two. This woman surveys the room with slow deliberation, approaches closely and sits directly on my left. A wave of honey perfume passes over me.

I dumbly peruse the sheaf of stapled papers before me, attention shattered. Her odor is pure sex. The exquisite woman – surely a goddess from Babette's pagan texts, rummages through her book bag, then turns and grabs my elbow.

"Hey, what's your name?" she asks.

"Ross,"

She smiles and holds out a hand, fingernails manicured and scarlet.

"Annakiya."

Her fingers squeeze, then slide over my knuckles. Surprised, I pull away.

"Are you a writer?" she asks.

"Sort of. There are some short story ideas kicking around my head. I like research papers also, that's mostly what I write these days."

Annakiya smiles, light hazel eyes studying me. "I'm a poet. Would you like to hear some of my poetry?"

"Sure."

"I think we should hang out after class," she continues, "maybe you can come visit at my place."

The tawny skin bulging above the neckline of her blouse is impossible to ignore. My pulse leaps. Before I can respond, the professor clears his throat.

"All right. It looks like we're all here. Let's start with introductions. We'll go around clockwise. Tell us where you come from, a few personal details and what subjects you enjoy reading."

When it's my turn I stand.

"My name is Ross Eliot. I'm from Seattle but spent the last year in Portland with several odd living arrangements. By trade I've usually worked as a roofer or forklift operator. Most literature I love has always been nonfiction but my favorite novel is <u>McTeague</u> by Frank Norris. It's fantastic because the characters are complicated, just like real life. You can't sympathize with anyone."

A couple people laugh, and the professor smiles. He motions to Annakiya. She rises. Every gaze locks on her.

"I'm Annakiya Singh. My father came from Nigeria and my mother is East Indian. I grew up in Portland but spent the last couple of years in Hawaii. The books I like best are usually poetry collections or works on spiritual philosophy. Oh, and I just met Ross here, but I'm very excited to spend more time with him. A lot more time ..."

My mouth gapes and both cheeks redden in a hot rush. I grin awkwardly, then look up at her. She winks. The men on my right cast incredulous stares.

Creative writing passes by in a thick haze. Afterward, the two of us walk to a nearby southbound bus stop on Albina Street. In heels, Annakiya must stand at least three inches taller than me, but her high coiled braids and scarf amplify this height even more. As soon as we board and sit down on a narrow bench seat, she pulls me close. Honey-scented body oil wraps around us like a protective fog. Her left hand grips my thigh, the right caresses my neck. Every survival instinct I possess screams something is amiss, but Annakiya's pheromones overpower all reason. My lips drag across her silky ear.

We step off downtown and she directs us toward another bus stop, arm still around me. I rest a hand on one curving hip. This transfer will take us into the upscale northwest district.

"My apartment isn't far," Annakiya observes, "but there's no way I could make it in these heels."

"Why do you wear them?" I ask.

She stares at me with a twinge of pity. "Flats just don't go with this outfit. Oh, look, a taxi! We can split it!"

She leans into the street and flags down a black Radio Cab. We climb in back and Annakiya gives the driver an address just off 23rd avenue. He looks rearward and examines her.

"You do realize that's only six blocks, lady."

"Yes," she replies indignantly, "I know where the hell I live."

The driver raises an eyebrow at me in the mirror. I look away. In a few minutes we stop before an immaculate older building, its façade a brushed gray. Annakiya opens her purse to reveal an obscene explosion of cash. I withdraw my wallet and count out half the tab. We exit into mid-afternoon sunlight and the cab growls off, searching for better fares.

Annakiya leads me through the lobby and into an elevator with draw cage doors. We reach the eighth floor and walk down a plush hallway. At her entryway, she fishes for keys amidst greenbacks dense enough they might escape and litter the floor. At last we enter. Inside, the space is quite elegant, with polished hardwood floors and tasteful art on every wall. Décor is minimal, mostly modern or faux antique. Annakiya gestures across the living room to a short hallway.

"My room is this way."

I follow her into a chamber overflowing with clothes. They spill from the half-open wardrobe, jut out of partially-closed drawers and strew the floor in piles. Panties, bras, corsets, skirts, teddies, yoga pants, blouses, dresses ... and mixed among them– money. Twenties and tens stand out amidst enough one dollar notes to wallpaper a theater. Annakiya waves me toward the bed and I push aside several plush pillows. There is a Benjamin Franklin crumpled underneath.

"So you're a ... dancer, then?" I ask.

"Yahs, an exotic dahnsah ... "she purrs with an affected accent, then laughs.

"Looks like you could use an accountant."

"Maybe. Do you like this shirt?" She holds up a sky blue garment. "Wait, let me try it on first."

Annakiya unbuttons her blouse in a businesslike manner and tosses it aside. She slowly bends close. Her golden skin glows and honey floods forward as she moves nearer. I avert my gaze from the spectacular breasts within her leopard print bra. She wants to be touched, nothing could be clearer – but something feels wrong. Every nerve tingles on red hot alert.

With a step back, Annakiya stretches into the new blouse and fastens it. Her expression is calculating. She spins around and strikes an exaggerated pose against the wall.

"How about now?"

I nod, then start as turning keys clatter from the other room. The front door closes and footsteps approach. Knuckles rap on the bedroom door.

"Sugar?" comes a male voice, "are you home?"

"Oh," Annakiya whispers in my ear, "that's my boyfriend." She straightens up. "Yes, baby!"

The door opens and a pink-faced man wearing athletic warm-ups enters. He appears in his mid-thirties and drips with perspiration. Annakiya offers her lips to him for a tender kiss.

"Baby, this is my gay friend Ross from school. We have a writing class together, he's going to help with my poetry."

The man offers a moist handshake. "Hey bro."

"Hi." I meet his eyes briefly, then lower my head.

"Damn, Suge, those kids at the basketball court wore me out. I am so fucking hungry, what have we got to eat?"

Annakiya shrugs. "There's some leftover Thai soup from the other night. It's probably still good."

The man brightens. "Oh, hell yeah, that was delicious." He spins on his heel and leaves.

"Well, I think I'll be on my way" I declare loudly, standing up. "We probably got enough homework done for now."

Annakiya walks me to the door and pulls close for an embrace.

"Gay friend Ross?" I whisper in her ear.

"What, you're not gay?" She shrugs. "Well, that's ok. See you in class soon."

Chapter 23

"It seemed to him that the whole world of politics and religion rushed to extremes; and that what was not extreme was inert and indifferent– dragging out, day by day, an existence without faith and without principle."

Octave Feuillet. Monsieur de Camors. 1867.

"Hey, do you wanna be a concentration camp guard?"

I consider this question from a tall youth with cropped sandy hair. His lips brush my cheek in the cellar of Klub Z, an underage gay dancehall downtown. A large white spiral painted on the concrete dance floor circles our boots as thunderous beats reverberate and bounce off graffiti spattered walls. Around us, a small crowd of goths move to the rhythm, raised arms nearly colliding with rusty pipes that cross the low ceiling.

"WHAT? Can't hear, too LOUD," I shout.

He gestures at a narrow staircase. I follow him– up and up, until different sounds drown out the abrasive basement tones. The large room we now enter is filled with glittery teenagers celebrating Saturday night. They bounce to upbeat techno music before a raised DJ booth. Drag queens pose on blocks and athletic dancers in bright costumes vogue along a low stage. We push through the crowd toward an exit. Warm bodies press against me, limbs slick with sweat.

Outside, a mid-October chill strips away the sour reek of perspiration and I zip up my hoodie. On the street corner, a queen shivers in her sequined dress. She takes a final puff of a cigarette, crushes it under stiletto heels and returns indoors. The tall youth, wearing only a tight black t-shirt and patched cargo pants, seems oblivious to the cold. He fixes me with curious eyes.

"I'm doing a performance here in a couple weeks. Not the usual drag bullshit. I want to act out a Holocaust love story between a concentration camp inmate and his guard. It requires several SS soldiers, would you be one?"

"Maybe. I am curious. What's your name?"

"Isaiah."

"Ross." I shake his hand.

"So, can you meet up soon and talk more? I've gotta take care of some business tonight."

"Probably. I'm fairly preoccupied with school. The idea is intriguing though. Where around do you hang out?"

"Mostly this part of town," Isaiah says, head swiveling. He is handsome, with an intense gaze. The black shirt clings to his spare build.

"Well, tomorrow night I have a postering mission up in Northwest. Do you want to come along? We can talk more then. Like about eight, does that work?"

"Sure. Meet me at my office on Stark Street."

"Where?"

Isaiah laughs. "Find me on the corner of Stark and Burnside. But hey, I gotta run. See you tomorrow."

Isaiah saunters off, footsteps careful and boots almost noiseless against concrete. His tall figure disappears in darkness.

The next evening I board the bus carrying a satchel filled with freshly photocopied political posters. The sky is overcast but rainless. I walk up Stark Street, Portland's linear gay district, passing bars, dance clubs and a bathhouse. Perhaps this strip is where Babette picked up clients as a teenage prostitute in the '40s, her English fragmentary, but improving.

Isaiah leans casually against a wall near Burnside, breath visible, still clad in the same dark shirt. We exchange nods. I gesture across the busy intersection.

"Want to walk up to 23rd street? My plan is postering along there and maybe 27th as well."

"Sure, let's do it."

We make our way west along Burnside for several blocks and turn right into a business district filled with clothing shops and boutiques. The telephone poles are covered with flyers advertising bands and local music shows. I remove a staple gun from my jacket pocket and pull out one poster showing the outline of a naked man tied to a giant dollar sign. Whip stripes trace across his back.

"Nice graphic!" Isaiah observes. He reads the text: 'Pro-Corporate Power, Pro-Militarism, Pro-Capitalism, Pro-U.S. Global Hegemony- The Republican and Democratic Parties.' Well, it's a little wordy for the size. Did you make this yourself?"

"Yeah, it's just cut and paste work. I did a whole series just in time for the presidential elections. So, what is this performance anyway?"

"Ok, here's what I have in mind. Usually on weekend nights the club kids put on drag shows upstairs. That's fine, but it's time us basement dwellers threw something a little more interesting. I talked the owner into letting me have fifteen minutes next Saturday. For the soundtrack we'll start out with a Coil song, one of the really slow creepy ones. As that begins, three Nazi SS soldiers enter. They drag me between them in a striped concentration camp inmate's uniform, big yellow Star of David patch and all that. They set me up before the stage and beat the hell out of me, I want that to look goddamn brutal. Then two march off and leave one behind. He can't help pitying me, all crumpled on the ground. The guard comes over and touches me to see if I'm still alive. Anyway, short version, the two of us make out and then perform a dance to the Tear Garden song 'In Search of my Rose,' you know that one, right?"

"Of course, a club classic–good choice." I staple another poster up. This one shows a screaming baby and declares: "The Democratic and Republican Duocracy– Break Their Grip on Power. Vote for a 3rd Party." Isaiah watches closely.

"That one is better. More minimal. Anyway, by the end, Nazi and Jew are entwined together, it'll be hot as fuck. Then the other soldiers come back and execute us both. We die in each other's arms under a fusillade of bullets. How do you like that?"

"Wow, pretty intense. I hope the crowd can handle it."

"True. They'd better! The owner wasn't an easy sell, but I told him I'm a fucking Jew and this is fucking art. After that he backed down."

"Count me in then. So, next Saturday, right?"

"Yeah, but we should get together soon for choreography. Are you free Wednesday afternoon?"

"I have classes until one, so any time after that. Oh, there's a political action at the Portland State campus later that day I want to check out, but there should be plenty of time."

"Excellent, let's meet at Klub Z around two-thirty."

We continue down 23rd and then double back, hitting poles on the opposite side. I am nearly out of posters by the time Burnside stretches before us again. Night has fallen and Isaiah's pale face glows under yellow streetlights. Our breath rushes in light billows of mist.

"Well, I should head back home. Do you live near here?" I ask.

Isaiah nods. "Yeah, I've got a squat close by. Thanks! This project will be super fun! I'll see you soon then."

His bony torso presses against me in a tight hug and we part ways.

Chapter 24

"Women who take malicious pleasure in making men suffer, sometimes go too far in the art of torture. When those whose hearts they have kept on the rack lose sight of them, they are remembered only by the torments they invented ; and when love goes, a kind of horror succeeds it."

Henri Rochefort. Mademoiselle Bismark. 1881.

The next evening our phone rings and Babette answers. She covers the receiver with a shaky hand.

"It's for you, someone whose name sounds like anachronism? Is that right?"

I laugh. "It's probably Annakiya. That girl from my class I told you about!"

"Oh, I must apologize," Babette turns back to the phone, "did I misunderstand? Is it Annakiya, not anachronism? ... I see ... of course ... beautiful name … West African? Ah! Yes ... Lovely. You know Wrahs from school then? ... Oh! Well, he is quite a dear ... No, I do not suspect homosexual really, not quite ... well ... nobody is perfect ... Ah, thank you, perhaps young Wrahs will invite you over sometime. Here, I give you him." She holds out the phone. I take it.

"Hey, Annakiya?"

"Ross? That was Babette right? She sounds like a riot, I'd love to meet her."

"I'm sure we could work that out sometime."

"So, do you have plans tonight?"

"Just homework."

"Let's meet up. We can talk about my poetry."

"Ok. Where?"

"How about the Red Sea, do you know it?"

"Reggae bar downtown, right? When have you in mind?"

"Oh, after I get off work around 9:30. You should come by the club where I'm working and we'll go together. It's the Porpoise. Up on Powell Boulevard in southeast, not far from you."

"Sure, is there a cover? I'm pretty broke."

"Not tonight ... shit, I'm up next on stage, gotta go, see you soon."

With a click she is gone.

Babette looks at me, bushy eyebrows raised. "That is your friend from writing class who dances, then?"

I nod. "She wants me to come by her work tonight. You'd like her, she's something like a character from the films you adore."

Babette smiles. "Be careful then. If this woman resembles those females whose wiles I appreciate, use caution indeed, though, tell me everything! But go, have fun while you still can. My heart is glad you take advantage of your youth."

I pat her hand. "You'll be the first to hear any scandalous details."

An hour later I step off my bus in southeast Portland and cross the street to a low building with purple neon signs. Light rain dimples puddles between cars in the half-full parking lot. Inside the entrance, a sallow pockmarked man checks my ID.

"That's three bucks, guy."

"Damn, I didn't think there was a cover. I'm just meeting my friend who dances here. Annakiya ... oh, she probably doesn't go by that, but she said ..."

The man rolls his eyes, then holds up three fingers. I hand over the bills. Dance music thumps, then lowers as a smooth-voiced DJ cuts in. Through the vestibule, about twenty men congregate, half circled before a small stage on one side. Christmas lights illuminate the DJ booth where a curly-haired man cuts short his patter on the microphone. I glimpse white skin and auburn hair as the last dancer flashes away behind a curtain. Cigarette smoke fills the room.

The bartender nods as I approach and pulls a pint of beer. Turning away from the stage, I remove Balzac's <u>Father Goriot</u> from my satchel and settle down on a high barstool. The music now rises again and my peripheral vision catches a pale blonde figure with arms raised. She reaches back, unhooking the straps of a red bra. I look down again at Babette's latest recommendation. There's just enough light to read, but then a shadow blots out the pages.

"Go ahead and look if you want. That's what she's there for."

I glance over. "Oh, hey Annakiya."

She stands beside me, luscious body wrapped inside a tight silvery dress. Instead of long braids, her hair is processed straight, the short bob slicked down with a severe part.

"I go by Indus here," she retorts sharply, "keep my real name quiet, ok?"

"Sure thing." I pause and chuckle. "S'pose I woulda guessed Kali instead."

"Oh, that's for weekends up at the Dancing Bare. It's a small town and I don't usually work the same clubs very long. I always switch up different names."

"Understood."

"Sorry, I'm going to be a little late. My last set is after Waterloo. Why are you hiding back here anyway? The action's up at the rack, you know!"

I frown. "Well, my finances are pretty low right now. I had enough for a couple drinks with you downtown but after one here plus the cover, I'll be lucky affording even one Pabst then."

Annakiya laughs. "Don't worry about later, I got you covered. But come over in a few minutes when I'm up."

She gestures where the topless blonde swings around a pole, legs bent out as she twirls.

"Waterloo, that's a great stripper name," I muse, "what an awesome theme. You could use Appomattox or Cannae, oh God, the best would be Passchendaele– fucking brutal ... but sexy as hell!"

Annakiya skewers me with a terse look. "You are an odd one." She stalks away.

I tip back a deep swallow of beer and resume reading. After one more song, Waterloo gathers her clothes, picks up bills scattered across the stage and withdraws.

The DJ switches into a more upbeat track, then fades it down.

"Gentlemen, haul out your wallets and hit the rack for Indus! Don't be cheap fellas, come on over!"

Beats pump up again and Annakiya enters the stage. She glances around, disapproval etched on her lovely face. She fixes me with a glare and leans near the DJ. He picks up his mic again.

"Guys, don't miss this next dancer. Indus needs your attention ... and your money! Come on up, especially you, sir, at the bar with a book. The public library's downtown but tonight you're at the Porpoise! Heeeeey ya!"

The men cheer and whistle. I sigh, mark my place in Balzac with a cocktail napkin and take a seat at the rack. Music rises while Annakiya walks in a casual circle around the pole. Her body sways with thick seduction that resonates to my core. I am not alone. "Yeah, BABY!" yells one fellow. Wallets crack open and bills line the wooden rail as she moves in sinuous grace across the stage. I take out my last three dollars and slap them down.

Annakiya pulls the shiny dress up over her head in one quick motion and stands before us, motionless. Only a pair of black panties stretch around curving hips, her tawny form a study of perfection. With the slow inevitability of a felled tree, she bends forward, leans out and downward until her soft cheek brushes against mine. Blood surges through my ears as honey penetrates every membrane. With serpent-like speed, she recoils into a new position on the hardwood, legs angled. I breathe again and my fists relax where fingernails have almost broken the skin.

After a two-song set, Annakiya rakes up bills that pile around her high heels and exits amidst hearty catcalls and applause. I return to my spot at the bar and attempt reading. Every nerve still twitches with a salty mixture of adrenaline and lust. Fifteen minutes later Annakiya appears beside me. Her head is wrapped in multicolored silk above a low-cut green dress.

"You ready?" I ask.

"Yeah, I need to drop off my clothes first." She gestures at a large suitcase, then beckons the bartender. "Hey, will you call us a cab?" He nods and smoothly pockets the wad of bills she thrusts at him. I follow her outside. We stand together in the parking lot. Chilly night breeze carries cigarette smoke from a nearby cluster of men who cast resentful stares in my direction. Annakiya unzips her luggage and removes a black jacket. She stretches into it and sighs.

"God, this has been the most ridiculous week. My boyfriend and I split up a few days ago. For now I'm staying in a motel. With all that drama there's no way to write poetry." She scans the street, lips curled.

I smile. "Maybe that's just the inspiration you need. Sometimes I feel my best writing came after breakups."

Annakiya shrugs. "I hope so. It's like my brain can't relax enough yet. I just get angry and need distraction … oh, here's our taxi!"

From the back seat of a Radio Cab, Annakiya provides directions for a dingy motel on east Burnside. After ten minutes, our driver turns into the parking lot. He swerves around broken bottles scattered on the pavement."

"Wait here a moment." Annakiya tells him. "We'll just drop my luggage off."

"Ok, lady," the driver responds, his eyes narrow with suspicion.

I open the door and move to take Annakiya's suitcase. She swats my hand away.

"No, I'm a strong Nigerian woman!"

We enter a small room completely filled with clothes, the same explosion witnessed at her previous apartment. In keeping with the theme, cash is strewn everywhere, from soiled carpet to unmade bed. Annakiya sets her luggage down and sifts through piles for a different pair of shoes. She straps new ones over delicately painted toenails and tosses the old aside.

It's nearly midnight by the time we are dropped off downtown at the Red Sea. Inside, reggae music crackles from large speakers through dense clouds of cigarette smoke. On a small corner stage, dreadlocked musicians dismantle equipment. Annakiya scans the room and immediately approaches a middle-aged black man in thick framed glasses alone at the bar.

"Hello there," she purrs, "would you like to buy me and my gay friend a drink?"

I shake the fellow's hand. He scarcely notices, eyes fixated on Annakiya's cleavage. With a flick of his wrist he beckons the bartender and orders two cocktails. Across the room a pair of young white women observe this interaction. They wrinkle their noses and huddle with two well-dressed black men in a side booth.

"Fucking bitches over there," Annakiya mutters as the drinks arrive. She takes a sip. "I know they'll start talkin' some shit." She pushes me toward the man with glasses. "Here, you guys hang out, I gotta deal with this."

I smile at the man but he ignores me and glances at his wristwatch with an exaggerated yawn. Dismissed, I look over where Annakiya has invited herself into the occupied booth. She cackles loudly at some comment. The women laugh too, but through stiff lips under icy stares. After a few minutes Annakiya saunters back and hails the bartender.

"Two more, thanks, these'll be on Andre's tab." She leans close. "Andre over there claims he's loaded but won't give me numbers. C'mon, anyone can play big shot with a credit card. His friend's the real deal, wallet stacked with cash and everything. More of an asshole though ...But hurry up, you're still on your first!"

I shake my head and raise the glass. "You are a real piece of work!"

Annakiya frowns. "I don't know what you mean. Anyway, keep an eye out for me. I'm going to keep moving." She gestures at a group of white men in athletic clothing around another table.

I throw up my hands. "Thanks for setting me up and all, but I'm not your bodyguard. I can't save you if you get into trouble here."

Annakiya smiles. "Don't worry. Everything will be fine."

The night flows on and drinks appear before me as if poured from an invisible spout. Intermittently, Annakiya flits by the bar with new intelligence about some man's financial situation. I'm fairly inebriated by the time she appears again, arms clasped around a tall black fellow in a dapper suit. He studies me indifferently through half-closed eyelids.

"Rossssssss," Annakiya announces, her voice hissing alcohol fumes, "I'm leaving with Jordan here. Ah, Sam ... Sam? No, Seth! Seth in the corner will drive you home."

I glance at a balding white man who sits by himself, expression forlorn, then back at Annakiya "Are you all good?"

She flashes a brilliant smile.

"I'm exquisite. Thanks for coming out. Talk to you soon. Good night!"

With a quick kiss on my cheek she is gone. I feel a shoulder tap. Seth's glum face hovers behind me.

"You ready

"Sure."

We exit and walk down the block to where a red Mustang is parked at the curb. He opens the passenger door courteously. I recline into supple leather and Seth starts the engine. It fires with a frustrated roar.

Where to, guy?"

"Head across the Ross Island Bridge, take a right on Milwaukie and my place is down Bybee, close by Reed College."

Seth pulls out with a jerk as he works the clutch but quickly brakes. The traffic light ahead is red. He sniffs. "I can't believe that girl. Look, I'm sorry, 'cos she's your friend, but what the hell! I tried to be nice, but all she cared about is how much money I make. What the hell!"

"Yeah, that's tough." I comment. The Mustang has a seat warmer switch and I flick it on.

Seth isn't finished. "I bought plenty of booze and somehow still end up driving her gay friend home. What am I doing wrong? No offense, bro," he offers.

"None taken."

"No really, I don't mind you gay people. Whatever you do in your personal life is fine. I can see why that girl hangs out with you. As a straight man, I know I couldn't be around her without a 24-hour hard-on." He half-laughs and wags his head.

Before long the Mustang halts on Tolman Street. I thank Seth and wobble inside. A light shines from the kitchen. Babette sits at the table, Maclean's magazine and glass of mineral water before her.

"Ah, my dear Wrahs. A late evening for you. I was just about to return upstairs. My sleep is so fitful these days. Are you alright?"

I nod, then grab onto the counter for support. "I'm fine, or will be as soon as my liver processes the forty or so drinks Annakiya hooked me up with. Luckily class tomorrow isn't until ten. It's been quite a night."

My professor shivers. "Surely you exaggerate. I am cold, but so desirous to hear about your time with that young lady."

"Well, ok, here goes, wow, you should have seen her operate." With no omissions, I describe Annakiya's manipulation of the men she encountered. Babette thrills with delight.

"I tell you," she enthuses, "this creature sounds like the ultimate woman in every extreme. Cunning and deceptive ... beautiful and cruel! Oh, be very careful with someone like this. I would love to meet her, but am almost afraid. Thank you so much for sharing these details. Oh, but I almost forgot. As you are aware, I adore train travel. Do you know the Coast Starlight?"

"No, what's that?"

"It is a luxury Amtrak route that runs down the West Coast. I discovered some time ago that frequent flyer miles from my air travel could be exchanged for deluxe accommodations as far south as Santa Barbara. Naomi seemed a good companion at the time, so I made reservations the 11th through 15th of December. She has now chosen a different path, so my question is, would you take her place during winter break?"

"Sounds wonderful."

"It will be a treat then." Babette replies. "The most modern sleeping car and all meals provided. I greatly look forward! Well, on such an auspicious note, I must depart for bed. Good night."

Chapter 25

"A man who's not interested in politics is not a man; be he ever so wise, he's still a bug that gnaws at its own guts..."

Max Aub. Field of Honour. 1943

"Hey, Christians! Da ya know why Jeezus got so much action? 'Caz he was hung like this!"

The tall drag queen in a long sequined dress leans back, arms outspread, and laughs. Outside Klub Z on Wednesday afternoon, dancehall kids cluster together amidst clouds of cigarettes smoke and gossip. The unit above is rented by a church. Several clean-cut young men file down the stairs amidst a barrage of raucous catcalls and whistles. I shoulder past the embarrassed youths and make my way inside.

It bustles with activity. Acne-stippled teenagers hammer together large set pieces while queens in various states of dress advise and assist one another, broad torsos compressed into sleek corsets. Voices filter through the din, some loud, others soft and feminine. Sawdust and heavy perfume fill the air.

I see Isaiah talking with a couple fellows toward the rear. One wears black leather and replies through multiple lip piercings, while the other is nattily attired in dark slacks and a suit jacket. They look over as I approach.

"Oh, hey Ross," Isaiah calls out. "This is Facer and John, your SS comrades."

I shake hands. Another figure appears at my elbow— medium build, olive skin and long black hair tumbling down his shoulders that frames delicate features.

"All right, you miserable Aryans," he declares. "I'm here to teach the master race how to dance."

"This is Buenaventura, he's helping us with choreography," Isaiah says, laughing. "There's a lot going on as you can see. Buena is part of the big horror program next weekend. They're acting out scenes from a bunch of different movies. You'll be Carrie, right?"

"Yeah, a bucket of blood dumped on me and everything," says Buenaventura, throwing up his hands in mock horror.

Isaiah continues. "But he's generously volunteered his skills to make our piece a real show stopper. So, we'll begin that in a minute. As far as costumes go, mine is almost done. You will all need black pants, black button-up shirts with lightning bolts on the collars, swastika armbands and guns. I already started the armbands, what can you guys manage? John, you said fake rifles were no problem."

John grimaces apologetically. "I could only find two."

Isaiah nods. "That's enough, no problem."

"Lightning bolt patches would be easy to sew," I offer, "and I'll even shave off my Chelsea bangs to look the part more."

"Excellent!" Isaiah beams. "So, let's block out the beginning sequence. John and Ross, you march on either side as we enter. Then, Facer, you smash my face with a rifle butt. I go down hard and you all kick me. Then drag my body in front of the stage. Afterward, John and Facer, you two stomp off. Ross– stay and guard."

The four of us rehearse this scenario several times, then Buenaventura signals stop.

"I think your scene is pretty solid so far. That beating looks killer, when you're all in costume the crowd will get chills. Let's move on to the central dance."

Buenaventura walks us through choreographed movements from beginning to end, then stands back, eyes observant.

"Come on, you've got to feel it!" he yells after our third time through. "This is total fucking subversive love here. Ross! When you grab that Jew for the first kiss, you need to make us feel passion. You're risking your life because he makes you hot, c'mon! Let's try it with music this time." He enters the DJ booth, a CD in hand.

As initial chords from "In Search of My Rose" begin, I bend down and grab Isaiah by the collar. His crumpled form lies stricken on the floor. My fist draws back, as if to smash him once more across the face. I hesitate, now conflicted. He reaches out and touches my hand. I recoil at first, then gently stroke his cheek. I raise him up, and we pull closer, bodies tentative, then break apart. The two of us circle, moving in rhythm until synthetic strings swell as we draw back together. My lips turn and meet Isaiah's. We hold tight until the final note fades.

"Beautiful!" shouts Buenaventura, "that's great!"

A round of applause spreads across the club. Everyone, from teenage queens to gutter punks have gathered. Isaiah and I take a bow.

"Ok, ok," Buenaventura cuts in, "we're on a schedule here. Let's keep at this. Now, from the top."

After another hour, the scene flows smoothly, and Isaiah calls it a wrap for the day. I locate my satchel under a pile of jackets by the stage and pull out several new propaganda flyers. As I flip through the sheets, a pair of scuffed Doc Martens boots step in front of me. I look up and see Buenaventura's curious face.

"What have you got there?"

"Oh, political posters I made. There's a Democratic Party fundraiser at Portland State this afternoon and local activists are crashing it. I'll pass these out in the crowd."

"Are you with some group?"

"I heard about it from Green Party folks. However, this project is just mine."

Buenaventura picks one up and reads aloud.

"Pro-War, Pro-Capitalist, Pro-US Global Hegemony. The Republicratic Party."

"Seriously, this presidential election is fucking bullshit!" says Isaiah, leanings over his shoulder. "How can people be so goddamn apathetic? Here, let me see these."

He grabs my stack of papers and takes them over to the partially-completed stage where a cluster of drag queens lounge.

"Girls," he announces, "check this out!"

"What's happening?" asks a thin queen leaning against stacked plywood. Stiff blonde waves cascade above her strapless red dress. "Is there some kind of protest going on?"

"Ross made these." Isaiah replies. "There's a political action going on at PSU."

The queen bats long eyelashes.

"What do you say, bitches? Portland State isn't far. Do you ladies want to go on a field trip? Here, give me some of those!"

Within minutes, I march amidst a small teenage militia along sidewalks through central downtown. My newly-minted comrades enthusiastically hand flyers out to startled bystanders or stick them under car windshield wipers. Boots clip along beside stiletto heels, allied in purpose under a cloudless sky. Distant drums beat with a dull throb.

Near the college, we pass increasing numbers of people, some preoccupied with schoolwork on benches, but others in groups that stare curiously toward the commotion. Finally our progress halts on the edge of a thick crowd filling the main campus block. It is decorated with large official banners for Oregon's Democratic Party.

VOTE AL GORE 2000
SUPPORT LOCAL DEMOCRATS
GORE/LIEBERMAN FOR A BETTER FUTURE

However, hanging out of windows and carried on poles are other signs made from cardboard and spray-paint.

U.S. OUT OF EVERYWHERE
END CORPORATE POLITICS
KILL THE MILITARY INDUSTRIAL DEATH MACHINE

I smile and hang back on the periphery. There are many Green party activists I recognize. Several energetically debate Democratic volunteers who sit, ashen faced, behind tables. There is a stage nearby where a rock band sets up instruments. Its members look surprised, then nervous as turmoil increases. A crescendo of noise erupts as about thirty people dressed in black round a corner into the main square. They march together with bandanas tied over stern faces, resolutely pounding large drums. One slender man with dark curly hair shouts through a megaphone covered in stickers. Feedback screeches.

"Don't give your money to Democrats! They're owned by

corporations just like Republicans!" A wave of cheers spreads through the mob.

Buenaventura stands beside me, face aglow.

"This is awesome!" he exclaims. "I'm so glad you got us out here!"

"What a turnout! I had no idea you club kids would be political at all."

"C'mon, we like to dance and put on shows, but that doesn't mean none of us give a shit about the world."

I grin. "Sorry I underestimated you. Oh, look, that guy onstage is talking."

A pale man with bleached hair has switched on his mic. "We're Everclear and we're going to play this afternoon raising money for Oregon's Democrats!"

A round of handclaps is quickly drowned out by boos and hisses. The man with the megaphone begins a rebuttal but I can't make out words. Buenaventura turns to me again.

"This is probably the worst audience they've ever had."

"Oh yeah? That guy yelling at them with a loudspeaker is Tre Arrow. He's one of the Green Party candidates this year."

The blonde man switches his mic back on. "Tre, if you make any noise through that thing during our set, I'll shove it up your ass!"

Buenaventura and I enter the crowd. Middle-aged men in suits argue with anarchist youths and gray-haired socialist organizers. Groups of kids wave giant puppets representing oil barons and war profiteers. Anti-capitalist signs overshadow the scene and Democrats quake before a horde of gutter punks and drag queens. Isaiah shoves past us, a few remaining flyers in his hands that he spreads across a long table set up for donations. The fragile young man behind it protests, his voice a high-pitched lisp.

"Bad faggot!" Isaiah thunders.

Further down the campus block, a bus pulls around and black armored police file out. They line up, riot batons at the ready. Many well prepared activists pull gas masks out of backpacks and satchels. Others simply wrap scarves around their heads. Buenaventura clutches my arm and pulls close.

"This is so exciting. Let me know the next time there's an

action. Also, we can talk more later, but after the performance with Isaiah, I have ideas for some other ones I'd like to cast you in."

I squeeze him back.

"Sounds like a good time."

Chapter 26

"It is a mere vulgar error that the blood is of any use in the system; the faster you draw it off the better."

Alain Rene Le Sage. Gil Blas. 1715.

On Friday morning, December 1st, the basement light switches on, and I sit up in bed with a start. Labored footsteps tread down the stairs, then well-worn slippers slap across smooth concrete. Through bleary vision my bedside clock reads 3:30AM. I've been asleep not even four hours. Knuckles rap urgently at the articulated streetcar door.

"Wrahs! Oh, Wrahs, are you awake?"

I rub crust from bloodshot eyes and groan. "Barely. What's going on?"

The door opens, and my professor staggers through on wobbly legs. She leans against the jamb, cheeks aflutter with light gasps. The sash around a maroon terrycloth bathrobe hangs loosely. Shaking hands gesture near her neck.

"Wrahs. I cannot … breathe … please … take me to the hospital."

Heart pounding, I fling warm covers away and grab a pair of cargo pants from the closest cardboard box behind Babette's enormous train table. After zipping up a black hoodie, I pull the straps on my tanker boots tight. No socks.

"Ok, let me help you up these stairs, take my arm. Here we go, one at a time...should we call an ambulance?"

"No...just drive." My professor leans heavily against me as I half lift her bulk upstairs and then outside to the Toyota. She wheezes loudly and rattles with shivers. There is barely enough light to see. Deep shadows flicker underneath the old gas lamp. Settling her in the passenger seat, I rush around and start the engine. It hiccups into life. Immediately the radio blares. I turn down Shostakovich and crank the heater on.

"Hold on, just a moment."

Darting inside, I find a replica Hudson Bay Company blanket folded across an ottoman in the living room. I hurry back and drape the heavy striped fabric around Babette. Misty breath fills the gap between us. She swivels her gaze my direction, eyes full of misery.

"St. Vincent's … do you know the way?"

I cock my head. "There are closer emergency rooms. That's almost in Beaverton!"

Her voice catches a fierce lungful of air. "No! Take me to the Catholics!"

"All right, all right!" I reverse onto Tolman Street and cruise through a stop sign, barely slowing down. At last the heater spurts warm air and my professor stirs.

"Wrahs … thank you so much … but there is one thing yet. My class this morning … I cannot tell the school … they would dismiss me. Will you teach it?"

My eyes open wide as I accelerate. "Babette! I can't lecture a college-level class. Which is it?"

Her throat rumbles. "Roles of women ... in the Middle Ages."

I slap the steering wheel with both hands and steal a look towards the passenger seat. "There's just no way I can fake that."

My professor's wan lips fracture into a faint smile. "Wrahs, Wrahs … then lecture about what you do know. My students are everything. I have complete faith you will succeed."

I sigh in surrender. "Sheesh, ok then, what time is your class?"

"10AM."

Twenty frantic minutes later I peel off Barnes Road and veer right at the "Emergency" sign in front of Providence St. Vincent. Babette fumbles with her seat belt but can't release the buckle. I climb out and run around to help. Her wide body supported against my shoulder, I stagger slowly through electronic doors. Just inside the vestibule, two crisp nurses hurry over with a wheelchair and help lower Babette down. She is ashen-faced, her wig askew under bright lights. One nurse moves behind, about to push my professor away, but Babette beckons. I lean close.

"I must go … Please know you mean the world to me. Come

visit this afternoon. Goodbye now."

Her frigid fingers squeeze my arm, but the pressure breaks as she is wheeled off. My own breath comes short and a chill runs through every nerve as they turn a corner and disappear. I glance up at a wall clock. Almost 4:30AM. My sockless toes curl inside boots that squeak against the slick floor as I return to the Toyota, its engine still running. An ambulance idles several car lengths behind. Numbly, I shift out of park and drive home.

It is early afternoon when I return. The hospital receptionist sighs wearily in response to my queries.

"No, sir, we do not have a Babette Ellsworth, Albert Ellsworth or Bobbie Ellsworth registered here."

"I'm sorry, this is a little complicated. Could you try Elizabeth Ellsworth?"

The woman types at her computer. "Ah, yes, there we are. Room 423."

I scribble this down on my hand with a permanent marker and head towards the elevator, stifling a yawn. Each limb hangs leaden with fatigue. I almost trip across an elderly woman who creaks behind her walker, hair thin and matted. Once the elevator chimes on my floor, I stride down hallways that seem almost desolate. At Room 423, I pull a thin curtain aside and peer around. My head jerks back in alarm, but I recover, yank the cloth back and burst through.

Blood. It pools on beige tiles, dots crumpled white bedclothes and the body of my professor, who lies diagonally on her back in bed. One bare foot press flat on the floor. She looks up through thick glasses underneath the grey wig, attached precariously to her head. Trembling hands clutch a blood-soaked towel between widespread legs. She spots my shocked face and drops the towel. A fresh wave of blood sluices down wobbling thighs and I run over, face drained.

"What happened? Can you talk? Are you all right?"

She moans and speaks, words blurred with anguish. I bend closer, straining to hear.

"I know I don't have much longer to live."

Both eyelids drift shut. In panic, I reach over to an emergency call button mounted on the wall and press it repeatedly. Nothing happens. My fist hammers, two, three, four times. Cursing, I run out into the hall. The distant figure of a nurse heads away with slow, measured paces.

"Help!" I shout. The woman looks at me and pauses. "Hey there, help! Please!" I repeat.

She turns in my direction. I retrace red smeared footprints and find Babette braced upright. Determination twists her broad face.

"No! No! No! Hold still. Lie down. You're going to be ok. Help is coming." At this, a hand flaked in clotted blood wraps around my forearm. The air hangs heavy and metallic.

"You have to get me out of here. I swear I can't stay a minute longer." Her voice rumbles low, lips close to my ear. "They put these things in me, I can't bear it. I tore them all out ... it is an absolute vision of hell."

I notice a small oozing wound on the inside of her left wrist and several clear plastic tubes trail along the floor. Voices sound nearby and three nurses bustle in. Two of them lower Babette back down, pressing a towel between her legs.

The third nurse pulls me aside. Her tone is brisk.

"Are you a relative?"

"Yes. Her grandson." I hope stress makes this sound convincing.

"We need to keep Dr. Ellsworth overnight. She can't leave like this. Look here what she's done to herself! A catheter tube must be deflated before it's removed from the urethra, but she ripped it out regardless. I don't want to sound callous, but your grandmother has been nothing but a terror for everyone. Please keep her under control."

"Like an animal," Babette croaks, "treated this way by you beasts!"

All three nurses turn and leave. I wet a fresh washcloth at the nearby sink and wipe crusted streaks from my professor's arms. Babette's expression softens, and she gazes at me soberly.

"You must take me out of here immediately. I know soon I can regain my strength. Enough at least for us to fly to Las Vegas. We will be married. You may keep living in my house and preserve the library and no one can stop you. All my books ..." Her voice drifts off.

She blinks behind thick glasses that magnify her lazy right eye hugely out of proportion. Its gaze wanders over my shoulder, as if plotting a next move. I press tense lips together and swallow. My two eyes meet her one, yet are still outnumbered.

"We shall be wed," she continues calmly, "and then so I never come back to a place like this, I will commit suicide. I have the pills. It will be quick."

"Babette!" I cry out. Stress and fatigue overwhelm me. Hot tears run down both cheeks.

My professor stares with mild concern as I sink into a chair, sobs ragged. The hospital spins around me, her room a blood spattered kaleidoscope. I choke down nausea, pull out a handkerchief and blow my nose.

Babette clears her throat. "Ahem. If I might suggest a first order of business, it would be obtaining a wheelchair. There are probably some out in the hallway."

I trumpet my nose again. "Sorry, this is a lot to handle right now. I've hardly slept, expected you to die at any moment this morning, taught my first college level class, and then ... this..." I gesture around the room. "Can I just wheel you out of here? Shouldn't you be discharged or something? Is really safe for you to leave?"

My professor waves a dismissive arm, then dabs at her crotch with the towel. "My bleeding has stopped. One valuable lesson I long ago discovered is not asking too many questions. Action. Just take action."

Outside the room I find a wheelchair and roll it back. Babette now sits up in bed. With a strong hoist from one side, I slide her onboard. She settles back and stretches.

"Thank you, Wrahs, I feel better already. Lying in this room like a cadaver on a slab was simply intolerable. Let us leave right now!"

I look down at her. "There's a plastic bag with your robe here, but let me drape one of these clean towels over you. With all that blood soaking your gown, I'm afraid it'll cause a scene on the way out."

"Ah, what excellent foresight, my appearance might raise

alarm."

With her condition thus disguised, I push my professor down the hallway to an elevator. We emerge in the busy lobby. Medical professionals scurry about and patients in various states sit or slowly push oxygen tanks. I thread Babette around these obstacles and through the front door with no questions asked. Outside, bright sunlight shining down on a clear, chilly afternoon makes me blink. Once she is transferred into the car, I roll her wheelchair back and leave it against a bike rack. As we drive off, my professor smiles with delight.

"You know, I simply feel wonderful. What an exquisite day! Have you eaten yet? I am famished!"

The Toyota throbs into high gear as I accelerate onto the freeway. "No, I didn't have time, preparing for your class and all. I came here right afterward. There's food at home. I'll make something there and then put you to bed."

"Bed! But I just escaped that dreadful fate! I have an idea, what about Wong's Garden on Woodstock? Where we first ate and talked so long ago ... let us stop there for lunch."

"Really? You've lost a lot of blood. I can't let you walk in looking like a massacre victim. They'll call the police, plus you're probably a major health code violation right now."

"Ah, true. But we still have my robe. I can cover myself and seem moderately respectable."

"Seriously, if you want Chinese, I'll order take-out once we're back."

Babette glares at me. "Wrahs! Take us there directly! *Vite, vite!*"

"Alright, calm down! You're the boss!"

Twenty minutes later I turn into Wong's parking lot and select a spot near the entrance. My professor braces against the door as she stands, face twisted with exertion. I furtively glance at passersby on the sidewalk and help pull her bathrobe over the soiled gown. Flaked blood still clings to Babette's wrinkled thighs, but the catheter wound seems staunched. I firmly tie the maroon sash and straighten her wig.

She raises quizzical eyebrows. "Am I presentable?"

"You'll be ok, just take this easy and lean on my arm. Ok,

watch your step, I'll hold the door for you, there, we're good!"

Inside, sesame oil from the kitchen fills my nostrils and a young waitress seats us. We slide on vinyl upholstery into a side window booth. The waitress swiftly returns to deposit a kettle and take our orders. Once she departs, I pour hot tea. Babette gulps hers down while I pause for mine to cool. She smacks her lips together and beams. The frail invalid who proposed marriage on her deathbed scarcely an hour before has dissipated like steam above my porcelain cup.

"So, Wrahs, how was class this morning?"

I laugh. "Oh, God. Well, given my lack of confident knowledge about women in the Middle Ages, I jumped ahead a few centuries and lectured on World War I, specifically Canada's role."

My professor chortles. "Did that go over well?"

"I think so. It's the subject I'd been reading lately and felt most confident talking about. You have a pretty good documentary in your collection too. I did as well as I could, then showed the video."

"You encountered no difficulties?"

"Not besides sleep deprivation. I explained you were ill and would probably be back on duty soon. Your students can really handle anything. They took the chronological leap forward in stride. Best of all, no one demanded my teaching credentials."

"Thank you so much, dear Wrahs. You have truly saved me this time."

"Well, next time, please provide more warning. This day just about killed me."

Babette shrugs. "You really are so melodramatic at times!" She takes another deep sip of tea.

When our waitress returns, she sets a bowl of soup before my professor and slides across orange chicken for me. With enthusiastic slurps from a large spoon, Babette dives in immediately. I break apart wooden chopsticks and sprinkle soy sauce over the rice mound on an adjacent plate. My boots squeak against the tile floor. I move them back and forth. It feels newly slick. I lift the tablecloth and gasp. Blood again. A thin stream courses down my professor's pale legs. It puddles on the floor.

"Babette," I whisper.

She takes another mouthful and wipes moist lips on her bathrobe sleeve.

"Yes?"

"You're bleeding again. It's everywhere. We need to get out of here now!"

"Oh!" She reaches down. The fingers come back dripping red.

I raise an arm and signal the waitress. She is slight, perhaps only a teenager, with short black hair and glasses.

"Could we get some paper napkins? There's a bit of a mess."

The girl nods, then looks more closely at my professor. Dark eyes widen. She brings up a hand to cover her mouth and pulls out a cellphone. Babette cries in alarm.

"Please, mademoiselle, this is no emergency! Just bring a few napkins to clean up and we can be on our way!"

The waitress retreats, lips curled with distress and nausea. After a moment she returns, stacked brown paper towels in her arms. I rise, bunch several together and hand them to my professor. The girl scowls at me before disappearing again. Babette looks up, face dismayed. I take in the bloody scene.

"Ok, hold these between your legs, keep the pressure up. Then stand so I can wipe underneath. I'll clean the seat and make a quick pass on the floor. We need to get moving before someone calls an ambulance and they haul you back. Also, get your wallet out, that poor girl deserves a serious tip."

Babette follows my instructions silently. We hurry out, half devoured remains of our meal abandoned. Back home, I rush her upstairs to the bedroom. There she stands, trembling as I remove the maroon bathrobe and thin hospital gown underneath. Naked, her exposed skin is veiny and gray. The bleeding has stopped, but red crust streaks down both legs.

"Do you want a shower?" I ask.

"No, I only need rest. Thank you for bringing me here."

"Ok, get some sleep then." I peel back the bed covers and tuck her in with a thick feather comforter on top.

My professor sighs. "This has been a tremendous day."

"No kidding."

Babette's eyelids droop and she reaches a hand caked with

dried blood from beneath the bedclothes. I grasp her rough fingers, sandpaper against my palm.

"Thank you so much, Wrahs. I don't know what I would do without you these days."

A fresh wave of tears flood down my cheeks.

Hours later, once evening has fallen, I drift into weary slumber. The night slips by, but despite deep fatigue, I wake with a start. Again, footsteps creak on the basement stairs. My clock reads a few minutes after 3:00AM. The steps continue, but now something is wrong. Babette would have turned on the light. These feet are unsure and ring out sharply in complete blackness. I freeze, ears alert.

With a creak of hinges, the streetcar door swings open. Hesitant shoes move across the threshold and pause. I hold my breath. Under the bed is a bowie knife. I slip my arm down, clutching the wooden handle. Tense fingers grip it tightly and prepare to unsheathe the blade. I hear an exhalation as something drops on the floor with a light thump. Elastic snaps and fabric whispers. A zipper clatters downward. Bare feet kick away shoes and approach my bed. There is a sudden rush of honey perfume. I release my knife and move back as someone naked, soft, and lushly fragrant slips beneath the covers.

"Annakiya?"

I press against her back, reach around and cup a warm breast in one hand. She arches her spine at the pressure. There is no mistaking that scent, or that height.

"Yeah, it's me. You're so hard to find down here. I couldn't locate a light switch. Thought I'd break my neck on those stairs."

"What are you doing here?"

"Oh, I had an awful night. Hardly made any money. Ended up in a car with two guys after my shift. I got a bad feeling, sometimes you can just tell. So, when we stopped at a red light, I jumped out and ran. They didn't follow. Abandoned a bag full of clothes to those assholes, they won't even appreciate the value. I walked down side streets for a while, just in case, then realized I'd wandered near your neighborhood. The porch light was on so I knocked. Babette must have been awake because she answered right away. Looked just like you described her. Anyway, she recognized me and said 'You must be Annakiya.' I asked for you and she replied you were asleep."

"I'm glad you're safe," I interrupt, "but you really can't come over here so late without warning ..."

Annakiya turns over and presses against my bare chest.

"Sorry," she breathes, "I won't make a habit of it."

I kiss her neck. "You're forgiven."

She pushes my head away.

"I'm not done telling you about tonight! So Babette invited me inside and said I could stay. Then she got a real sly look in her eye. 'Oh, Annakiya, you are so beautiful and I am so cold, please come share my bed tonight' she said.

"Damn!" I exclaim, "That's bold!"

"I told her of course, I'd spend the night with her, but after I used the toilet. She pointed out the bathroom. I waited inside until she gave up and went upstairs. Then I ran down here." Annakiya laughs.

My mouth moves close to her ear. "Babette's a lecherous old biddy, but I gotta hand it to her– what balls, even if she did have them cut off!"

"God, that's gross!"

"Not as gross as what happened earlier. I broke her out of the hospital. She was bleeding everywhere from yanking out a catheter tube. It tore the hell out of her vagina. With all the blood loss it's amazing she has energy to move, let alone attempt a seduction. She seemed near death, I thought she might expire right in front of me. Then she asked me to marry her ..."

"Wait – so, you're engaged?"

"No, I don't think so. I didn't accept."

"You told her no?"

"I couldn't say anything. What do you do when someone like her proposes marriage from a pool of blood? We've become so close ... the idea she might die was too much, I just burst into tears. She hasn't mentioned it again. I know I won't bring it up!"

We lie together in darkness. Annakiya shudders. I nuzzle fragrant skin. It tastes intoxicating under my lips. To hold her at last feels unreal, as if the moon was truly clenched in my teeth. I bite down gently on a soft earlobe. There is no response.

Annakiya's exquisite bosom rises and falls with slow even breaths. I sigh, and soon exhaustion overtakes me as well.

At 6:30 my alarm clock shrieks and I jolt awake. Annakiya's body is wrapped around me, legs and arms entangled with mine. I switch off the noise. It would be heaven to stay with her like this, but the restaurant where I've picked up a few hours dishwashing opens in an hour. Carefully, I extricate myself and get dressed. Annakiya remains curled under the blankets, her delicious form insensible. I tiptoe upstairs and check on Babette. My professor lies prostrate. Heavy snores rumble from pillows mounded around her head.

Shortly after noon I return home, fingers dry and cracked from soapy dishwater. The driveway is empty. Babette must have awoke and attended mass. Hopefully nothing more energetic. I open the front door. Annakiya stands before the dining room table, cell phone in hand.

"Oh!" she exclaims, "I just called a taxi. Should be here any minute."

"Right on. When did you get up?"

"A few hours ago. I came upstairs as Babette cooked breakfast. She didn't mention anything about last night. Just asked if I'd like some food. Well, I said yes, so she gave me a plate of eggs and toast, then sat in the chair across from me, her bathrobe open and fake pussy exposed, just staring at me. The eggs were runny. Oh, God, those runny, runny eggs!" She shivers at the memory and looks down at her phone. It tinkles.

"That's my cab, it must be out front." She opens the door and peers out. "Thanks for everything. We'll talk soon. Oh, I still can't get it out of my mind, those runny eggs!"

I close the door behind her. Clocks tick away their steady chorus. Dishes from yesterday are piled in the sink. My veteran hands make short work of these with sponge and soap. Afterward I am sitting with a copy of Maclean's when the front door opens and Babette bursts inside. She enters the kitchen, all smiles. I reflexively check exposed ankles below her skirt but see no blood.

"Oh, Wrahs," she begins, "today I attended late mass and heard the timeliest sermon of my life. Sexual temptation! Such an appropriate subject after encountering your friend last night. She was all you described and more, be quite careful with this one."

I nod in agreement.

"But still ..." my professor pauses and frowns, "her abilities are not yet fully realized. A woman with her potential could be so much more. Living in cheap motels, as you say, and her predations limited to men who frequent dance parlors, well, mere fox hunts. Annakiya is a caliber suitable for big game."

"She's only twenty-one," I observe.

Babette shrugs. "Her skills lack temper and are not aimed for long-term success. She is like a wild beast whose destructive powers rage in all directions without focus. I certainly hope you maintain enough distance from such a creature for your own safety."

"I'll do my best."

My professor's grin relaxes and she sits down.

"So, I am very excited about our upcoming train trip to Santa Barbara. Some time back on the rails will do me no end of good. Also, there is a very special concert in Yakima next weekend. Do you think we might drive up together Saturday afternoon and then return Sunday?"

"Certainly."

Babette beams. "Ah, I promise a performance you will not regret. In the meantime, perhaps today you could assist tidying my quarters? The amount of blood I lost appears rather significant."

I sigh. "Yeah, let's get that over with."

Upstairs, I find my professor's sheets stiff and crusted. Underneath soiled bedclothes, stains even penetrate the mattress. I swallow hard and flip it upside down. Sheets, blankets, pillowcases and Babette's bathrobe go down the laundry chute. Fortunately her carpet is scarlet already.

The bathroom is another matter. Dried blood spatters everything, from yellow tile floor to porcelain toilet. With a pail of bleach water at my side, I scrub every surface until no traces remain, from floor grout to bidet. As I finish wiping down the sink, stairs creak and Babette's broad reflection appears in the mirror.

"Thank you, Wrahs, I really don't know how I made such a mess."

I pour out my bucket and water gurgles down the bath tub

drain in a dark spiral.

"Seriously, let's not do this again."

Chapter 27

"... I belong to a third, distinct sex, which as yet has no name, higher or lower, more defective or Superior; I have the body and soul of a woman, the mind and power of a man, and I have too little of both to be able to pair with either."

Theophile Gautier. Mademoiselle de Maupin. 1836.

Late next Saturday morning, my professor and I drive east. It's a cold December day and few vehicles share the road. We reach Yakima by midafternoon and check into her customary Howard Johnson room. I set down our luggage and stretch. My professor looks outside where steam billows from the nearby hot tub.

"There is no better way to relax after long hours on the road than a soak," she proclaims. "Will you join me?"

I unzip the front pocket of my backpack and remove a pair of bathing trunks.

"Of course, I even brought proper attire this time."

Babette chuckles. "You and your petite bourgeois morality. The Presbyterian church must be so proud."

I laugh. "Ha! If anyone complained about you, they'd hear a story about French culture shock. When guys like me get naked in public, people just call the police. No thanks. A soak does sound wonderful though."

Babette strips down to red lacey panties and together we walk outside. Freezing central Washington wind swirls through the empty courtyard. I hurriedly remove the Jacuzzi cover and climb in. My professor follows. I recline on one side, filled with ecstasy as hot water circulates around us. Bubbles rumble with deep bass tones as they explode when my ears dip below the surface. Babette grimaces, her glasses an opaque mask from condensation.

"This machine could hardly melt ice cubes. Ah well, perhaps it will improve. At any rate, tonight we have a splendid program.

The featured musician is named Awadagin Pratt. A musical genius, he performs on piano as well as violin. This will be my first time seeing him in person, if what people say is true, this should be a tremendous event."

"But you've heard him before?"

"Oh, yes! They play him often on my radio station and his technique is tremendous! A true master. We are so lucky to have him perform here."

"Right on. You always know the good ones."

I raise a hand out of the water to wipe away perspiration. Dead skin hangs in a strip from my thumb. I peel it free. Another piece comes loose. As I remove it, my whole arm appears covered with flaking layers. Panic rushes through me.

"Babette!" I exclaim, "There's something wrong!"

"What do you mean?"

"My skin is coming off! See!"

"That looks awful, is it just your arm?"

"I don't know, oh, my other hand also. What the hell? ... Wait ..." I squint into the depths. "I think I see something down there."

I find a button for an underwater light, press it, and immediately recoil. The entire tub teems with strange particles. Some dance in slow motion around our legs, others float along the surface.

"Babette! There's something horrible in here with us, it looks like an armada of jellyfish or something!"

My professor glances over, her face aghast. "Oh no, Wrahs, I am so sorry. My vagina bled again this morning so I packed my panties with tissue paper to soak it up. They may be disintegrating." She reaches down and tugs at her underwear. A cloud of pinkish wisps billow forth, backlit under the glare.

My stomach somersaults. "Christ!" I stand upright into the cold air, but am instantly coated by a slick bloody film. I leap out of the tub and reach our room with frigid strides. Tissue covers me scalp to toes in a thin sheen of ersatz menstrual mucus. Gagging, I climb into the shower and crank it full blast. A tiny bar of hotel soap provides just enough lather to remove the slime. Head, neck, torso, everywhere– urgent hands scrub each centimeter of flesh. At last I lean against the smooth plastic wall and simply let hot water flow over my body. Babette wanted a chauffeur and household helper. This is not what I signed up for.

Several minutes later, I turn off the tap and step out onto cold tiles. The exhaust fan whirs loudly. Once dried, I wrap a towel around my waist and re-enter the hotel room. Babette sits on the nearest bed, her round face filled with concern.

"Wrahs, I really am sorry, how negligent of me."

I grit my teeth. "It's ok, I'm fine now. You should go wash also."

"All right. Afterward we shall have a delicious meal here. You will enjoy that, *oui*?"

"True, lunch was some time ago."

While she showers, I dress and then slowly turn the worn pages of Mademoiselle de Maupin, an old French novel by Theophile Gautier. The antique pages smell reassuring and my appetite gradually triumphs over nausea. Upon returning, Babette grins to see me thusly engaged. She flings aside her towel, sits down and stretches into thigh-high stockings.

"You know, Wrahs, my heart explodes with delight that you appreciate my library. Oh, Gautier especially! Everyone has forgotten these classics, even in France! Well, I do my best, but students ... they prefer the same old rubbish. It makes me long for death. However, when these stories live again in your hands, oh, such a joy!"

Once she dresses, we walk down to the dining room where a buffet awaits. There are only three tables occupied in the large room decorated with agricultural themed photographs. I select mashed potatoes, some dinner rolls, squint darkly at wilted greens in the salad bowl and finally accept several slices of chicken breast from a bored man who stands with carving knife in hand toward the end. We sit and Babette continues her exultation of Awadagin Pratt's musical career between bites of food. Through a wide window, dusk sets in, the low sun casting amber fractals on simulated wooden panels.

After a desert of ice cream, we make out way to the Capitol Theatre and take seats in my professor's accustomed spot, halfway down on the right. A full house chatters and well-groomed attendees flip program pages with the massed rustle of doves at roost. After a lengthy wait, the brocade curtains part, revealing a grand piano. The crowd is silent until Pratt enters from stage right. He wears a colorful vest with striped pants and thick dreadlocks hang heavily behind. Smiling cheeks beam above a bushy black beard. He sits down gently and waits, hands poised above the keys.

With a rush, the orchestra begins to play, but Pratt holds back – it almost seems he has forgotten, until BOOM! his fingers crash down in a thunderous cascade of notes. My skin tingles. He is electric, hair swaying with every measure. A tornado loosed across Central Washington could not equal this powerful display. I look over at Babette. She leans forward in her seat, eyes wide and mouth parted.

After ten minutes, the first piece ends and my professor leaps to her feet, applauding furiously. Others clap as well, but no one else rises. Babette stands alone, her bulky shape above me silhouetted against the ornate gilded ceiling. She curls a baleful lip in my direction, then turns, facing the audience behind us.

"Are you people dead?" she shouts. Her arms beckon upwards. Hundreds of heads turn.

I jump immediately beside her and as if on cue, our entire section rises. Within seconds, the whole audience joins in. If Pratt summoned tornadoes from his fingertips, it is returned with hurricane force as hundreds of hands collide again and again. The ovation continues until every finger smarts. It seems our applause will never end. When we sit once again, the concert continues. Babette trembles beside me, enraptured and eyes aglow. Almost two hours later the curtain drops for a last time.

"Oh, Wrahs, did I not promise you an unforgettable evening?" my professor asks, as we file towards the exit.

"Absolutely!"

She bobs her head. "I must congratulate Mr. Pratt in person."

We descend to a wide ornate chamber in the lower levels. Well-wishers pack tightly around a long table. There, Pratt sits before a forest of outreaching hands, face open and genial. Babette moves near a booth where CDs are arranged for sale. She purchases one and opens the plastic case eagerly.

"Perhaps he will sign this!" she gushes and pushes other massed admirers aside with urgent shoulders. Several well-heeled patrons scowl but she ignores them. I hang close behind as my professor penetrates the dense crowd and looms over Pratt.

"Oh, sir," she cries, "your performance tonight was beyond words. I cannot express myself, but please know it has been exquisite. Would you autograph this recording for me?"

Pratt beams up at her. "Thank you, how kind. What is your name?"

"Babette."

He removes the cover and scribbles on it with a permanent marker. My professor takes it back and presses the paper against her bosom.

"Thank you, Mr. Pratt. Nothing could surpass this experience. My very best regards."

Chapter 28

"Do you know last year, when I thought I was going to have a child, I'd decided to have it brought up a Catholic? I hadn't thought about religion before; I haven't since; but just at that time, when I was waiting for the birth, I thought "That's one thing I can give her. It doesn't seem to have done me much good, but my child shall have it."

Evelyn Waugh. Brideshead Revisited. 1945.

A week later back in Portland, we wake early and I help Babette pack for our winter vacation California trip. She fills her plaid luggage with everything five days traveling will require; sweaters, skirts, blouses and several wigs that she stores inside round Tupperware containers. We take a taxi down to the train station in Northwest Portland, an elegant structure whose tall central tower dominates the industrial district skyline. Despite thick clouds overhead, ample light flows through immense windows at one end and my boots echo against white marble. We exit to a covered platform where passenger cars line up behind a sleek locomotive. Babette grips my arm with excitement.

"A Talgo engine! Oh, these trains are Spanish and very good, the height of comfort, you will see. What a way to travel!"

Onboard, our sleeping quarters are indeed luxurious, with bunk bed, table, and a bathroom with shower stall. I stow our bags and gaze outside through glass flecked by chilly December drizzle. After a series of slight jolts, the train moves forward. We pick up speed and the platform rolls away as steel wheels vibrate under our feet. They shudder with a steady clickety-click. My professor smiles. Her eyes assume a faraway glint.

"You must understand, for me this is the most beautiful sound in the world. I can feel my French mother's arms around me again and tell she is happy at last. To be free and on our way somewhere new, it's a marvelous sensation."

I look at her closely. "She really was incredible, your mother Germaine."

Babette nods. "A true woman in every regard. It is she I compare your friend Annakiya against. Both possess the instincts of a snake, but my mother honed her powers and perfected them to their fullest. If Annakiya ever develops such skills ... well, we should all live in fear."

I chuckle. "That's probably true. Oh, look. Here's a printed schedule of activities. After lunch there's wine and cheese tasting in the lounge car. They probably don't have it moldy the way you prefer, but might still be fun."

Babette shrugs absently. Her gaze passes over industrial buildings and green patches that lurch by outside

After digesting our midday meal, we walk down to an elegant car with open glass ceilings that arch above comfortably upholstered seats. It is thinly filled with passengers who nibble small blocks of cheese on toothpicks and sip wine from long stemmed glasses. A red-haired man sits near the entry and dabs his fiery mustache with a napkin. He glowers at the smaller fellow across from him and pounds his fist stridently. "Absolutely not! Those are the only suitable subjects for conversation on a train, by God! Religion and politics! There's no escape, so you might as well get it out of the way!"

Babette chortles. "You are so correct, sir," she admonishes. The red-haired man grins widely.

We pick seats near the center and a waiter brings by selections of cheeses and wines. Babette reaches for both. I accept only the proffered glass.

My professor scowls. "To think I should spend my days with an infidel who refuses cheese, the finest fruits of God's creation. How low can one descend?"

I shrug. "It makes me ill. Sorry."

She devours a yellow chunk on her small sampler plate and washes it down with red wine. We must be well into southern Oregon by now. Outside, thick woods stretch to our left and flashes of rocky coast flicker between evergreens on the right. The train rattles along, to and fro, a baby's cradle rocking on iron tracks.

Behind us, the two men argue loudly. Babette opens her purse and removes a leather case. She unzips it, revealing a book.

"Did I show you my recent gift from the Canadian nuns?"

I shake my head. She smiles and holds the black volume out.

"The Rule of St. Benedict. This lays out Benedict's expectations for communal living, just the thing to inspire Brides of Christ like me. Look how they dedicated it on the Feast of St. Joseph! See what nice things the sisters wrote! 'I wish you many blessings in your chosen monastic life,' and here's another. 'Love + Blessings to you, Elizabeth as you climb to ever loftier summits!' Oh, these women are too much! Are you curious about my convent?"

I nod.

Babette settles back and bites down on another cheese wedge, this one pale with dark flecks. Crumbs speckle her purple sweater.

"It is quite impressive. Twelve foot high walls surround the grounds. Inside, we nuns live under a regimented system; strictly scheduled prayers, mealtimes, chores and so forth. Only Mother Superior leaves, purchasing what food cannot be grown in the garden or deal otherwise with the secular world."

"What about you?" I ask. "She permits a great deal of latitude, most of your time spent in Portland and everything."

My professor clears her throat and reaches for the wine again. "Ahem, Mother Superior and I have a special understanding in that regard. My status as a full- fledged nun is, shall we say ... pending."

I frown at this.

Babette continues. "Mother Superior, you see, is in some ways a rather similar creature to myself. We have formed a relationship as kindred spirits of sorts. Her past is quite unusual. A French-Canadian, she grew up very religious and always attended Catholic schools. From a young age, she excelled at swimming, to the point where Canada's Olympic team showed interest. Such opportunity filled her with absolute joy and she thanked God for his generous favor.

"Now, this occurred at a time during the 1960s when people became more aware of artificial means by which athletes might compete at higher levels. For the first time in her life, young

Mother Superior faced a thorough medical examination. She appeared perfectly normal under initial inspection, but eventually doctors asked for the date of her last period. 'What do you mean?' she asked. 'Your period,' they repeated, 'when did you last bleed?' Well, she understood nothing! Sexual education was not emphasized in religious schools and this poor girl passed through adolescence with no idea such a thing as menstruation existed!

"Surprised, the doctors subjected her to various tests and at last made a discovery. Mother Superior's chromosomes were not XX but XY, that of males. It is a rare genetic anomaly, but on occasions people may externally resemble one sex while internally the opposite is their biological reality. Despite breasts and a vagina, she possessed no uterus. The women's Olympic team would not accept her."

"What a shock that must have been," I interrupt.

Babette swallows another chunk of cheese. Our train jolts slightly around a curve. The noisy men behind us have resolved their disagreement and signal for more wine.

"Just imagine, for a promising athlete to have the chance of a lifetime snatched away because of something beyond all control and furthermore, that they never knew could possibly exist. Well, as you likely guessed, this girl became more religious in her sorrow and eventually entered the Order of St. Benedict. This trauma from early life became an ocean of resentment, and she rules our convent with bitter resolve."

"You should see her cruelty toward the younger sisters. One nun who prepared food in the kitchen angered her for some reason. So, Mother Superior came to supervise and brought me along as sport. She tasted a soup under preparation. 'Oh, no, this is terribly bland, it needs more salt.' The dutiful girl added some. 'What an awful concoction, it needs more!' Again the sister poured additional salt. This continued until her soup tasted nothing so much as the Dead Sea. Then at dinner, everyone complained at being served such an inedible briny repast. Mother Superior scolded the cook and sent her to bed early with no dinner. The rest of us did the best we could, but also ended our day hungry. Mother Superior seemed unconcerned by this discomfort– and no wonder, for she keeps a small refrigerator in her chambers!"

I finish the rest of my wine and rise, locating another glass, this time a white. I return and sit down across from Babette. Sweet fluid tips down my throat.

"This woman sounds like a complete tyrant." I comment. "It's no surprise you admire her."

Babette chuckles. "Yes, it's true, I do very much. So, our days are quite regimented. We wake at 5AM for lauds, those are morning prayers, take breakfast at 7 while Mother Superior reads from scripture, then go about daily tasks with several more breaks for additional prayer. During this time communication is quite restricted. We speak only to each other as necessary. The day ends after evening devotions and dinner, around 9. Now, physical contact is strictly forbidden, but with one exception. On our way to bed, each nun is permitted a brief embrace with the other sisters as they file out. It is very ritualized. We exchange a quick prayer, though I always make more of this, perhaps a subtle squeeze of their hand. So far no one has responded.

"Then, in our cells we have only a few minutes before the lights are turned out. It is against the rules to bring electronic devices, but I have a portable compact disc player and tiny earphones that are not easily seen, especially in a darkened chamber. You see, Mother Superior makes regular nocturnal inspections. These rooms have no doors and periodically she walks down the hallways, lamp in hand, to check and make sure all is well. We must sleep on our backs with both arms on top of the covers. This, of course, reduces temptation for fleshly pleasure, which strike most often at late hours.

"I am always a model of perfection in this regard when her passing light illuminates the chamber. But what Mother Superior cannot see are concealed earphones and the music machine under my pillow. I lie in darkness, but Mozart and Furtwaengler and our friend Awadagin Pratt join me while the other nuns slumber. Oh, such moments are indescribable joy!"

She takes a small sip of wine and smiles, still on her first glass. I look to my right where rocky crags meet water frothy with whitecaps. The ocean stretches forever and merges at last into grey clouds. Seagulls circle above crashing surf, beady eyes in search of their next meal. Far out, the low outline of a barge moves slowly behind its tug.

I shake my head. "You understand, this sounds like pure torture."

Babette smiles. "That it is. But for me, the most sublime depravity. I cannot expect you would understand. However..." she lowers her voice confidentially and bends closer, "I have a scheme. My plan is so ambitious I hardly dare speak it out loud– the seduction of Mother Superior!"

"Oh? Is that all?" I ask nonchalantly.

My professor's lips widen further. "Listen! Late one night I will rise, make sure all others are asleep, then walk carefully to the chapel. When Mother Superior makes her next bed check, she will notice my absence. Her first thought should be the lavatory. Next she might suspect the kitchen but on her way, observe the chapel door left wide open. There I will wait... kneeling: a passionate mass of spiritual energy in thrall before the altar. Perhaps she may call out, but my devout form shall remain still. Mother Superior must approach closely to see what is afoot and it is then I will make my move." She leans back, satisfied.

I scratch my forehead. "There are problems here. Mother Superior's potential willingness for romance aside, she knows your health is fragile. What if upon discovering you aren't in the bathroom, she panics and rousts the whole convent?"

Babette's smile sags. "This is true, my plan requires risks. I should have remembered there is no joy in life you cannot destroy, Wrahs."

We sit in silence, tracks clicking away and coastal scenery in motion. The argumentative pair behind us now speak with jovial tones as the wine smoothes frayed tempers. My professor brushes her mouth with a napkin, eyes downcast.

"Sorry to criticize your plans," I offer. "It's still probably worth an attempt."

Babette sighs. "What a day. I remain glad you came on this trip, Wrahs, despite your ability to ruin my dreams. But now I feel tired and must take a nap. Please wake me if I do not get up before dinner."

She stands and makes her way back toward our sleeper car

Chapter 29

"And yet I must own my wickedness. I was in love with the wench, though her morals were not strictly pure. She scandalized with so winning a malignity that one liked her the better for it."

Alain Rene Le Sage. Gil Blas. 1715.

It is a cold mid-January evening after our return to Portland when I encounter Salazar's roommate Zoya out dancing in the Klub Z basement. She spins on stiletto heels and dreadlocks fly with fury above a tight blue dress. When the music merges into another track I pull her aside.

"Hey, how's things at the House of Many Pleasures?"

She shrugs and leans close. "Fine, not much happening with Sallie back in L.A. for a while. He should return sometime late spring. We should talk later. Anyway, I can hardly hear you ... oh, Tones on Tail is coming up. I gotta do this one."

She regains the dance floor and glides across painted concrete. Her muscular arms sweep in wide powerful movements. Damp with perspiration, the dress clings to her compact form with every motion. I can't look away. A brush against my elbow breaks this trance. Buenaventura stands nearby, the whites of his eyes aglow under black lights.

"Hey you!" He gives me a hug. "So, check this out, I want to do my own show upstairs."

"Let's go someplace I can understand you."

We vacate the humid basement and step outside. Blasts of icy wind cut down the street with merciless effect. It penetrates my hoodie and dries every sweat droplet in an instant. Drag queens and teenage goths mingle around us, hand rollies or clove cigarettes clutched in frigid fingers.

"So, I was really inspired by your production with Isaiah," Buenaventura begins. "I have an idea for one we could do together.

So, imagine this with Portishead's song 'Glory Box' as the soundtrack. I'll be a woman married to an abusive man– that's you! He beats her but she's still in love with him. They dance together, and it turns into a rape scene. Afterwards he's full of remorse but she murders him. It'll be totally fierce."

"Sure," I agree, "That could be fun."

"Lovely!" Buenaventura beams. "So, do you want to come over and practice at my house this week? There's time. We're not scheduled until early February."

"How about Friday? I just have a morning class, not much otherwise."

Buenaventura nods. "Ok, I'll write down directions later. Let's go back inside, I'm freezing my ass off out here."

We file through the teenage pack with tobacco lips and glitter spangled cheeks. Soon subterranean warmth absorbs us once more and our limbs move to the harsh music until beats blur together in a synthetic hallucination.

The next afternoon I knock loudly on Babette's study door. French dialogue blasts from the TV.

"*Oui!*" she calls.

I penetrate a solid wall of tropical heat. The space heater runs full bore and my professor sits pensively, an afghan covering her knees.

"Quick, shut the door, you'll end my life with that horrible chill!"

I close it and sit down on a small couch between stacked Jules Verne novels. Quebec evening news chatters away. Babette stares at the screen with dissatisfaction and grimaces. She turns the volume down. "Look at this! British authorities have placed poor General Pinochet under house arrest! What an indignity!"

I snort in disbelief. "Poor General Pinochet? You know what his regime did to Chile!"

Babette frowns and her maroon bathrobe slips back, revealing one round breast. She scratches her belly with one hand. "Oh, poor Wrahs, it always surprises you thatI really am quite a conservative."

I look at my professor, half exposed, her wig pushed back at an awkward angle. My mouth tries to form a retort but instead I laugh.

"What is so funny?" Babette exclaims. The large crucifix around her neck wobbles as she turns toward me.

I can't control myself and nearly fall out of the couch in hysterics. The old Verne paperbacks tumble over.

"It's true ..." I reply at last. "No, it's absolutely true, and that's why it's hilarious."

Babette snorts with annoyance. "Please, be careful there! I sometimes think I will never understand young people."

I reach down and collect her scattered books. "Sorry. Oh, speaking of young people, it looks like I'll be doing another performance at the club where I dance downtown. It's with Buenaventura, the one who choreographed my first show there. Instead of a concentration camp love story, this one is about spousal abuse."

"What charming topics. You should invite this young fellow over for dinner sometime. He sounds quite delightful."

"Yeah," I agree. "You probably would like him. I'll ask if he'd enjoy that, maybe after our event."

I hear the kitchen telephone ring. It sounds strange, higher pitched than usual.

Babette sits up straight and pushes aside her afghan. "Oh, hurry Wrahs, that may be my cousin in France, I am eager to speak with her."

I enter the kitchen but pause. This ring is indeed different, shriller– almost distorted. I stare at the caller ID box. Instead of green numbers and French text, the LED screen now glows red and pulsates with every urgent tone. 999-999-9999 flashes across it again and again. My professor now stands behind me. I turn around.

"Babette, were you expecting a call from Satan?"

"What?" She looks closer at the machine. "Oh dear! Perhaps you should answer it."

"All right." I pick up the receiver. With a series of light clicks the line goes dead. I shrug and set it back. My professor purses her lips, inspects the caller ID, then suddenly cries out in alarm.

"*Mon dieu*! Look at this! It says UNKNOWN! There is no more French, that should be *INCONNUE* ... you know, we always suspected the devil to be an Englishman, what a catastrophe!"

"Don't worry, I can reset it. Hold on ... just a few selections ... English, Spanish or wait– now French. There, look, its back in your language of God again."

"Thank you, Wrahs. You can't imagine what terror I just suffered. The idea of that machine speaking a mongrel tongue at me every day."

The phone rings again, this time a normal tone. I pick it up.

"Hello?"

"Ross? It's Annakiya."

"Oh, hey."

"Are you free tonight?"

I glance over. "Babette, do we have Scrabble plans this evening? Annakiya wants to hang out."

My professor shakes her head. "No, you should go, please enjoy yourself."

"Looks like I'm not required here. What's happening?"

"Do you want to meet at the Galaxy? You know, that bar across Burnside from my motel?"

"Sure. When around do you think?"

"Well, it's seven-thirty now, how about we meet in an hour? I can send one of my boys over."

"Your boys?"

"You know, the stripper shuttle boys. They drive girls between clubs and other places. A person can make a decent living at that. There's one who never charges since he hopes I'll fuck him someday. I like sending him on errands."

"Well, all right then."

Annakiya laughs. "Look for him in forty minutes."

"Ok, see you soon."

Around the appointed time, our doorbell rings. Outside stands a slight man whose pale features glow under the porch light. Crooked teeth grit together in a scowl. He says nothing and jerks his head. I follow him to an older minivan parked out front, and we drive off. The vehicle reeks of stale cigarette smoke and a small tray overflows with butts, some well anointed with bright lipstick. Ten minutes later my silent driver pulls into the Galaxy's parking lot. Blue neon reflects off the stubby hood.

"Thanks," I offer.

He snorts in dismissal. I reach for my wallet to find a tip but he shakes his head.

The minivan roars off, fan belt screeching. I walk inside and scan the room. It's fairly large and semi-deserted. Patrons nurses beers in front of video poker machines or fondle scratch tickets around wood veneer tables. Annakiya sits at the bar between two older bearded men, both talking at once. She is uncharacteristically dressed down in workout gear, a half-consumed cocktail before her. She sees me and smiles. The men glare. Annakiya turns away from them to give me a hug.

"Let's grab a booth," she says.

I order a drink and join her in back.

"So, ever get any poetry written?" I ask.

"No, not really. There's so much going on these days, I can never concentrate. How do you manage writing?"

"It's not hard in Babette's basement. There's usually peace and quiet, plus her library is just around the corner if I need reference on just about any subject. Of course, I'm not composing poetry, research papers are what I love."

"God, that sounds so boring. How's Babette anyway?"

"She's back to normal as if nothing ever happened. Maybe it's all the mineral water she drinks. I'll bet her circulatory system runs on that instead of blood."

Annakiya smirks. "So, when's the wedding?"

"Oh my God, shut up! I'm pretty sure it was just Babette's crazy talking."

"Can I be a bridesmaid?"

"How about this, if I actually marry Babette, you can be a bridesmaid and jump naked out of the wedding cake, but remember, on our wedding night it'll be you she wants, not me."

Annakiya laughs and turns her head. Abruptly she sits up straight. "Oh, check out that guy. I spy a hottie!"

I crane my neck. "Where?"

"Don't be so obvious! In the corner booth."

I look again. "That fellow in back with his girlfriend?"

"Come on, do you really think they're together?"

My eyebrows lift. "They're holding hands."

"He's too cute to be with her. I'm much better looking."

I shrug and take a sip of my drink.

The girl, a slightly plump brunette with braids, stands up and walks past our booth. She heads towards the restroom. Annakiya quickly stands.

"Watch out for that bitch and cover me."

"Annakiya!" I hiss, "I'm not your goddamn security guard ... this isn't war – fuck!"

It's too late, Annakiya is already out of earshot. She approaches the man and sits down. Their heads bend close. I take a deep swallow of my sour cocktail and sigh, swirling ice cubes with a thin black straw. Before a minute passes Annakiya saunters back, her expression thoughtful.

"So, how'd it go?" I ask.

She purses her mouth. "Not such a winner close up. Pockmarks, bad teeth. He gave me a number pretty quick. That is his girlfriend but he's willing to trade up. This could be fun."

"What could be fun?"

"Oh ... almost anything really."

After a moment, the brunette returns. As she nears us, Annakiya snakes out an arm to grab her elbow.

"Excuse me," she begins, voice hesitant. "I'm so embarrassed. But is that your boyfriend? He came over and hit on me just now, it didn't seem right. Is this his number?"

Annakiya hands over a torn piece of notebook paper. The girl takes it and stares. Every drop of blood in her round cheeks drains away. She tries to speak but only stutters, face slack.

"I'm so sorry." Annakiya commiserates. "Men are just pigs."

I kick her shoe under the table.

The girl's eyes water and jaw muscles tighten. With a dull crackle, the paper crumples up in her fist. She makes a beeline for her boyfriend and fling the wad at him. It bounces off his chest.

"You fucking bastard!" she screams, face awash with tears.

The man mumbles in retort, palms upturned helplessly. Set with fury, the brunette grabs her boyfriend and leads him outside, abandoning mugs of beer and a half-full pitcher. From the parking lot an engine roars into life like a guttural curse, then quickly fades. Annakiya still watches the door, her calm smile brilliant.

"That was a shitty thing to do!" I exclaim.

"What do you mean? That girl owes me a favor!"

"Maybe, but if her man was hotter you'd have taken him away, at least long enough to prove you could without even dressing up."

Annakiya nods. "Yeah, it's true. But still, I did a public service. You can't say that's nothing. Plus ..." her eyes fix mine with a knowing glint, "you enjoyed it too. Don't act all high and mighty."

"I suppose I wouldn't spend time with you if I wasn't at least somewhat a cruelty voyeur. Still, damn ... that poor girl."

A hum reverberates from Annakiya's purse, and she glances inside.

"Just a second, Ross, I gotta take this." She speaks quickly into her cell, eyes darting with mischief. After a moment the phone snaps closed.

"So," Annakiya leans toward me, "that was a guy who visited work yesterday. He asked how much money for sex and I said $700. Hell, my phone number cost him fifty. Anyway, it's a deal. He'll be at my motel in twenty minutes."

"Damn," I choke, "well, have fun with Mr. Big Spender. Catch you later then."

"Oh no," Annakiya contradicts, "It's not like that. Once he's here I'll tell him he can't fuck me, but for four-hundred I'll strip and let him jerk off."

I shrug. "Well, like I said, have fun with that. Thanks for getting me out of the house a bit this evening."

Her brow contorts with indignation. "You'd just abandon me?"

I nod vigorously. "What do you want? I said before I wasn't your security guard. This guy will be royally pissed you're running a cock tease scam."

Annakiya pouts out her lower lip. "You'll feel sorry if you read about me in the papers tomorrow, raped and murdered with my body all chopped up."

I sigh. "That's not likely. What could you even want me to do?"

She drums long fingernails against the table. "How about

this. You hide in the shower stall. If there's trouble, burst out and help."

"No!" I exclaim. "That's a terrible idea!"

"We'll have a code arranged. You can eavesdrop and tell if things are ok."

"For real, no."

"C'mon, I'll even give you a cut. How about sixty bucks? That's fair– you're not even the one who gets naked."

"Oh my fucking God, Annakiya, clothes won't help since I'll get shot first."

She shakes her head. "I doubt he carries a gun."

"Yeah, well, you don't know for sure."

"Ross, you're such a worrier! This will be great. We'll have fun, make some money and you can feel good not letting me get killed!"

"Seriously, I don't know why I'm even considering this..." I look at my pocket watch, then crunch a melting ice cube. "Oh, all right, what the hell."

Annakiya grins. "Let's scramble."

We exit the bar and jaywalk across Burnside to her motel. A home bum shivers against the wall and we ignore his request for change. Inside her room I survey the usual mess. Clothes, money, fast food wrappers, soda cans, cosmetic tubes and jars.

"First of all, that cash has got to go," I announce. "Plus we should straighten everything. You want the impression a seven-hundred dollar hooker lives here."

Annakiya stuffs clothes under the bed while I grab bills with both fists. This cash I shove behind spirituality books and poetry collections on a shelf. Crusty liquid eyeliner bottles, tortilla chip bags and torn magazine pages fly into the garbage can. Once that fills, I cram more trash inside a plastic grocery sack and tie it shut. Annakiya organizes scattered VHS tapes under the wall-mounted television and picks broken glass shards from a smashed wine glass out of stained carpeting.

"This lighting won't do," I muse. Two floor lamps glare through torn shades that cast blotchy patterns on the wall.

"Yeah," Annakiya agrees, "let's improvise."

She stretches a leopard print top over one and steps back.

Half the room softens into an amber glow.

"Nice," I observe, "we just need something for the other one. What about this?" I hold up a pink hoodie.

"Maybe ... no, too thick. Oh, my peach blouse might work, it's a bit sheer, heeeeeey, look at that. And the cherry on top of the cake? I've got a stick of incense."

She lights this in a ceramic holder and places it on the bookshelf. Aromatic smoke corkscrews upward.

"This is sexy as hell!" Annakiya proclaims. She glances in a small wall mirror. "Fuck, but I'm not."

With a fluid motion she tears off the t-shirt and hops out of her sweatpants, nothing underneath. Low light plays over every curve, from her luscious breasts to perfect buttocks. Anxiety in my brain disappears as lust expands, filling every lobe. I breathe deep and slowly exhale. This is no time for distraction. A blue towel hangs nearby and I cover the wine stain with it. Turning back, my loins jolt uncontrollably. Annakiya rummages under her bed, thighs spread and smooth bottom arched. After a moment she withdraws, black bra and leopard print panties in hand.

"These don't match," she remarks, "but no one will complain about that."

Annakiya slips on the underwear, fastens her bra and zips up a crumpled red dress. Oriental dragon motifs writhe across it in gold thread.

"Ok, now my makeup needs a retouch and we're set. Come on, see where your security station is."

We enter the small bathroom and Annakiya refines her face with eyebrow pencil, mascara and lipstick.

"Your shower curtain isn't much coverage," I point out, "what if this guy wants to take a leak? He'll see me for sure."

"Still such a worrier. Just stay back in the corner."

"So, what's our code phrase? Would 'help, I'm about to get stabbed' be good?"

"Always so dramatic, Ross, you really spend too much time around drag queens."

"Well, this is the first time I feared for my life with you."

"How about this– at first sign of trouble I'll use the word 'chartreuse.' Just a heads up something is amiss. Then if I need you to barge in and kick ass, I'll call on Tara to protect me. That's the creator goddess of protection."

I nod. "Got it."

As she speaks, low rumbles thump outside and bass notes rattle every window. I duck my head around the doorframe. Widely-spaced headlamps from a large vehicle glare through thin curtains.

He's here!" Annakiya hisses. "Get back, I'll leave the door ajar."

I retreat and switch the lights out. My boots squeak as I step into the plastic bathtub and freeze amidst almost total darkness. The incense smell fades, replaced by a mixture of grout mold and mouthwash. I tense up, every nerve twitching. From outside, the car stereo pounds, then falls silent. A metal door slams. Good, just one. *But what if friends wait in his backseat?*

A sharp knock rings out and the motel door creaks open. I hear muffled greetings. A man is talking, deep voice gruff. The words aren't distinct. Then he shouts "Fuck!" and something thumps.

"Chill out, will ya!" Annakiya cries loudly. She continues, but the rest I can't make out. Was that "end the ruse?" "Good news?" "Chartreuse?" Either way, I'm on alert. Blood tingles through every vein and adrenaline pulses, head to fingertips.

How much time has passed? Five minutes? Fifteen? The grout molt is suffocating. I detect nothing— then Puff Daddy blasts on Annakiya's boom box. I strain anguished ears and suddenly recognize call letters from a local R&B radio station. Now a TLC track starts. Fingernails dig into my palms. I'll never hear anything until it's too late. Each second scrapes by until, mid-song, the music cuts. There is a murmur of talk, then the door slams.

I slowly step out onto warped linoleum. The car engine starts outside and tires screech as it roars away. Annakiya stands in the main room beside her discarded dress, bra in one hand. She holds a large fan of bills across her bosom. Amused eyelashes flutter at me with triumph. "Check this!" she calls and hurls the money upward. Bills cascades down in a whirlwind. "Guy wasn't happy at first, but he settled. I didn't even have a chance to strip down all the way. He shot his load in a hurry and wanted to get the hell out."

"Did you sound the chartreuse alarm? I couldn't hear shit."

Annakiya nods. "He got pissed at first and kicked a chair. I said something about my dress being chartreuse. It's not, of course, but that fool didn't know. Got him calmed down pretty quick after that. Here, take a cut for all your hard work!" She kneels down and scoops three twenties off the floor.

I take the cash and fold it away. Both hands still slightly shake. I run them across the stubble of my shaved head. "So, just a typical night for you, then?"

"...280, 300, 320, 340, ok..." Annakiya looks up from counting. "You should relax, Ross! Everything worked out fine ... great even. This girl's gotta pay bills somehow."

Chapter 30

"So, when a man is pierced by the shafts of Venus, whether they are launched by a lad with womanish limbs or a woman radiating love from her whole body, he strives toward the source of the wound and craves to be united with it and to transmit something of his own substance from body to body."

Titus Lucretius Carus. <u>On the Nature of the Universe.</u> circa 54 BCE.

"Hey, Nazi-tranny wrangler! Over here!"

It is a clear sunny day in mid-February and Buenaventura hails me outside the downtown public library. His breath floats in the air but a slight trace of perspiration still lingers on his brow from ballet practice. We embrace and he grips my arm as we walk toward a #19 bus stop, our boots in sync down the sidewalk.

"I'm so excited to meet Babette!" he chirps. "After everything I've heard ... do you think she'll like me?"

I laugh. "Not if you call her a Nazi-tranny!"

A half hour later we arrive at Tolman Street. Inside, the odor of onion nearly overpowers us. I try to lead Buenaventura further, but he tarries behind, wide eyes absorbing the clocks, antique furniture and rusty rifle.

I take his hand. "Come on, let me introduce you." In the kitchen, my professor bustles about, _Larouse Gastronomique_ propped open amidst garlic cloves, onion peelings and an entire defrosted duck. She looks up as we enter.

"Babette, this is Burneventura."

"_¿Usted es vegetariano?_" she asks.

Buenaventura shakes his head. "No."

"Well, one can't assume. Ah, but I will reluctantly persevere in English for the sake of poor monolingual Wrahs here."

I shrug. "Sorry for the grave language deficiency. Can we

help?"

"Absolutely!" Babette sets Buenaventura to work chopping celery while I peel potatoes. Once boiled, my professor bids me slice and fry them in oil with parsley. She splits the duck into quarters and sets each simmering on the stovetop with generous quantities of tomato sauce, celery and onion. As they bubble away, she leans against the counter and fixes Buenaventura with curious eyes.

"So, Wrahs here told me you have family in Mexico."

Buenaventura nods. "Yeah, I was born here but my family comes from the central region. We visit every couple years."

Babette smiles with delight. "Oh, I adore Mexico. In the past I led tours everywhere from Baja California to Mexico City and Oaxaca. Well, the history is so fascinating. Americans know none of it! An entire country just hours away that might be another planet for all people care. Such a shame. But look how this relationship with Europe began!"

The oven emits spurts of steam as my professor launches into a lecture on Hernando Cortes and his conquest of the Aztec Empire. Tomato sauce spatters her apron when she gestures enthusiastically with a wooden spoon. Buenaventura engages her, full of questions. I watch silently and set the kitchen table with fine china, enjoying their congeniality. At last each dish is ready, and we sit down together.

"Fantastic!" exclaims Buenaventura. "Everything smells and looks delicious! Thank you, Babette and Ross, for inviting me over."

My professor waves a generous hand. "It is nothing. I quite enjoy your company. Consider yourself a welcome guest anytime. But no more delay, let us eat!"

Her prompt is unnecessary. We tear into the duck, pausing for bites of red rice and stewed vegetables. Before long our bellies are completely stuffed. I pop the cork on a bottle of Samos dessert wine and fill glasses. Babette turns up her palm in refusal, but Buenaventura accepts a blue tinted goblet.

"Would you like to see some pictures from our last show?" he asks my professor. "I just got prints today."

"Why certainly," Babette replies. She dabs her lips with a red serviette.

Buenaventura reaches into his backpack and pulls out a packet of photographs.

"Ok, these first ones are from a noise music performance Ross helped out with. You can see one guy on guitar, another behind a synthesizer and that's him with hammers and scrap metal."

My professor squints. "Wrahs, what on earth are you wearing?"

I laugh. "Orange coveralls and a gas mask. Very fashion forward, don't you think?"

Babette rolls her eyes and crosses herself with exaggerated motions.

Buenaventura flips through more shots. "Here they started losing the crowd," he note, "so Ross threw a metal toaster in front of the audience and attacked it. Here's a good one of him punching the thing. Didn't it just tear up your knuckles?"

"They are still bruised." I admit.

"How avant-garde," Babette comments dryly.

Buenaventura moves along to several from our dance piece. "So, you can see the way I set up our relationship. Ross, as my husband, is completely unappreciative, even though I try pleasing him!"

Babette grins at this. "Very typical among males in general, and of course Wrahs in particular."

"Hey now!" I interrupt. The others laugh.

"Ok, ok," Buenaventura continues, "then he hurls me down onstage and rapes me. It was super brutal, really got a strong reaction."

My professor snatches the picture. In it, Buenaventura lies helplessly on his back, blue velvet dress pulled up. I straddle him, teeth bared in a snarl.

"Oh!" Babette exclaims. "Your true nature revealed! What an image! Thank you very much for sharing these with me. I must retire now; company taxes me terribly. Buenaventura, you are such a dear. As I said, please feel welcome anytime. I wish you both a pleasant evening."

She stands and leaves, steps slow and hesitant to the stairs.

Soon Mendelssohn throbs from above.

Buenaventura smiles across the table at me and sips his wine. "Wow, you didn't exaggerate. Babette is a trip! Just like you described and then some."

I rub my jaw and stretch. "Yeah, she's pretty great, not to mention a total handful. Liked you though."

"Oh, you think so? Awesome! This was so fun! Well, can I help clean up?"

"Sure, thanks."

We carry engraved plates, ornate bowls, a gold-rimmed serving platter and crystal glasses to the sink. I wash while Buenaventura dries. The hum of Babette's orchestra upstairs accompanies our work. Next he wipes down each counter with a sponge and I take out the recycling. Back inside, I drain my wine glass, then fill it again. The bottle is still half full.

"Well, Buena, do you want a tour of the library?"

"Absolutely!"

I lead the way downstairs, Samos in hand, and show Buenaventura my professor's literature shrine. He trails his fingers across antique bindings that contain late eighteenth-century translations of Latin classics, old French picaresque novels and at last the World War II section where Hitler's *Mein Kampf* sits surrounded by related biographies and texts. His eyes narrow.

"So it's true then."

"What is?"

"What people say..."

"Oh? What do people say?"

"Like I was joking about earlier, that you live with an old Nazi tranny. Everyone suspects you're her boy toy."

I chuckle. "Hardly. She's a menace to the ladies but not me."

"But, is she a Nazi?"

"Well, are you in a hurry to leave?"

Buenaventura shakes his head.

I turn up the gas fireplace and move piled copies of *Le Figaro*, a conservative French political magazines from the orange couch.

"Well, sit down then, I'll tell you what I know. Here, have some more wine."

He leans back and takes a drink as I begin. More than two hours later Buenaventura still sits beside me. His eyes are wide and reflect the warm glow from flames hissing over iron logs.

"It's unbelievable! You're so fortunate to be part of this."

"Yeah, it's been ... an experience."

"You didn't really answer my original question though."

"Oh, is she a Nazi? Well, technically no. She was too young during the war and not being German that wasn't possible. However, I suspect she would have joined, given a chance. It's hard explaining but I'll try. Are you familiar with Hans-Jürgen Massaquoi at all?"

Buenaventura shakes his head.

"He's an African-American writer who grew up in Germany during the same time period as Babette. Massaquoi experienced discrimination, but in many ways less than if he'd lived in Alabama. However, National Socialist race laws kept him out of the Hitler Youth and military service. He was just as patriotic as any other German so it's not surprising Massaquoi wanted to join both. The thing is, he admired Hitler and Nazism because he lived insulated from their most negative aspects. In parts of Germany where significant black minorities existed, they were killed, but Massaquoi never heard about that until many years later.

"Babette is a similar creature. When she was young, Stalin wiped out Ukrainians by the millions in the Soviet Union. Her family lived just across the Spanish border where accounts of Communist atrocities during the civil war were fresh. Then, because southern France was unoccupied much of the war, things went well for the Bonnefonts until Germany started losing. It seemed as if Hitler was the savior of western civilization.

"Then you have the fact she's a historian. Once you discover what horrible things people have done to each other over millennia, it's hard viewing any one group as the embodiment of evil. If people fixated on atrocities Great Britain carried out in South Asia for instance, the Union Jack would be as reviled as a swastika. We just live in a racist society that counts brown people and their lives as less valuable currency than Europeans. Babette selectively views Hitler as great, just like the English selectively revere Queen Victoria."

Buenaventura sets down his empty glass. "This has been overwhelming."

I divide scant remaining splashes of sweet wine between us. "Sorry, I didn't mean for this evening to become only history lectures."

"Oh no, that's fine. So, you live down here also, is that right?"

"True. My quarters are in the pantry. I'll show you."

Buenaventura follows me through the folding glass door into my chamber and looks around curiously.

"Wow, look at all those canned goods! Oh my God, another whole shelf ... you really are prepared down here."

I throw my arms wide. "You should have seen it before the purge."

"This train table is awesome. Does it work?"

"Probably. It looks like all the equipment is set up. I don't mess with Babette's trains. You can tell she spent a ton of time on the papier-mâché mountain and everything."

"This is just incredible. It must be like living in a museum. I mean, you don't have a ton of room down here, but it's cozy. How long have you stayed here anyway?"

I think for a moment. "About a year and a half by now."

Buenaventura glances at my alarm clock. It reads 10:40. "I should probably leave soon. The busses don't run very late out in southeast where I live."

"Stay if you like."

"That would be nice, thanks."

"You can sleep in my room, or the library couch folds out too."

"I don't mind it here."

Buenaventura sits down on my bed and slips off Doc Martens boots. I walk upstairs to brush my teeth. By the time I return, he is snuggled under warm blankets. Long black hair covers the pillow and his clothes are neatly folded on the floor. I undress, switch out the lights and climb in beside him. We lie silent for a moment, then move closer. Buenaventura takes my right hand and clasps it to his bare chest. A rough odor fills my lungs. He turns around and warm breath caresses me. Tender lips crush against mine and his back flexes as we cling together.

Chapter 31

"... in a word, after having first been a woman, she then, after wavering, after toying with androgyny, seemed to make up her mind, to define herself, to become a man completely."

J.K. Huysmans. Against Nature. 1884

Babette sits in the study, a thin smile on her lips. She holds printed e-mails in shaky hands. I lean against the doorframe. Outside, shafts of afternoon sunlight break through late March clouds. Dark-feathered crows dip thirsty beaks into the full birdbath and water from recent rain sparkles on grape vine leaves. My professor emits a short laugh and looks up.

"Ha! Well...well...well. Now Wrahs, did you read this?"

"Yeah. It looks as though Mother Superior is concerned about who controls the convent. I'm a little confused. Wouldn't that be Pope John Paul II?"

She grins. "Of course, but things are always a little more complicated. You see, I have made a strategic investment and will become half owner of the property when it clears."

"Is this part of your grand seduction plot?"

Her smile deepens. "We shall see. Right now I have an immediate request. Please come upstairs and assist with a reply on that infernal machine."

I sit at the computer and Babette peers over my shoulder. She recites.

Dear Mother Superior,

Please do not fret regarding legal ownership of your property. While it shall become a joint venture between the two of us, the demise of any one party will absolutely revert full share to the survivor. As you know, my health is quite fragile these days and only God knows how many more years remain me on this mortal coil. Please view our financial arrangement as a gift to Our Lord through you and every good work the convent performs in His spirit. I shall visit very soon. Please give my best wishes to the other sisters.

In the devoted path of Christ,

Sister Elizabeth

I type out the final sentences. "Ok, does that look correct?"

My professor squints at the screen. "Yes, excellent. Do you find my religious language excessive?"

"Seems kinda over the top, but considering your audience it's probably fine." I click send. "Consider it sealed and delivered."

Babette shakes her head. "God, what a world we live in. Oh, I should also let you know Naomi Fields will move back soon, probably next weekend."

"Really? I'm surprised. Your last several fights were pretty epic!"

"Oh, we have our squabbles, but I really enjoy that girl's company. We apologized and want our relationship renewed with more understanding. I know I can be a trial at times."

"Hardly a trial– you're more like an international tribunal."

"Wrahs! You beast! I earlier possessed half a mind to take you out for lunch at the golf course ... now I have quite lost my appetite!"

"That's fine. I'm sure there's some cheese moldering away in the kitchen for when it returns."

"Well, that is unfortunately not the case. I must replenish my cheese supply and so will overlook this harsh criticism. Perhaps you might drive me to the store. Then we can eat out afterward."

I grin. "Sounds like a plan. I'll remember your tender feelings in the future."

The next Saturday Naomi appears on our doorstep, old Buick parked in front of the hedge. It is stuffed with boxes. I step outside to greet her.

"So ... can't stay away, eh?"

She sets a bag full of clothes down, and we hug.

"Well, you know how it is. There is no one like Bobbie."

Her fine red hair is cut slightly different, now with short bangs. Otherwise Naomi seems the same, her face friendly, though slightly guarded. Babette now descends the staircase and raises expectant arms outward. I turn away while the two embrace and help carry more things inside.

That evening all three of us play Scrabble. Our laughter fills the house, though Babette decisively wins every game. Once she departs for bed, I gather up tiles from the final defeat, Naomi raises a thin eyebrow at me across the kitchen table.

"So, what's the real deal around here?" she asks.

"Oh, God. Lucky you missed the catastrophe in December. I took Babette to St. Vincent Hospital early one morning, taught a college level class, then broke her out after she improperly removed a catheter tube and bled everywhere. That's about when she proposed marriage."

Naomi chuckles. "I moved out just in time!"

I laugh as well. "Sure, it's funny now. At the time I thought she'd drop dead right in front of me. What else ...oh, her driving is still terrible. Last week she backed into the neighbor's truck across the street again. I think it must be at least the third time since I've lived here."

"Don't you chauffeur?"

"Usually. But when I'm at school or elsewhere, there's no stopping her."

"So what's up with you then? Besides the engagement to Babette, I mean."

"Hey, shut up! Mostly schoolwork and some odd jobs on the side. I've got a few friends I see, make it out dancing whenever possible and still smash capitalism when there's time."

Naomi smirks and stands up. She rummages for cocktail mixer in a cupboard. "Sounds like your same old routine then. Dating anyone?"

"Well, I don't know. It's usually complicated"

"Girls? Boys?"

"I said shut up!"

She pours herself a drink and settles back down. "Like it matters to me. Anyway, Bobbie does pass on the occasional rumor."

I smile. "It's good having you back, Naomi."

Our household dynamic holds stable for several months. We watch mystery films in the evenings or play board games together. Babette takes us out to eat often and sometimes on weekend trips to Yakima for classical music performances. With enough credits earned at Portland Community College, I transfer to Portland State University and enroll as a history major. One sunny Wednesday in late April I come home from school and find Naomi stubbing out a cigarette with her heel on the front sidewalk. She glances over anxiously. I set down my satchel and frown.

"You smoke?"

Naomi sighs. "Not ordinarily. Bobbie hates the smell. Today things have me a bit on edge."

"How do you mean?" I ask.

Naomi jerks her head toward the house. "Just don't know what's gotten into her lately. Bobbie's agitated. Got a serious bee in her bonnet."

I laugh. "More like a hornet's nest, and I think she was born with it."

Naomi wrinkles her nose. "I don't know. Today we went out for lunch at the gold course and she absolutely tormented our waitress. Ordered something, then sent it back, claiming it was wrong. She pulled the same trick with dessert, then complained about awful service. Just about had the poor girl in tears. I told her to stop but she just laughed at what fun it was."

"I don't see why she'd be so capricious like that."

Naomi smoothes a lock of hair behind one ear. "It was really sad. Just keep on your toes. I know she dislikes how much time you spend away these days."

"That's news. I usually get a comment about how much she wants me to enjoy my youth or something."

"Well, remember, what our friend says and thinks are often quite different."

"Yeah. Oh, I'm visiting Seattle briefly this weekend. My friend James is on his way through town after a trip to California on Friday and will pick me up. I'll hop a Greyhound back Sunday."

"That's your blond friend who visited the winter before last, right?"

"Yeah, him and Babette totally hit it off. They both love Scrabble, and he's a plant expert so together there were plenty of observations about how I could maintain the yard better."

Naomi exhales and pops a mint in her mouth. "Well, as long as you're just gone a couple days, I can probably hold down the fort. Like I've said before, Bobbie's on much better behavior around you."

"Understood. Don't worry. I'm pretty sure we can handle her together."

Smoke spirals up from the crushed cigarette butt. Through an open upstairs window, strains of Tchaikovsky's *Romeo and Juliet* overture float by on a light breeze. Every yard is filled with hopeful blooms and newly sprouted greenery. The heady scent of cultivation and warm soil surrounds us as majestic notes rise and fall inside.

Next Friday I return from class to find James enjoying early afternoon tea and cookies with Babette and Naomi in the backyard. The sun is warm, and they sit around the small patio table, umbrella raised. My friend waves, his face all smiles.

"Hey, I made it here a couple hours ago and found some excellent hospitality."

Babette gestures at him with her cup. "Young James offered sage advice on the tomahtoes I wish to grow this summer. He really is a wellspring of botanical knowledge."

I nod. "Hopefully he can be a remote resource. I'm a better forklift operator than gardener. It's about all I can do maintaining things as they are."

James takes a sip of his tea. "Seriously. Babette showed us pictures from years ago when she did all the yard work. There was even a newspaper spread on her flowers!"

My professor purses her lips and half laughs. "Quite. Sadly those days are long gone. So, what do you two have planned for today?"'

James looks at me questioningly. "Well, I'd like to make Seattle tonight, but there's no hurry. It's been a while since I last visited so perhaps we could spend the afternoon sightseeing.

Maybe drive up Council Crest, get a view of the city, walk around downtown, find some food and then head north."

I shade my eyes against sunlight that angles past the overhead canopy. "Sounds good."

Babette clears her throat. "Would you perhaps enjoy supper here? I could prepare something, a pork roast?"

James bobs his head. "That sounds delicious. What time would you like us back?"

My professor throws up her hands. "Oh, return whenever you like. It is not important."

"We should have some idea," I cut in, "what, six or seven maybe?"

"Now, now," Babette tuts, "if you are late, we will keep the food warm. Please go, enjoy yourselves today." She waves us off.

Dismissed, James and I climb into his rusty Datsun pickup. Over the Willamette River we pass through southwest Portland, where buildings give way to evergreen trees and eventually a winding road leads upward. The motor strains in protest, around and around and around. We park at the hilltop summit and step outside into warm dry air. It's a complete panorama. The entire river valley stretches out before us. Snowcapped Mt. Hood dominates the eastern skyline and Mt. St. Helens' shattered hulk lies north in Washington State. We stand awed.

I point down towards the sluggish blue ribbon splitting Portland in half. "That second closest span is the Ross Island Bridge, a bit over from that you can see Reed College. The big green area nearby is Eastmooreland, my neighborhood."

James squints. "You're really sold on this town, aren't you?"

"Yeah, I love it. Who knows what'll happen though. It's still about a year until graduation. Makes sense if I stay with Babette long enough to afford my bachelor's degree."

"Can things last? You said she's had a lot of drama with Naomi."

"True. Their situation is different though. I've made a bunch of friends here, go out all the time and Babette doesn't mind. Poor Naomi takes an evening off, and they argue over it for days. I've stayed much more independent."

"So, would you care for Babette beyond graduation if she

asked?"

The breeze picks up and several dandelion puffs float by us. They drift over the city to disappear against white clouds moving in from the east.

"I don't know. Babette's become like family. Of course, her adventures are a rush, you just never know what scheme might come along next."

James shrugs lazily. "Well, as far as our scheme today, you just want to stay low key and hang out up here for a while? We could also catch a movie or grab a beer somewhere."

"No reason we can't do both. *Gladiator* is at the cheap theaters. I've wanted to check that out since Babette can't shut up about Roman times. I read a review that said it has Marcus Aurelius in it, he's her messiah more or less."

"Yeah, let's do that."

We drive down from Council Crest and share a pitcher of beer in the darkened Laurelhurst Theater. Every other row of seats has been torn out and replaced with long tables for drinks and food. Glasses clink along with battle cries as gladiators hack each other to bits and Marcus Aurelius is deposed by his conniving son.

The film lasts longer than expected and my pocket watch reads 7:10 when we leave. Our drive back to Tolman Street takes another fifteen minutes. Inside the house, garlic and heavy meat aromas fill the air. On the kitchen counter lies a half-devoured pork roast and beside it, two pans of garlic potatoes. I bring my nose close and sniff, then peer out the window. Babette and Naomi sit around the small patio table, empty plates before them.

"Well, they didn't keep it warm, but there's some good food here." I observe.

James moves toward the door. "Let's tell Babette about seeing her messiah on the big screen. She'll be excited about that!"

We step outside with wide smiles but my professor's icy glare freezes us in our tracks.

"I have never seen such disrespectful behavior!" she erupts. "Preparing a delicious dinner and then watching it sit uneaten by people who cannot be bothered to arrive in a timely fashion!"

"Babette!" I interject, "you said we shouldn't worry!"

"Excuses!" she thunders. "After everything I have done for

you, this is unacceptable! I have never felt so insulted!"

I glance at Naomi. She looks away, eyes downcast.

James shuffles his feet. "I'm sorry. We clearly misunderstood."

Babette scowls. "If you must eat, there is cold food."

James and I retreat to the kitchen. "What was that about?" he asks. "Seriously, I heard her say it didn't matter when we came back, right?"

"Yeah, I don't know. She hasn't been like this before. Sure, we've disagreed but Babette's never raised her voice. It's how she gets with Naomi."

James looks at the pork. "If I wasn't so hungry I'd suggest we find dinner elsewhere."

"Let's just eat and hit the road, maybe she'll cool down while I'm in Seattle."

We help ourselves to meat and potatoes. Even tepid, my professor's cooking is spectacular. I cut slices off the roast and savor each bite. Outside, the sunlight fades, casting amber speckles through tree leaves. After a few minutes, Babette's heavy tread sounds through the back door. Her slippers smack kitchen linoleum. She pauses, then leans against the counter, face lined and weary.

"I am sorry." She looks from James's face to mine. "It was wrong shouting like that. Wrahs, you have been such a help, and James, I adore you as well. Please forgive me. I haven't felt well lately. My health is unstable, but that should be no excuse."

"Oh, Babette! That's fine, don't worry about it," I tell her.

"Really, don't feel bad," James cuts in, "it was just a mistake."

Babette flashes a wan smile. "Understand my intent was not malevolent. At any rate, I need rest and will go upstairs to relax."

I nod. "Ok, goodbye then. I'll call from Seattle and check how you're doing."

My professor drops her gaze briefly. "Thank you, how considerate. I bid you both adieu." She turns away and leaves the room.

James looks at me. "So, how ready are you? We have a late drive ahead."

"More or less. There are just a few things I need from the basement."

Naomi appears from outside with a handful of dishware. She deposits them in the sink and beckons at me.

"Did Bobbie mention the Jacuzzi?"

"No."

"She said earlier that it smells strange. Maybe the chlorine level needs adjustment or something. I don't know, it's not my department."

"Ok, hold on, James, let me check that. It'll just take a few minutes."

From the broom closet I grab a box of chemicals and walk outside. Low hanging branches camouflage the green veiled alcove and a small unseen spider web catches my face with a tiny snap as miniature filaments tear. I lift the plastic cover and steam billows up, more aromatic than usual.

I dip testing strips into the water and compare colors against a cardboard chart. As suspected, the balance is off kilter. I measure powders into a plastic cup, pour them in and stir with my arm.

After a couple minutes, I repeat the test. This time every colored stripe reaches the right level. Hopefully that smell will dissipate by the next time Babette wants a soak. I return inside and put the chemicals away but something seems wrong. All is strangely still. Each main floor light blazes but only clocks sound. Tick, tock, tick, tock, tick, tock. I pass through the kitchen and almost collide with Naomi in the dining room. She stares at me, eyes wide.

"Ross!" she whispers urgently. "Bobbie just came downstairs and tore poor James apart for no reason at all! She sent him away ... and he left! I've never seen her so vicious!"

"What the hell! She only just apologized to us!" I exclaim. "Where did he go?"

"She was like a rabid animal! Just unreal! Go find James, I think he must be outside ... then come back."

I rush out the front door as an engine grinds behind the hedge. It doesn't quite catch. My friend sits at the wheel of his Datsun and tries again. This time it rumbles into life. He rolls down the driver's side window as I approach.

"James, what on earth happened?"

He slaps the dashboard helplessly. "I don't know. After you went outside, Babette came downstairs. She yelled at me, said I was a bad influencer, no longer welcome in her house and that you should leave as well. It was awful, just out of nowhere."

"Ok, this needs to get sorted out. Will you wait a minute?"

I spin on my heel and return inside. Naomi sits at the kitchen table, a tumbler already half emptied before her. She looks up when I enter.

"Did you find James?"

"Yeah, he didn't get far. So, what's this about Babette wanting me to leave?"

"That's what she said."

"Did she mean gone tonight? When I return from Seattle? What's going on?"

Naomi takes a deep gulp of her drink. "You'd better talk with her personally. Poor James, that was no way to treat a guest." She wipes her eyes with the back of a hand.

"Ok, thanks. I'll see if I can do."

Heart heavy, I mount the staircase. Every step creaks in a familiar way under reluctant boots. No sound emanates from Babette's room, but a faint glow filters through the open doorway. I pause atop the landing and take a couple breaths. My knuckles tap gently against the doorjamb. Still nothing. I peek through and spy my professor on the edge her bed, bathrobe untied and wig in her hands.

"Babette? Can we talk?"

Her breath comes slow, face slack and head hung. I enter the chamber. It is thick with perfume and menthol skin ointment. In one corner lurks General Bonnefont's old wooden chest with the large toy tanker truck on top and model Stuka dive bomber. I sit down beside her. At last Babette looks over at me. She swallows, features lit soft by the dim nightstand lamp. I bite my lip and meet her gaze.

"Do you really want me to go?"

Babette's jaw twitches. Her one focused eye holds me, then turns away.

"No, Wrahs. I do not wish that." She touches her temple. "No apologies can undo my actions tonight. I behaved shamefully, and there is no excuse. Do you think James will forgive me?"

"Well, I don't know. You should probably wait and try an apology later. He seems pretty shook up."

"Ah, time often heals. But do you understand my greatest fear? Solitude! Naomi is flighty, she may stay or she may go, so when I feel as though I cannot rely on you, my mind reacts with fright. I lose all control! With ill health it is important I am not left alone. Do you see that?"

I place a hand on her broad shoulder. "Babette, of course I understand that. But I need defined expectations. If it concerns you I have friends and sometimes stay out all night, tell me. This can't work if you play games or keep things to yourself and then blow up without warning."

Babette picks up a half-full glass of mineral water from her nightstand and sets it down empty.

"My nature does not welcome introspection ... but the reality is I sometimes find myself in the midst of some act or speech that from within feels repellent, yet I cannot stop. I am captive, watching helplessly! Tonight was a terrible example more than once and I feel embarrassed to have spoken harshly at poor James who did nothing wrong. Oh, the look on his face haunts me so. But I couldn't stop ... the venom erupted without mercy and nothing can take it back." She reaches out and squeezes my hand.

I smile at her. "There are things we all regret. But ... I need to make sure we're on the same page if you really want me here."

Babette's face furrows. "I wish you would remain. Just please remember, more time may be asked of you as my conditions require it. Know I appreciate everything you have done for me and want to leave this sorry incident far behind. Have a good time in Seattle. Oh, do give James my apologies!"

Chapter 32

"Long have I trodden the stage of life in masquerade; and I may call myself doubly happy, in the spiritual rewards of virtue, and the temporal indulgences of the opposite side. Between ourselves, mine is the system of all mankind in the long run. Real virtue is a very expensive article; plated goods look just as well and are within the reach of all purchasers."

Alain Rene Le Sage. Gil Blas. 1715.

It is a rainy Saturday morning in early May when a car door slams outside. I spread butter across charred slabs of toast as Babette enters, flushed with excitement. Her wig wilts from moisture and water drips on the linoleum.

"Wrahs, Wrahs! At mass today the priest informed us about a film just now released. It is very wicked and portrays the Catholic Church in quite a negative light. Have you heard of this? It is called *Chocolat.*"

I shake my head and crunch into a blackened slice of bread.

"Anyhow," she continues. "We were informed everyone should discourage their friends and families from viewing such rubbish. Afterward, I discussed this news with the old biddies and we all agreed it is so unfair how movies portray Catholicism. An absolute social disgrace! You can perhaps guess my agenda this afternoon, if you are free."

"Want me to check matinee times?" I ask, reaching for the paper.

"Yes! I will invite a colleague of mine named Alice who might enjoy it as well. She is very nice, from the mathematics department. You will like her I am sure."

I flip through the entertainment section while Babette dials her telephone. About an hour later the doorbell rings. I find a middle-aged woman with wavy grey hair on the doorstep. She reaches out a firm hand and we shake.

"You must be Ross then? Bobbie speaks of you often."

I step back and allow her inside. "Yeah, that's me. Chauffeur, cook, and housekeeper to the finest local history professors. Specializing in hospital breakouts. I don't know how it'll all fit on my resume."

Alice laughs. "Well, I understand you've been a great help. Bobbie can be difficult, but I know she appreciates everything."

Babette bustles past me and embraces her friend. "What is this? I overheard an avalanche of lies and calumnies concerning my character! What a disgrace, after all these years! Anyhow, come to the kitchen for a moment, we have time. Would you like some tea? The kettle is already hot. Isn't mint your favorite?"

Alice nods and we follow Babette, who furiously ransacks the tea cupboard. She fills three mug with steaming water. I select black chai.

"What's this film about?" Alice asks me. "Bobbie would say nothing except her church completely disapproves ... that was enough enticement to get me here, but have you read a review or anything?"

"I found one. It's set in rural France during the 1950s and about a woman who makes chocolate that has weird effects on her whole village. It keeps people from focusing on spiritual matters so local Catholic authorities try to shut her down. It got a lot of stars, should be worthwhile."

"Sounds good then ... oh, thanks, Bobbie." Alice accepts a pungent cup emblazoned with Canadian railroad logos. "So, how's the history department these days?"

Babette rolls her eyes. "You know how it is. I avoid my supervisors whenever possible but the students are still a joy. But what about over in mathematics? Just last week I heard some rumors..."

The two professors gossip until every drop of tea is gone. Then we scramble outside between raindrops and climb into the Toyota, Babette taking shotgun and Alice the rear. I drive east on Woodstock, take a left at 82nd and soon reach the Century Eastport cinema complex. Babette pays for all three tickets. Together, we step into a dim theater less than half-filled. It's still early. After several minutes seated while advertisements scroll across the big screen, my professor stirs.

"Excuse me, I must use the lavatory. You two troublemakers, behave yourselves!" She gets up and heads toward a green illuminated exit sign.

Alice laughs. "Oh, Bobbie, stop!"

A couple behind us crunch popcorn loudly and giggle. Once my professor is out of earshot, I turn curiously. "So, you've worked with Babette for some time, right? Did you know her when she was Albert?"

Alice exhales deeply. "Well, that's a little complicated. I've taught at the school for over twenty years and always knew Albert Ellsworth casually. Of course everyone knew him, he was one of the original professors hired when Portland Community College opened. An intimidating mind– his memory still astonishes. But we were never close. You see, Albert was the sort of man who loved to shock people. He would explain obscure parts of world history and revel in each lewd detail. Albert might take someone aside and discuss aspects of grand intellectual theory with complete eloquence but then simplify it down to some perverted quip. Many people appreciated this but I found it, well ... creepy."

"What changed for you?"

"It was the sex reassignment, as simple as that. Why, just last week Bobbie approached me and began a discussion she turned into some joke about two traveling salesmen and a blow-up dolly. Now, years ago, from a balding middle-aged male professor, I found that sort of thing in complete bad taste, but when an elderly woman spat out the punch line, it became hilarious!"

"God, I can imagine."

Alice chuckles. "Exactly. Oh, no one enjoyed making people uncomfortable more than him. One colleagues told me he first heard about the sex change when Albert burst into his office and proclaimed with no segue at all 'I am going to become a woman! The surgery is planned– I shall live as a lesbian!' Nothing subtle about that character. Oh, but she isn't as sly as she thinks. Recently we talked at school and somehow the conversation turned to Hitler. She let slip some coy remark, then tried covering it up. I just laughed at her, I said, 'Bobbie, you don't fool anybody. We all know you're a dirty Nazi!' Of course she pretended to be so offended by that!"

"How did people react? I mean on campus, with the gender change?"

"Well, that happened in 1994. In some ways it's quite sad. I think Albert expected many old friends wouldn't accept this new identity and turned against them preemptively. I know several and it's still a hurtful subject. He didn't give them a chance, just cut people out of his life without explanation. Albert always possessed a vindictive streak, that wasn't new, but striking at those closest to him ... well, just cruel. Tragic, even.

"Anyhow, over the last few years Bobbie has shown more interest in me personally. I enjoy our activities together, but always keep my guard up, if you understand. It's hard knowing exactly where one stands with her at any given time. She speaks highly of you, that's why I'm being so honest here. This isn't original advice I'm sure, since you've lived with her for quite some time, but ... be careful."

"Thanks, I appreciate it."

Just then overhead lights lower and Babette's bulky silhouette lurches up the aisle toward us, backlit by the glowing screen. She sits down and settles back. We hush as previews begin.

Chapter 33

"Why, aren't the good things of this world made for our common enjoyment, every lovely thing free for the taking? . . . What is lovelier than water? Yet it flows for us all. Is love therefore exempt from the universal law, a bliss to be stolen and hid, and not our common reward?"

Petronius Arbiter. The Satyricon. circa 100 CE.

The next Friday evening I catch a bus down to Union Jack's, a strip bar on East Burnside. Zoya stands outside, her skinny Capri 120 clenched between lips tinted blue under neon. She gives me a hug.

"Hey, were you waiting long?" I ask.

"No, just a few minutes. Thanks for meeting up with me. It's odd, I can dance at a gothic club full of strangers but going in here alone spooks me. I gotta get used to that if I ever want to strip myself though. So, you think Annakiya can pass along information about the industry then? I'm so burned out on childcare."

"If anyone could it's her. I think that girl's worked every joint in the Portland metro area."

"Well, thanks for introducing us last month. She seems like a lot of fun."

"Annakiya's a trip, that's definitely true. You done with that smoke? Let's go in."

A bearded man just inside the door checks our IDs, and we enter. The main room is medium sized, with a center bar and two stages at either end. Red lights tint every surface. Mid tempo electronic beats pulse from the DJ booth and shiny metal poles reach over fourteen feet to the ceiling.

A small girl with creamy white skin covered in black tribal tattoos wraps muscled thighs partway up one pole and pauses. She leans back slowly, her body an arc, dark hair trailing; then suddenly–*wham*– performs a cartwheel and lands perfectly on high heels. I elbow Zoya who nods in approval. The dancer's top is already removed, and horizontal steel barbells pierce her nipples. She jerks at a sleek black thong. Lower, lower ... then with a final tug it's gone. Bills fly and applause echoes from the rack.

I move forward and point to an empty table. "Wanna stake this out while I pick up drinks?"

"Yeah, get me a Guinness." Zoya passes me some cash.

I order the dark stout plus an IPA for myself from a raven-haired bartender whose silver bracelets jingle as she pulls each tap. The chamber is still only half full, but customers file in steadily. I carry our drinks back and set the frosted glasses down. Zoya sips at the thick head on her pint.

"So, do you have any experience with the industry?" I ask.

"Not really. The daycare center I'm at now is ok but pays shit. I love dancing anyway and this city is packed with strip clubs. It's just a matter of time before I get enough courage."

Just then Annakiya cruises over, long black hair extensions cascading in Medusa-like tendrils. A tight gold dress showcases her figure above fishnets and tall heels.

"I'm glad you both showed up!" she exclaims. "It's been so boring here tonight."

Zoya smiles. "Girl, we wouldn't miss it!"

"God, it'll be nice having an audience who doesn't keep their nose buried in a book." She winks at me. "Zoya, I expect much better etiquette from you."

The DJ switches to an upbeat hip-hop track, then dips the volume.

"Everybody, come on, next up we have the lovely Manasa for your viewing pleasure. Pay close attention and check this foxy lady!" Music swells once more.

Annakiya reaches for my beer and steals a quick gulp. "Shit, that's me! Gotta go!"

She disappears and a moment later emerges onstage. Zoya sets down her Guinness and watches, fixated. Patrons move forward, crowding the rack. Annakiya circles the metal pole, one hand braced against it. Face impassive, she sways hips slowly to the beat and peels her gold dress off with one sure motion. Long braids whip back as she flings it aside. Clad only in fishnets and red lace panties, Annakiya works the stage, perfect breasts suspended above upturned faces and open wallets.

Zoya kicks my boot. "Don't forget to breathe."

"Hey, you gotta admit, she's something."

"True, but it's not dancing. Her body is just such a force by itself she doesn't have to."

We stare together in silence until two songs later when Annakiya's set concludes. Zoya looks over at me.

"Well, I can't say if my mind is made up about joining this industry, but what a show. That girl is spectacular."

"No doubt. Unfortunately she's equal parts trouble."

"Well, a package like that can't just circulate through life without causing waves. Say, why does she care if you read anyway?"

I laugh. "Annakiya gets offended if I'm distracted when there's important naked time afoot."

Zoya grins mischievously. "I've got a coloring book from work in my bag. Want to kill time until she's on again?"

"Sure."

Zoya pulls out a large book with fanciful fairy tale illustrations on the cover. She tears out two pages, then extracts a box of crayons from her backpack. The familiar childhood odor mixes with cigarette smoke and antiseptic spray.

"Hansel and Gretel lost in the woods," I muse... "Let's see, unfortunately the poor rascals ate psychotropic mushrooms and now these trees are fuchsia!" With thick marks I fill in the foliage.

Zoya laughs. "Nice. Of course, under this lighting you can hardly tell. Look, I've got the witch in front of her oven. She needs better shoes. I'll draw some good heels. Not useful for pursuing little ones through the woods, but much more glamorous."

As we color away, the dark-haired dancer from earlier approaches. She pulls over a chair and sits down. The black thong is back in place around her narrow hips but nothing else covers her except swirled patterns of ink.

"Hey!" she comments, "that looks like fun!"

Zoya tears out another page. "Here you go. Try Jack and the Beanstalk. See, that giant looks kinda mean, but he actually just wants to be friends."

The girl picks through our crayon box and pulls out burnt umber. Small unrestrained breasts bounce near my elbow with each stroke.

"You're so right," she enthuses. "Jack shouldn't be scared. That giant is just baking him a delicious chocolate cake! Oh, this is great. I haven't colored in years. I'm Melody, by the way." She looks over at Zoya's progress. "That's so cool. You know any self-respecting witch wouldn't be caught dead in bad shoes."

Another dancer stops and surveys our table. She studies my page, frowning.

"Why are those trees all weird?"

Before anyone can reply, Annakiya storms over, hair aswirl.

"What's going on here? Can't you bitches make your own friends? These are mine!" The second girl gives her a sharp glance, sniffs loudly and moves on. Annakiya isn't finished "Melody!" she hisses, "Get your ass onstage or hustle a lap dance! Ross and Zoya! You can't make art projects here! That's so disrespectful!"

Melody drops her gaze and leaves. Annakiya takes the vacated chair, eyes fiery. Zoya pats her arm.

"Calm down, girl! She wasn't causing trouble. Neither are we. It's just a coloring book."

Annakiya drums long fingernails on the table. "Look, I'm a bit on edge right now. I got kicked out of my room this morning and don't have a place to live. It's got me in a real pissy mood. Anyway, thanks for coming out. I'm gonna hop backstage, catch up with you two later."

She stalks away. Zoya raises a thin plucked eyebrow. "You warned me. Trouble."

I almost choke on my beer. "You haven't seen anything yet."

"Shame she lost her place."

"Yeah, that was a motel just up the street from here on Burnside. Can't say it's a shocker. Girl makes enough money, though. She'll find something else soon."

We stash the coloring book away and buy another round of drinks. When Annakiya returns after her next set, she seems less agitated.

"If you need somewhere to stay tonight, there's room at the

House of Many Pleasures," Zoya offers.

Annakiya sighs. "I don't know. I saw it once before. Your apartment is pretty disgusting."

"True, but mostly on Sal's side. Mine's not as bad."

"Well, how about I come over and think about it. There's nothing else going on. My shift is done in less than an hour."

Zoya and I make our final beers last until after Annakiya's last set concludes. Once she has changed into casual warm-ups and tipped out bartenders, the DJ and doorman, all three of us file outside. Above, the dark sky is overcast. I glance at my pocket watch. Almost midnight. Wind rushes down the street, air moist and chilly. A yellow Broadway cap pulls up before the club. Its driver gets out and hoists Annakiya's large suitcase into the trunk.

"Well, see you two later," I call.

Annakiya turns, dismayed. "Don't leave! Come on!"

Zoya wrinkles her nose at me.

I shoulder my satchel. "No, that's fine, I can still catch a bus home."

Annakiya stamps her foot. "Ross, don't run off, you're sticking with us." She beckons firmly. Zoya tenses her lips and climbs into the taxi.

I frown. "Well, if it's what you want, all right."

We slide along the vinyl rear seat. Outside, rain begins falling; dull, heavy drops that thump on the roof as our cab rolls down Burnside to the Civic apartments. It halts in front, and we pool money together. Outside, the downpour picks up with a frenzy as gutters overflow, creating small rivers that rush down the sidewalk.

Zoya opens her door. "Ok, ready, one, two, three!" We burst out into the weather. I accept Annakiya's suitcase from the cabbie and lug it along behind. The two girls are well ahead, laughing as their shoes kick up spray from puddles. Zoya keys the lobby open and ushers us inside. It smells like a meth lab flooded. We hurry down the hallway and inside her apartment, thoroughly soaked. I wipe my face. Droplets flick across empty Mountain Dew bottles and shag tobacco wrappers. Salazar is nowhere to be seen.

We enter Zoya's room and I rest Annakiya's suitcase on stacked fashion magazines. The raised bed is still a giant nest.

Sheets, blankets and a large quilt swirl amidst garments that almost seem knotted together. Zoya strips off her moist hoodie, revealing a snug halter top underneath. She hops aboard the bed and tosses out several large books with illustrations of 1920s pin-ups. They land in a half-full clothes hamper.

"Come on up, girl," she invites Annakiya.

"Ok, but your bed is ... complicated. I'm afraid I'll break something."

"You'll be fine. Just step on my sewing machine box for a little boost."

Annakiya follows these instructions and mounts the milk crate platform. She looks suddenly weary.

"God, I don't know why, all my energy's gone. Plus everything is wet. I'm going to get pneumonia." She wriggles out of the workout gear and shivers in leopard print underwear.

Zoya pulls a blanket over her. "That's all right. You can crash here. Ross, there's space on the floor in Sal's room if you move some crap out of the way. I don't recommend the chamber under his bed. It smells moldy."

"No!" Annakiya cuts in, voice petulant. "Ross should join us. He can be fun."

Zoya tosses her head and skewers me with a calculated stare. "Well, ok. Hey, Ross, there's a Japan record by my turntable. Queue that and hit the lights, ok?"

I slip *Gentlemen Take Polaroids* out of its sleeve and drop the needle. It crackles for a moment, then synth pop music flutters, a delicate blend of synthesizers and guitars. I turn down the volume slightly and flick a switch by the door. We are plunged into darkness. One of the girls mutters softly. I remove boots and mechanic shirt, then shrug off braces suspending my pants. They fall on the floor with a light thud.

As my eyed adjust, I try to step on the sewing machine box but crack a toe against something hard. A curse escapes and both girls giggle. I rub the injured foot and try again. This time my vault is successful. An arm holds the blanket open for me. I crawl underneath and embrace the feminine form. Annakiya? I press against her and feel another limb. Zoya? Japan plays on. All three of us lie stock still in thick blackness. Four songs later, the machine switches off with a click.

We are on one other in an instant. My lips move against Annakiya's neck and Zoya's fingers trail across her from the other side. Hands grasp, stroke and explore. The temperature rises and moans resound beneath undulating fabric. Skin catches against teeth against hair against muscle. My heart pounds and blood rushes through every extremity.

Then all ceases. I freeze in surprise. Annakiya's hands relax and fall away. Her breath comes slow and even. Still, a grip around my arm increases its pressure slightly. I run hesitant fingers over tight knuckles.

"Ross?"

"Zoya?"

"I think we lost Annakiya."

"Yeah, she's out."

We lie silently, connected pulses in disjointed rhythm. After a moment her clutch moves lower, fingernails sifting through hair on my forearm. I wait several seconds, then shift over Annakiya's comatose body to brace squarely above Zoya. Muscular arms encircle my torso and pull me down where our lips meet in a long kiss. I draw back and chuckle slightly.

"What's that?" she asks.

"This isn't your first choice but perhaps I can suffice for now."

She laughs. "You'll do as a consolation prize."

The two of us cling together and the nest envelops our mingled forms. A police car screams past outside the window but we pay it no heed. The night passes by as nocturnal traffic rushes down Burnside under pelting rain.

A different shriek of alarm wakes me. Annakiya is kneeling above us, her face a furious mask. She yanks the covers away, exposing Zoya and me, naked and intertwined.

"How could you!" she cries.

Zoya draws a blanket back to cover us. "Calm down, girl. You were asleep."

Annakiya's lips curl in disgust. She jumps out of bed and searches for clothes amidst the mess. Tawny skin once more covered by warm-ups, she storms from the room, suitcase on rollers behind her. Stomping feet echo down the hallway. I sigh. My eyes meet Zoya's.

"Do you know the time?"

She points out an alarm clock partially covered by the strap of a brassiere. It reads 6:15AM.

"Talk about a lucky break. I've got work in forty-five minutes. Picked up some weekend dishwashing shifts downtown."

Zoya yawns and pulls at me. "Come back for a moment."

I kiss her cheek, then earlobe and lips.

"No really, I've got to run. But, you're awesome. I've wanted this for a long time."

Her dark eyes lower. "Thanks. You know, I think we should hang out more."

"Absolutely. I'll see you soon."

Outside, the morning shines clear and brisk. I walk down Burnside, my hoodie zipped up against the early chill. Everything feels hopeful under a newly risen sun.

Chapter 34

"I began by desiring to be another man; then, on reflecting that I might by analogy foresee what I should feel, and thus not experience the surprise and the change that I had looked for, I would have preferred to be a woman."

Theophile Gautier. Mademoiselle de Maupin. 1836.

Naomi bursts into tears and embraces me on a late June afternoon. I set down the last box to hug her back. The old Buick is stuffed with possessions, from passenger seats to trunk. Her wet face presses against mine. I exhale humid air full of lawnmower fumes from neighborhood yards.

"I'm sorry you two can't get along. It's probably better this way."

Naomi releases me, then rubs her eyes and strokes fingers through fine copper hair.

"There's just no living with that woman. Unpredictable and possessive as sin. I should be apologizing to YOU– she's all yours now."

"Yeah. Well, good luck. I hope things work out. You could use time with fewer leashes."

"Absolutely. Ok, I really should go and stop making a scene like this."

"Good luck, then."

Her gaze lowers. "Take care, Ross."

As Naomi's car disappears at the end of Tolman Street, a postal truck turns our corner and pulls up in front of me. The carrier hops out, a stack of mail in hand. She recognizes me and smiles, handing over the pile. Bills, medical notices, advertisements and a small package for Babette. This I examine closely. The return address is British Columbian. I carry it inside.

My professor sits at the kitchen table, shaking her head. She looks up as I enter, face stern.

"I do not understand that girl. Naomi had every opportunity with me to pursue her education but threw it all away. *C'est la vie*, we are finished. She will not be welcome in this house again."

"This came for you," I say, handing her the small parcel.

She fondles brown paper edges and hums a Dvořák melody. It slips through her shaky hands and slaps onto the Formica. With a frown, she slides the package toward me.

"Please, see if your nimble fingers will open this."

I tear off sticky packing tape and find a rectangular shape wrapped in yellow tissue paper. Babette nods for me to continue. Beneath this layer is the framed photograph of a smiling pink-cheeked woman with short grey curls. She appears in late middle age and is dressed formally. Steel blue eyes glint behind large glasses.

"Is this Mother Superior?" I ask, holding the photo up. Babette snatches it away.

"Oh God, that snake wishes to keep her sight on me, even from afar!"

She lays the picture face down and crosses herself, up down, left right.

"So, do you want me to put it on the mantelpiece then?" I ask, straight faced.

"Heavens, no!"

"Oh, I see, you'd like it up in your room? The nightstand, perhaps?"

"Wrahs! Don't be a beast! I want that thing kept as far away as possible. Please put it somewhere in the basement where I shall never come across it in a hundred years!" My professor glowers and turns away.

"At any rate, speaking of Canadian matters," she continues, "I should mention that in two weeks a friend from British Columbia will visit for the weekend. Unfortunately, she is Anglo-Canadian and shares your vile language. I suggest you use it with her as minimally as possible."

It is a hot Friday afternoon two weeks later when I come home and find Babette outside with her guest on the patio, sun umbrella open for shade. Before them are delicate tea cups with matching saucers. Babette beckons, the gesture curt.

"Wrahs, Wrahs, come here, I would like you to meet my friend Bonnie Church. She drove down from British Columbia and will stay overnight."

I approach and take the woman's hand. She is probably in her early forties, short hair curly and brown with hints of grey. A floral sundress reveals freckled skin on her neck and shoulders. Our gaze meets but she quickly looks away.

"Very nice meeting you, Bonnie" I begin.

She opens her mouth for reply, but is cut off.

"There!" Babette announces, "You two have been introduced. That is all social convention requires. I do not believe further communication should be necessary. Oh, but join us for dinner at seven, Wrahs. I have defrosted some chicken. You are welcome to eat with us– in complete silence."

I nod, lips clamped. Bonnie frowns up at me, hazel eyes curious.

That evening Babette cooks with a frenzy. I find her in the kitchen, _Larousse Gastronomique_ open and numerous vegetables on the cutting board. She chops away, the sharp knife a blur. Bonnie sits at the table with a glass of wine. I silently fetch a broom to sweep up cucumber stem ends and leafy carrot tops that spangle the floor. My professor looks over benignly.

"Ah Wrahs, thank you. Some vegetables never hold still. But you may appreciate this. Tonight I make _etuvee de poulet Panurge!_ That is braised chicken in the style of Panurge. Have you read Rabelais yet? His story of Gargantua and Pantagruel? No? Well, a pity. Panurge is one of the main characters. A thief, liar and absolute coward. If you refuse to read Rabelais, the least you can do is assist me with this delicious meal." The dour mood from earlier has disappeared. Her feet almost skip as she moves.

"I offered to help!" Bonnie calls out.

Babette shakes her head. "No! You are a guest! Have some more wine! Wrahs, please finish these carrots and cucumbers, oh, do we have onions? Excellent ... they should be quite thin. Like parchment paper! Afterwards, could you bake some of your delicious fruit scones? We have apples, _oui?_"

I take the sharp knife and slice onions as directed. My professor busies herself preparing a chicken she cuts into pieces, then sears with butter on the stove. Steam rises and fat crackles against the hot metal. Once everything simmers away, she sets the dining table with a blue and white service from the china cabinet. Each dish displays detailed engravings of old castles and idyllic country sides.

"These are all scenes from rural England! What lovely landscapes. We shall use them tonight in honor of an Anglo-Canadian visitor." Her face glows.

Bonnie watches me dice green apples and mix up dough for the scones. I form eight triangular pieces on an oiled pan, then brush each lightly with milk and sugar. Once the oven reaches 400 degrees, I place them on the middle rack. Twenty minutes later the pan is filled with golden topped pastries.

Babette looks over my shoulder approvingly. "Wonderful. Desert can cool while we eat. Oh, Bonnie! Everything is ready, please come dine," she calls out.

We sit around the table, our plates overflowing. Bonnie and I tuck in with silent enthusiasm, however Babette maintains a constant monologue, hands aflutter. The genius of Francois Rabelais … a lewd anecdote about President Calvin Coolidge visiting a poultry farm … Haida Indian tribes on Canada's West coast. She pauses only to swallow bites of food, then gestures with her empty fork. Once Panurge's chicken is gone, I retrieve my warm scones and present them with flair on a blue engraved platter. Bonnie eats a whole piece but my professor merely nibbles the corner of one. She dabs her lips with a checkered serviette and leans back. The wooden chair creaks in protest.

"I am sorry. My energy has sadly flown. I must retire for the evening. Bonnie, it is my greatest wish you do so as well. Wrahs, why don't you visit that Zoya girl you enjoy so much lately?"

Her slippers tread upstairs. Napoleon III's bust fixes me with a severe stare. The clocks tick away in conspiratorial concert. Bonnie sets down a wine glass and our eyes meet.

"Is there a bar nearby?" she asks, voice low.

"Yeah, let's wait a little until Babette falls asleep. That'll give me time to clean up."

I hand wash my professor's British service; platters, bowls and plates. Once the drying rack is filled with blue china, I climb halfway up the stairs and listen. Heavy snores emanate from above. I descend and nod at Bonnie, who waits by the front door, a green knit sweater now covering her shoulders.

Outside, she unlocks a silver Honda 4-door parked on the street. As the engine starts, I glance up at Babette's window. The glass remains dark. We drive down Holgate to the Semaphore Lounge, just a few minutes away. Neon signs glare in the evening dusk. "Play Lotto Here." "Ice Cold Schlitz."

"This fine with you?" I ask. "A little divey, but it's close."

Bonnie shrugs. "No problem. We're not here for ambiance."

The two of us enter and select a booth near the back. "Gimme Shelter" plays on the jukebox. Around us patrons exhale smoke, guzzle pints, and slump before video poker screens. A rotund waitress with bleached blonde hair and dark roots cruises by.

I glance at Bonnie. "Do you want to share a pitcher?"

She nods.

"We'd like a pitcher of Pabst." I order. The waitress turns on her heel and disappears behind the bar.

Once she is gone, Bonnie shoots me a serious look, hazel eyes wide. "Oh my God, Ross, what have I gotten into?"

I frown. "Maybe we can figure it out. What are you doing here anyway? How did you meet Babette?"

She toys with a cardboard coaster on edge, then slaps it down. "It happened several months ago. She's been kind ...very kind, but everything is so strange. I know she doesn't want us talking. It doesn't make sense, God, nothing makes sense after meeting her!"

I laugh. "Yeah, same story here."

She fumbles in her purse for a cigarette as our beer arrives. I slowly fill two glasses at an angle from the cold plastic pitcher.

"So, what happened exactly?" I ask.

She takes a first sip, then licks foam off her upper lip. "Well, I live in Nanaimo, British Columbia and work at a funeral home. Last March, Babette showed up and opened an account, saying she spent much time in B.C. and wanted arrangements in case she died away from home. I set her up with a cremation package; she prepaid the whole thing, no big deal.

"Then we fell into conversation. One thing led to another and before I knew it, Babette invited me out for lunch. I agreed, and, well, it turned into a friendship. She visits often, sometimes for quite a while. But something seems odd. May I ask ... is she ... was she ..." Her voice lowers.

"Did she used to be a man, is that what you're asking?"

Bonnie nods. She twirls her cigarette, still unlit.

I tip back my glass and swallow. "The answer is yes. She was born male, lived as Albert Ellsworth until 1994, then underwent sex reassignment surgery. Voila: Babette."

Bonnie exhales. "Ok, ok, as I suspected. But it's so hard to tell! There's just something about her, well, many things. I feel rude asking, eh?"

"It IS a sensitive subject. So," I lean forward, "what next?"

She strikes a match. The cherry on her Marlboro crackles into life. "Right, well, it all began innocently, but now things have changed. That's why Babette invited me here, to talk serious business. Do you know about the convent?"

"The convent!" I exclaim. "Does it really have high stone walls and long dark hallways like some gothic novel?"

Bonnie laughs. "No, there isn't any wall. I've never been inside, but the place is just a big house. Plus of course, not an actual convent."

My face falls. "Oh! It's not? Damn, that's an image I really cherished. So, what do you mean, not really a convent?"

"I mean, not an official Benedictine group affiliated with the Catholic Church. Don't be disappointed though. It's creepier than any real convent. The place is full of women who pretend they're nuns. It's a community that replicates monastic life but without official Catholic status. I suppose there wasn't a way Babette could join any real convent so she picked the next best thing."

"What about Mother Superior?" I ask.

Bonnie blanches and takes a long drag. Smoke rises between her lips, circling above our heads in a ragged halo. "Oh, that woman is real. The fact I may have to deal with her someday makes my blood run cold."

"Why would you?"

"Well, Babette wants me legally in charge of her Canadian

affairs. You know she's Canadian, right?"

"Canadian? I had no idea! Everything I've seen suggests she's an American citizen. Do you mean, like, some kind of dual nationality?"

Bonnie lifts her glass again. "Maybe. So, can you tell me Babette's story? What am I getting involved with here?" Her voice trembles. "That woman paid off half my house! She must want something very serious from me!"

"Your house? Wow!" I finish my pint. "We're going to need a few more of these. I'll start with a motorcycle trip but the tale– such as it is– really began in the rural Northwest over seventy years ago..."

An hour later, I conclude a condensed version of my professor's past and our adventures together. Germaine Bonnefont and 1920s Yakima. Felix Yusupov and WWII France. Judge Shoemaker and Billie's house on Tolman Street. St. Agatha Catholic Church and the Rajneesh Puram. Bonnie stares, her expression drained. The ashtray is loaded with cigarette butts.

"I just don't know," she declares. "This is all so incredible. I don't think I'd believe any of it if she hadn't stood in front of me, flesh and blood. Can you verify these things?"

"Much of it. There are lots of pictures. Whether from a kidnapping or not, it does look like she was born in central Washington, then grew up amidst French high society. The rest fits. You perhaps saw a picture of her on the mantelpiece as a young woman? That was Albert in drag, probably back in the 1950s."

Bonnie stubs out her last Marlboro. "Well, we should get back before Babette wakes and throws a fit. Thanks for telling me all this."

"Hey, no problem. I'm glad you illuminated some parts for me as well."

We pay our tab and drive home. The mossy yard gnome regards us with disapproval. Inside, Bonnie gives me a quick hug, then slips off her shoes and heads upstairs, stockinged feet clandestine. I pick up the kitchen phone and dial.

Zoya answers. "Hello?" Jazz horns trumpet in the background from Sal's stereo.

"Hey, it's me. Got the night off from Babette duties. Can I

come over?"

Even across town, I can feel her smile. "Absolutely!" she replies.

I grin as well. "Ok, the next bus comes soon. See you in a few." The receiver clicks.

After grabbing an overnight kit with toothbrush, dental floss and deodorant, I exit into the tranquil night. My boots clip down the sidewalk at double pace and a crescent moon shines through patchy clouds. Just as I reach the stop by Reed College, wide headlights crest the hill at 39th and Woodstock. Number 19 is right on time. Everything must be falling together.

Chapter 35

"In place of quiet, we must be plunged into confusion; instead of listening to the ticking of clocks, we must hear the thunder of cannon...instead of smelling flowers and incense, we must smell powder."

Émile Erckmann & Alexandre Chatrian. <u>Waterloo</u>. 1865

As summer 2001 passes, Babette and I make many more trips together. We visit Shaniko and Fossil again, then Crater Lake and even Cowichan Bay in British Columbia, though she divulges no more details regarding the convent, and we give Nanaimo a wide berth. Her constitution is fabulous– indeed Babette feels well enough to spend September 5th through the 25th with family in France. I drive to the airport and pull up before the Lufthansa drop off.

"Do you need help inside?" I ask.

My professor gestures at a single piece of plaid luggage in back. "No, no. I am traveling very light. The suitcase has wheels so your assistance will not be required. Truly, I feel reborn these days, do not worry about me at all. Please, enjoy yourself while I am gone."

I squeeze her hand. "Ok, I'm glad. Well, have a fun time then."

Babette lightly steps out of the idling car and retrieves her suitcase. The door slams. After a casual wave, she merges with other travelers who march along toward their gates. A bored faced traffic officer directs my way back out into traffic and I drive home.

And then the house is my own.

Several days later, Zoya comes over for dinner. Eager to impress her, I select <u>The Art of Cuisine</u> and follow instructions preparing a lamb shank with peppermint and potatoes. We set places for ourselves at the patio table and dine off exquisite tableware. A light breeze moves around us, lazy and full as the sun lowers. Everything turns out delicious. For dessert, we pick sweet Muscat grapes from a vine twining along the garage. Zoya bites one in half and contemplates the remainder. Her dark brown eyes meet mine.

"Let's use your hot tub."

We undress in the living room, and she wraps her dreadlocks up in a long floral scarf. Outside, the two of us scamper naked behind thick bushes. I flip the Jacuzzi cover open and steam explodes, filling the natural alcove. It rises up through Japanese maple and rhododendron branches. Zoya climbs the wooden steps ahead of me and dips shapely legs beneath the water. Her cat's eye glasses immediately fog over. She sets them on the plastic edge. Immersed beside her, my toes glide against a smooth thigh. She grins, then moves close and embraces me. Long fingernails scratch my back. I smile with delight.

"Zoya, I love playing house with you. And it's impossible not to say ... Zoya. I love you."

She pulls her face back and looks deeply into my eyes. Amber shadows highlight contours along her cheeks and nose. "I love you, too," she says, and kisses me, full mouth pressed against mine.

We sit quietly entwined, soaking in the heat and sublime symmetry of the moment as sleepy birds chirp to one another and a neighborhood cat rustles foliage nearby. Final golden rays filter between green leaves overhead. The air carries a faint scent of wood smoke.

Finally Zoya speaks again.

"Let's get married."

"What!" I sit up straight and almost topple her over. "You're not serious, right?"

Zoya pushes away, raising an elegantly arched eyebrow. "Why not?"

"Well ... look at us! You earn minimum wage part time at a daycare and illegally sublet a tenement. I'm a college student dependent on an old French-Nazi-atheist-nun."

Zoya shakes her head. "I don't mean immediately. It's not like I expect you to carry me over the threshold of your basement pantry. But think about it. Babette is what, mid-seventies? Sure, her health seems sketchy, but who knows, she could last another twenty years. I know you feel loyal, but would you stay here forever?" She playfully flicks droplets at my face. The sharp scent of chlorine brings me to attention.

"True, I don't want to wake up someday, realize I'm forty and still Babette's chauffeur. But you're right, I do feel loyalty after all she's done for me. Would you wait, say, a couple years?"

Zoya's cheeks crinkle and her chin dips below the surface. "Yes. I would indeed, Mister."

"All right. But we can't let Babette know."

"Exactly. She might stalk me." Water swirls as Zoya pulls close. Warm lips graze my ear. "Then it's done ... we're engaged."

I stroke her supple shoulders, then move lower, caressing each hip. We melt together as light wanes and the alcove softens into darkness. Roman numerals on the sundial fade, now meaningless crepuscular sentinels. Nothing could eclipse this place and time. One by one, shadows merge until night unfolds completely around us.

An hour later, we reluctantly extract ourselves from the tub and catch a bus across town to the Civic apartments as Zoya works early. We sit in back, silently holding hands while other late riders stretch weary limbs or bury faces in newspapers. Once curled up in her elevated nest, despite loud thumping bass from Sal's stereo next door, sleep claims us quickly.

The next morning Zoya's urgent voice awakens me. "Ross, get up! We're under attack!" Her stiff forefinger jabs at my ribs.

"What the hell are you taking about?" I mutter. Along Burnside, traffic growls past just outside the window. Harsh daylight leaks through torn blinds. I squint and rub crust from my eyes.

"It's a fucking attack! You need to see this. Oh my God!"

She turns up the volume on an ancient rabbit-ear Zenith in the corner. I roll over to view better. There are sirens, panicked screams and orange explosions. At this I sit bolt upright. Airplanes are crashing, over and over again, into the World Trade Center towers. Next, ABC anchorman Peter Jennings comes on, sober faced. "*There is chaos in New York at the moment, there have been two incidents ... the City of New York is ordering major evacuations...*

We stare, riveted to the screen.

Chapter 36

"Thus far we have been a great country rather than a great people. The unbelievably rich heritage of land and raw materials which had fallen into the lap of our fathers has often made us forget that it was luck rather than merit which is making us the wealthiest and most powerful nation in the world."

Hendrik van Loon. The Story of America. 1927.

Left right, left right, left right. A column of military personnel marches through the airport and civilians scurry out of their way. Sitting against a wall, I pull my boots back and make room. Babette's flight from France has been delayed several times but now, sixteen days after 9/11, she returns to a different America. Everyone is extremely tense. Security operatives don't bother disguising suspicious gazes as I turn pages in a nineteenth-century Octave Feuillete novel, every paragraph or so scanning for my professor at the gate.

At last her bushy wig appears, but moving unexpectedly fast in a wheelchair, neck bent as she chatters with the young woman pushing behind. I slam my book shut and jump up to trot beside them. Babette beams at me, then signals halt. I take her hand. The fingers are chilly but press back.

"Thanks, but I can handle things now," I tell the woman.

She nods gratefully and pats Babette's shoulder, "You take care now," she says, and turns away.

"Thanks so much for your help," calls my professor. Then her eyes meet mine with a warm smile. "Oh, Wrahs, what is that you were reading? Feuilette? Oh, Monsieur de Camors is his masterpiece. A pure tragic genius. But what about Jean-Paul Sartre? It torturers me Nausea still gathers dust in the library!"

"Glad to see you too. Don't worry, I'll tackle Nausea eventually. How was the flight? Are you ok?"

"Ah, yes, this machine seems a bit dramatic, but I am fine. Splendid in fact. But you see, at my age any mention of ill health brings such attention! Not because people care about elders, but through horror I might drop dead on their watch. Attendants hurried me off the plane so fast my wig nearly flew away! Please, I would rather walk, not be perambulated like some invalid."

Babette rises to her feet. She moves stiffly but soon steps alongside me with little difficulty. I abandon the wheelchair against a wall. We ride an escalator down to find her baggage carousel. It rotates but is still empty. Anxious passengers gather in small groups, watching closely. Another group of uniformed men stomp down the terminal past us, faces stern.

"Quite a time to visit France." I observe.

Babette shakes her head. "Americans. They have been so isolated from tragedy, even a small taste feels like civilization is ending. Wrahs, do you know the significance of September 11th in history?"

I nod. "Yeah, it's when the US helped put your Chilean friend General Pinochet in power. That was 1973, right?"

My professor chuckles. "Correct. I will not re-open arguments where we disagree. However, what springs to my mind is September 11th, 1944. On that date, British airplanes leveled a German town called Darmstadt to the ground with firebombs. Over ten-thousand people burned alive. There was no particular military necessity. Then remember Darmstadt was only one of many cities destroyed this way. But you know, despite other hardships, I doubt survivors expressed such ridiculous hand-wringing as Americans do today! It is all I have seen on the news... they ask why why why? God, it drives me mad! How many decades have I taught history? But people here still feel nothing from the past affects them. They ask why– and no one gives them an answer! Well, in Europe, where everyone understand well the repercussions of international empires, there is no mystery, but Americans are completely lost! As a public educator my entire life, I find it hard not taking this tragic spectacle personally. Perhaps it is I who sought to grasp the moon with my teeth! One thing is clear, we are in for a long dark night. Of course, when I say we, I mean you. I will be dead!" She cackles loudly. A young couple with their toddler nearby give us pained looks.

"Well, don't some people have all the luck!" I retort. "Are you sure this is the right place?"

"Ah, yes, I believe so. Look out for my plaid suitcase."

"Don't worry, I remember it."

Babette sighs. "Alas, to fret is useless. If my years teaching did good or ill, little can change it now. Oh, but look, there comes my luggage. You know, it is so useful having plaid things ... everyone can tell what you seek, no matter the color. Please, fetch it and let us be gone from this place."

We drive home and my professor immediately collapses exhausted into bed.

The new school year begins with a full load of history classes at Portland State and Babette's Saturday morning tours. Despite a tight schedule, I still manage the occasional night with Zoya. Bonnie Church often calls from Canada and my professor spends much time on the telephone speaking with her in hushed tones. Around mid-December, I am sorting mail in the kitchen when Babette comes downstairs, face pensive and maroon bathrobe open. She sits across from me at the table.

"Ah, Wrahs, have you a moment?"

"Certainly." I pass her several letters and bills.

She frowns, pushing them aside. "It is my daughters. They wish me to spend Christmas with them but such times are really never pleasant. I know your family celebrates the holidays. Do you think I might visit Seattle with you this year?"

I consider her request for a moment, then reply slowly. "My parents would agree if I asked."

Babette brightens.

"However," I continue, "you would need to be on good behavior."

She nods. "Naturally."

At this I can't help but laugh. "That's what I'm afraid of, your nature! I mean extremely good behavior. We attend midnight service on Christmas Eve, spend the next day with my grandparents and it's very traditional. No religious debates, no shocking people and I would also appreciate if you kept your clothes on the whole time."

Babette flings up both hands in protest, then firmly ties the sash of her robe in a bow. "I really find such admonishments unnecessary. Perhaps you have believed some vicious rumors!"

I grin, but my eyes narrow. "Don't cause trouble for me. I mean it."

On December 23rd, we ride Amtrak north together, though Babette plans on returning alone while I stay a few days longer. With unprecedented deference, my professor indeed keeps most inappropriate comments to herself over the holidays and, at other times, only a sharp glare keeps her in line.

The day after Christmas, I borrow my parents' Jetta and drive Babette to the train station downtown. She sits silently beside me, lips thin and tight. It's a blustery day and rain whips across the windshield. I pull up at the terminal, step out and unload her luggage. Babette still waits, frozen in place until I tap on the passenger window. She grimaces, climbs out and adjusts a thick red knit scarf around her neck. I extend the handle on her plaid rolling suitcase. My professor reaches for it, then lets her arm drop.

"Do you need help inside?" I look into her face.

She stares back vacantly through water-spattered glasses.

"With your bag," I prod, "can you pull it alone?"

"Oh, that. Yes, I will be fine." Her one focused eye tracks mine, then looks away.

"Are you ok?"

She clutches my arm, mouth trembling. "Do you know? When you first moved into my house, that I would test you? I left money around obvious places and then waited, in hope you might take it or steal from me other ways. I never detected any such thing. Can you imagine how infuriating that was? To live with someone I could find no advantage over?" She takes a breath. "Oh, it nearly killed me. But despite it all, these last years I really have become quite fond of you. I will even admit ... that I love you."

"Oh!" I move forward and wrap my arms around her broad torso. "I love you too."

It is the first time we have ever held one another. She smells of medical ointment and damp wool. I squeeze tightly, then release her, but the single eye still stares deeply into mine. Babette looks lost and a little scared.

"You'll be fine," I say, patting her shoulder. "In just a couple days I'll be back in Portland. You can humiliate me with Scrabble every night."

At last she smiles. "Yes, we shall do just that. Goodbye for now, dear Wrahs."

She turns and I watch her slowly drag the plaid suitcase through an automatic door into the terminal.

Chapter 37

"There are few women worthy of the name who are not ready to put into action all the words which passion has caused to bubble from their lips. If they speak of flight, they are ready for exile. If they talk of dying, they are ready for death. Men are far less consistent with their ideas."

Octave Feuilette. <u>Monsieur de Camors.</u> 1867.

It is a mid-January afternoon when I enter the kitchen, stomach growling, and overhear Babette in animated telephone conversation. "Yes ... well, we shall see ... Oh, I am delighted also! ... Alright then, let us speak again soon." She hangs up and swivels around, face contemplative. I pick through the refrigerator for sandwich ingredients and select leftover chicken in a covered glass bowl.

"There has been ... an unexpected development," she begins slowly.

I nod, slicing pieces off a thick rye loaf.

"It has recently come to my attention that I possess a long-lost sister," my professor continues, "and the two of us just now discovered one another."

"Really?" I lay cold meat slabs on the bread and open a jar of pickles.

"This woman's name is Rosalyn," she continues, "I would very much like to meet her in person. She is somewhat younger than myself and lives in Florida. I am so curious about what she looks like. Rosalyn sent a picture. It might arrive any day."

I slice a pickle and inhale the briny odor, then look up. Babette watches, eyes narrowed.

"Won't you congratulate me? Ah, such lackluster enthusiasm is deplorable. Perhaps that Zoya girl lingers on your mind. Or is it Buenaventura? I quite understand, they are both lovely."

I grin. "That is totally true, also– totally none of your business!"

She chortles with delight. "Oh, Wrahs, so sorry to intrude on your personal affairs! But would you be a dear and check the electronic mail upstairs when you can?"

"Sure, just let me eat first."

"That is fine, take your time. But this winter weather petrifies me to the marrow. I will be in the study where it is warm. Come find me there." She turns away and soon French news reverberates from the other room.

I sit down and chew my sandwich slowly. *A long-lost sister?* Well, at this point, why not? The wallpaper sailors and semaphore signals float beneath orange enameled pots. Outside, a light drizzle agitates puddles on the back patio. Once my food is devoured, I head upstairs. The computer slowly sputters into life and its dial-up service activates with a long staccato twitter. Babette's email inbox contains just one new message. It is from Mother Superior. I click it open. Alarm constricts my throat. Wasting no time, I switch on the printer and run a copy, then scamper downstairs. My professor sits in the study, afghan over her legs and space heater cranked high.

"*Oui?*" she asks. "Anything interesting?"

I read out loud:

Date: 1/15/02
Subject: Genesis 3:13-15

The woman said, "The serpent tricked me and I ate." The Lord God said to the serpent, "Because you have done this, cursed are you among all creatures; upon your belly you shall go, and dust you shall eat all the days of your life. I will put enmity between you and the woman, and between your offspring and hers; he will crush your head, and you will strike his heel."

I am of two minds as to what I will do with a folder I have here containing copies of your papers. Perhaps give them to the lady who is now half-owner of my house, or perhaps send them to a trusted ally or the clergy in Portland, or perhaps to your college. I have shared these happenings with all interested people here and in Portland, so the name Elizabeth, aka Albert aka Bobette or whomever it is now should be well known. Lie down with serpents, one had better be vaccinated against venom.

Babette's eyes sparkle and she jumps to her feet. The afghan falls away unnoticed.

"Aha! Our game is afoot!"

"That letter gave me chills. Do you really know what you're doing mixed up in all this?" I exclaim.

My professor smiles. "Wrahs, Wrahs, please do not worry. I have everything under control. Will you come and assist with my reply?"

"All right," I agree, "but if this nun shows up at the front door with a shotgun, you're on your own."

She laughs. "I find that unlikely. Come along."

Back at the keyboard, Babette stands behind me, almost bouncing with excitement.

"Do you have some macabre Biblical quotation in mind?" I ask.

"Really, I do not think anything so dramatic is necessary."

She begins dictating:

Dear Mother Superior,

I was absolutely astonished by your e-mail, its contents and its veiled threats. You should certainly be ashamed of yourself and I never thought you would stoop so low. It was the parish of St. Agatha that advised me to change the title of the property so that I became half-owner and the intent was to give my half title to the parish. Once this was done by their lawyers and accountant, the parish decided that it was too far away and when they examined the property they thought it was not suitable for their needs. So, I was left with a half title which I had not desired and therefore decided to give it away without any payment whatsoever just to get rid of it.

Conversations with you have always consisted of insults, accusations and threats and any possibility of discussion with you was completely impossible. Therefore, what I did was give the title of my house in Portland to St. Agatha parish in lieu of the half-

ownership of the property in Nanaimo. As you can see, I benefited nothing and neither did I want to. Why you make these wholesale condemnations and threats is absolutely unfathomable.

The Catholic Church, Revenue Canada and the US Government all have documents as to my changes of identity and have presented no objection. My status is therefore totally honest and clear. I pay my taxes in Canada as well as everywhere else in an honest way. I regret that you should have such personal feelings and thoughts as though I'm trying to gain something for nothing which as you see is absolutely not the case. Should you have been less accusing and more human it would have been possible to have a civilized and intelligent conversation.

While I have undergone four heart operations and my chronic leukemia has deteriorated considerably, it has been my purpose to divest myself of all assets in stocks, bonds, property, etc. I don't know what else I could have done and I am truly sorry for your most amazing reaction which was beyond my control. Should you have doubts about anything I am telling you, the financial administrator of St. Agatha in Portland could clarify matters. I know that reconciliation is not one of your strengths, but I hold absolutely no grudges.

Since you do mention threats, I have papers showing that you fraudulently extinguished the mortgage with your trust company in Toronto, made a new title in my name only, which was not recorded, and made a bill of sale creating a new title by which we were joint tenants. My lawyer told me what you had done was absolutely illegal and could actually bring you to justice, although I would certainly have no desire to do that.

Sincerely,
Sister Elizabeth

"Ok, is this how you want it?"

My professor squints at the screen. "It looks perfect. Thank you."

I click send.

"Is my message on its way?"

"Consider it delivered."

Babette looks down at me, her countenance grave. "For some time I have contemplated instructions in the event of my death. Will you hear them?"

I frown. "Of course, but why now? You seem a picture of vitality these days. Solo international travel, working full time and when did I last beat you at Scrabble? It's difficult to even remember!"

She smiles, though only slightly. "Indulge me."

"All right."

"For the sake of speculation, imagine you wake tomorrow, late, as is your wont, but I remain upstairs. Upon investigation you find my cold body, a study of rigor mortis. This is tragic naturally, but save your tears, important tasks await. The absolute first thing you must do is call Bonnie Church in Canada. Even if carrion birds feast on my eyeballs, do not brush them away, telephone Bonnie Church immediately, is that clear? Her number is in my directory."

"Notify Bonnie, yes."

"Good. Next, Wilhelm's funeral home, you know the one, on Milwaukie Avenue? I purchased cremation services there years ago. They will burn my corpse into cinders and mail the ashes to Canada. In Nanaimo, Bonnie shall scatter me throughout the convent garden. An obituary is already on file, the funeral home knows when it should run.

"Then, exactly four days after I have expired, call my attorney, Deborah Gray. She will communicate with the executor, who is a trusted colleague of mine, then conclude any family matters. As far as relatives go, if any show up at the house, do not let them in. Say: leave at once or I will call the police!"

I swallow hard. "Uh, Babette, that might be difficult."

"No! You simply tell them GO AWAY!"

"Ok, Ok."

"Next, destroy all paperwork that relates to Canada. Documents, cards, letters, ticket stubs– anything that indicates I have even visited there. Use the calcinator, it will leave no trace."

I throw up my arms. "This house is a dozen museums. How could I ever sift through all your files? It would take years!"

Babette smiles. "Exactly. Destroy what you can. Everything else will remain buried long enough for my purposes. The rest may become clear in time. But tell nobody about Canada. Especially not my lawyer. Are these wishes understood?"

"Yes, but you don't make things easy."

"Good. Oh, I think I just heard mail fall through the slot."

She shuffles downstairs and I follow. Indeed, a small pile of letters lies on the carpet. My professor sifts through them, musing to herself.

"Let me see, advertisements, the water bill, oh, a letter from your parents ... how nice, my doctor, what can she want? Aha!" She hands the stack over but clutches one small envelope to her breast. With a rush, she turns and disappears into the study.

I sit down at the dining room table and open my parents' letter. Some *New Yorker* cartoons, a disapproving newspaper editorial about Portland anti-war protests and their usual chitchat note. Just then Babette's bare feet come slapping past into the kitchen. She grabs up the phone and punches in numbers.

"Hello? Rosalyn? Yes, this is Elizabeth. I just received your wonderful letter ... Oh, thank you so much ... Not at all. But you know, the picture you sent is just a head shot. I really wanted something perhaps a little more, well ... physically descriptive ... No, I don't mean to complain, it is quite nice ... As far as you coming here ... oh ... all right, we can discuss that some other time ... Goodbye then."

My professor pads out, her frown severe. I look away and continue reading the article. She stalks wordlessly by and slams the door to her study.

The next morning before World Geography class, I check her e-mail account again, with more than slight apprehension, but only a short message from Rosalyn awaits. I print it out and knock on the master bedroom door.

"Yes? Come in." Babette invites

She sits on the edge of her blue chaise lounge, wig in one hand. The other picks at dry patches on her scalp.

"Nothing more from Mother Superior, but Rosalyn sent something brief. Do you want to hear it?" I ask, leaning against the door jamb.

"Please read."

I begin:

Dear Elizabeth. I feel a little overwhelmed. It means so much to me that we have become acquainted after all this time. You want to meet me and I want that also, but maybe it's still too soon. I just feel like sometimes all you care about is what I look like. If that's what's most important to you, perhaps the time isn't right.

Yours,
Rosalyn.

"Oh no!" Babette cries.

She drops her wig on the crimson carpet and pushes past me. Her bald pate bobs as she descends the stairs two at a time. "Be careful!" I call, running after. She ignores me, hurries to the phone and dials. Impatient fingers rattle the Formica counter until it picks up.

"Rosalyn!" she barks, "I want you to visit Portland. I don't care if you look like a fat pig! Don't worry, I will pay for everything, just say you'll come. We shall conclude details later, just agree please! … Yes, you say? Oh, wonderful, I am so delighted. All right, talk soon, my dear."

Babette sets down the telephone and beams. Short grey hair wisps above her ears and neck. A trickle of blood gleams on the shiny crown where she scratched away a scab. The thin red line winds downward, disappearing amidst bushy tufts.

Chapter 38

"... men will always have the desire to appear more than they are, and women to hide what they are."

Charles Paul de Kock. <u>The Barber of Paris</u>. 1826

"Alright, watch this." I place my word on the Scrabble board. "S-T-O-M-P. Only eight points, but with a *mot compte triple* that's twenty-four."

I add this number to our tally sheet. It's late afternoon on Thursday, February 14th and I sit across the kitchen table from my professor, a half completed game between us. She fidgets with her square wooden tiles; for once, I actually lead in points. 198 to 167. Dim winter light through open curtains illuminates the room.

Babette sighs, lips pursed. "What an awful choice. I feel it describes the weight of your boots on my poor neck. Surely you have not added the numbers correctly."

I grin triumphantly. "If you want a recount, be my guest."

She takes a drink of mineral water. "No, no, that would only revisit my agony. But listen, I hear a knock, it must be our guest." She half-rises, then settles back. "Ahem, Wrahs, would you be so good as to answer? Let me ... collect myself a moment."

"Ok. Don't cheat and look at my letters."

I approach the door and open it wide. Cold wind swirls past me, ruffling the grey hair of a woman who stands alone on the porch, a brown suitcase beside her. At the curb, a yellow Broadway cab shifts into gear and pulls away down Tolman Street. Something is wrong. I squint, focusing on my professor's face. At least it looks like her face. The same round head and unmistakable features look back. I stare, as surely as the day I moved in, surprised by Babette standing naked where I now hesitate. Details begin breaking through. This woman is shorter, with a slighter build; her form more feminine. Before either of us can speak, Babette shoulders me aside.

"Rosalyn! Come in, come in! Wrahs, don't just loiter there, be a good host and put on water for tea. Would you like tea, Rosalyn?"

The woman steps inside and sets down her luggage. She looks around, then nods at each of us. My professor reaches out, clasping her hand, then pulls close for an awkward hug.

"Elizabeth!" Rosalyn murmurs, her voice hesitant. "It's so good seeing you ... to meet you finally."

Quietly, I turn and set a kettle on the stove. Low conversation sounds from the hallway. After a few moments, Babette enters the kitchen, long-lost sister in tow.

"Ah, Rosalyn, I would like you to meet Wrahs. He lives in the pantry downstairs and helps me with daily activities. I really don't know how I could manage otherwise these days." Babette reaches into a cupboard and takes down two gold rimmed china tea cups.

I shake Rosalyn's hand. "Pleased to meet you. I made the guest bedroom upstairs all ready."

She fixes me with mild blue eyes. "Thank you. This is a strange time for us, but I appreciate your hospitality ... it's, well ... hard finding words..."

My professor clears her throat. "Ahem, thank you, Wrahs, I do not believe you will be required the rest of today. Please put away that deplorable game. We shall play again when I feel more competitive. Why don't you visit that Zoya girl this evening? Tomorrow, however, I have invited several students over for dinner and a film afterward. Your assistance will be greatly appreciated then." She turns away. "Now Rosalyn, which tea would you like, we have quite a selection! Oh, I must give you a tour of my library..."

I sigh, fold the Scrabble board and tilt our tiles back into the box. My winning words disintegrate, now a meaningless jumble. Behind me, the two women pick through packets and Babette launches into a long anecdote about the British East India Company. Rosalyn looks perplexed, but once the kettle whistles, holds out her cup. She follows my professor downstairs, steeping tea in hand. I stash our Scrabble game in a closet and dial The

House of Many Pleasures. Zoya answers after a few rings.

"Hello?"

"Hey, it's me. I got the night off, can I come over?"

"Definitely. Sal planned a Star Trek marathon later, but we can do something else if that sounds lame."

I grin. "Actually, after a week immersed in books for my 20th Century Intellectual History class and Jules Simenon mystery shows every evening, Star Trek sounds great. Babette's been on a Maigret kick lately."

"Who?"

Oh, an old French detective series. It's good stuff but I could use a break."

"Right on. Hey, do you think you'll have tomorrow night free also? Dawn is throwing an '80s theme party. It should be fun. I'm going as Grace Jones. Not sure about Sal, he might be Nina Hagen."

"Wow, that sounds awesome. Maybe I can borrow one of Babette's wigs. Think that would do for Blanche on the Golden Girls?"

Zoya laughs. "Oh my God, I wish!"

"Right. Ok, well, I'll be over in a bit then."

An hour later, Sal answers my knock at his apartment door. He is uncharacteristically dressed down with dark stubble and hair wound up in a black beret. Behind him on the elevated bed are piled videotapes. I step inside, and my boots crunch a Styrofoam Chinese take-out box. Chow mein oozes onto the carpet.

"Sorry!" I apologize. "Didn't see it down there."

Sal frowns. "So that's where the smell was coming from!"

Zoya's door opens, and she approaches for an embrace but stops short. "Sall-eeee! I told you to throw your cheapie Chinese out! That's fucking disgusting!"

"All right, all right!" Sal scoops up the decomposing food, opens a window and tosses it outside. From the sidewalk, one story below, comes a light plop.

Zoya rolls her eyes. "Great. Anyway, how are you Ross? What's up at home?" She hugs me, then draws back for a short, sweet kiss.

I sit down on a low plastic milk crate and draw up my knees.

"Well, just when I think it can't get any weirder. Babette's long lost sister arrived today. Here's the thing. They're almost identical. I mean, I've seen pictures of her daughters, there's a definite similarity, but this is just creepy."

Sal thumbs through a container of records. "Who even has long lost sisters anyway?"

I shrug. "Europeans apparently. It's just like her old French novels I've been reading. They all have plot twists where the protagonist discovers some sworn enemy is actually the brother of his fiancé."

Zoya smiles. "At least your life is never boring."

I reach out and stroke her leg. "Seriously. Hey, let's start the Trek. I could handle turning my brain off for a little while."

Sal selects a videotape, and we all climb up on top of his bed. Soon, all thoughts of long lost relatives are light years from my mind.

The next afternoon I catch a bus home and begin entertainment preparations. Babette has already laid out a fresh scarlet tablecloth in the dining room. We augment this with ferns and other greenery picked from the garden in vases. I set places for six, using blue and yellow Spode Bluebird china. My professor nods and presses her palms together approvingly.

"Excellent. We should expect guests around seven o'clock. After dinner, I will show one of my favorite films, 'Babette's Feast.' You remember it, don't you?"

"Of course."

"Do you mind seeing it again?"

"Well, my friend Dawn is throwing a party. Since you seem so preoccupied with Rosalyn, I thought it might be a good night to stay out again."

"That is fine, at least we saw it together before. Oh, such a wonderful story, the way Babette gives up everything she has for one last fantastic meal. At any rate, here is my idea for our actual feast. I have filet mignon steaks frozen downstairs. They would taste delicious in teriyaki sauce. Do you think we have some?"

My eyebrows raise. "If you mean multiple gallon jugs, then yes."

Babette grits her teeth. "I see. An observation not without

barbs. Perhaps you could retrieve the meat and defrost it while I suffer in silence? I would retire upstairs to repair my wounded feelings but Rosalyn waits with a book of hers ... something about ancient astronauts ... don't you dare laugh! Really, this visit is not at all what I expected."

I grin "That lecture on the role of tea trading in the British Empire wasn't up her alley, huh? She flies back Sunday. I'm sure you can get along until then."

My professor bobs her head. "True. I have little reason to complain. This reunion is such ... well, a difficult experience. Nothing could have prepared me." She looks over my shoulder. "Ah, Rosalyn! Would you assist us preparing dinner?"

I turn and see her sister who stands behind me, book in hand. She sets it down awkwardly.

"Here," I offer, "there are some potatoes we need peeled."

"Thanks," she says softly, "I'd like helping."

I find Rosalyn a potato peeler and set her to work, then fetch steaks from downstairs. As the meat softens in a tub of water, I pour vegetable oil into a bowl. When the potatoes are done, we roll them in oil and shake on garlic salt.

She smiles at this. "Oh, such a mess! Good thing I packed several shirts, it's all over my sleeves now!"

I hand her a dishtowel. "Don't fret, both you and dinner are well seasoned. There should be enough greens to make a decent salad as well, let me check." I open the refrigerator.

"Don't touch my fruit!" calls out Babette.

"What's that?"

"My canned fruit. It was very expensive. I saw you eying it with sheer greed!"

I notice a glass jar above the vegetable crisper. Multicolored sections of mango, peach and whole cherries float in clear syrup. "Do you mean this?" I hold it out.

"Yes! Put them back at once!"

"Ok, Ok, don't worry. Nobody will eat your fancy fruit."

At 6:15 I slide our garlic potatoes into the convection oven and switch it on. The machine emits a high-pitched whine. On the stovetop, meat bubbles away under tinfoil in two metal pans. Soon delicious aromas thicken the air.

Twenty minutes later the doorbell rings and I answer. It's Angela, the chubby blonde woman who attended our first dinner party. It seems so long ago now. She steps inside, and I take her parka to hang up.

"Wow!" she exclaims. "I wish I could keep my apartment this warm. Feels like ninety degrees in here."

I nod. "You're close, we do peg it at eighty-eight. Babette likes the temperature Mediterranean."

Angela smiles. "Well, she's earned it. So, how are you doing? I never see you on campus anymore."

"Oh, that's because I transferred to Portland State about a year ago. Just working in a history degree there. That's fine, but you know, I do kinda miss Portland Community. It's much smaller and more laid back..."

Just then my professor bustles in, Rosalyn close behind her. "Angela!" she cries, "so pleased you made it. This is my sister Rosalyn. Visiting all the way from Florida!" Babette gushes onward with delight "Angela takes all of my classes and tours. She was on my last trip to the high desert. Wasn't that wonderful? Such a shame my health no longer permits longer excursions. Come into the living room. I must put on some music."

We follow, and Babette flips through her classical records. "Bruckner? No, not tonight. Mozart ... perhaps .... let me see here, Brahms ... dear, dear me...oh, is that the doorbell? Wrahs, please go answer!"

I discover two young men on the porch, one with dark curly hair, the other taller; a long ponytail down his back. "Looking for the Ellsworth dinner party and international cinema spectacular?" I inquire. "Then you found the right spot."

They step past me and look around with wondering eyes at the artifacts, from old rusty rifle to antique clockwork. My professor has finally settled on an LP in the other room. I recognize a favorite, Walter Gieseking playing Debussy.

The shorter man holds out his hand. "Andreas Gianopolous" he declares. We shake. The other man is still distracted by Babette's Quebec clock.

"God, just look at this, Andy, you can see its mechanism through the glass!" He straightens up. "Sorry ... these pieces are amazing. I'm Brian. Are you from one of Dr. Ellsworth's other classes?"

I shake his hand as well. "My name's Ross. Former student, now basement resident. Here, come along."

They trail behind me into the parlor where Babette stands before her grand painting of the Château du Lac, hands aflutter in the midst of a story.

"...you see, Felix Yusupov possessed quite a complicated sexual life and later claimed Rasputin came to the Yusupov palace in hopes of seducing his wife Irina– except everyone knew she was at some dacha in the countryside. Some historians wonder if he actually lured Rasputin there by suggesting a homosexual liaison and then murdered the man. We will never know ... oh, Andreas and Brian! This is wonderful, welcome to my house! Wrahs, open some wine and fetch glasses please."

I twist my heel against the carpet. "Ok, do you have a ... preference?"

"Yes! You can find a red burgundy in my study. It is exquisite... the spirit of 'Babette's Feast' decrees we cannot drink anything less tonight."

I head toward the study as my professor makes introductions all around. Beside folders of historical articles on her writing desk sits an unopened bottle. I half expect it to be Ripple but the label is French. It looks expensive. In the kitchen I tear off foil around the neck, twist down a corkscrew and pull. It bursts free with a light pop. The scent is delicious; rich and fruity, yet slightly tart. From a cupboard I select crystal goblets, set them in a row, then fill each halfway. As I finish, Babette leads her guests through the door. She picks up a glass.

"Ah, excellent. Thank you Wrahs! Everybody take one ... we must drink a toast! But to what?"

"We should drink to your health, Dr. Ellsworth!" suggests Angela.

Babette chuckles. "Oh no, my health is too poor. Let us toast our gathering tonight ... to special times with friends!"

"Perfect!" agrees Andreas. We all drink deeply.

Angela shakes her head. "You know, I thought nothing could surpass the fancy old wine you served at that one dinner, but this is fantastic."

I choke a little and frown. My professor glares at me, then inspects our steaks cooking away on the stovetop. "Ahem ... I think these are done. Are you all ready to eat?"

Everyone sits down and I carry in food on ornate serving platters. It takes several trips. Once everything is ready I take a seat between Angela and Brian. Rosalyn sits across from me, back stiff. I meet her mild blue eyes and nod. She allows a slight smile back.

Babette looks around with satisfaction. "Thanks to you all for coming. As I mentioned before, later we shall view a film called 'Babette's Feast.' It tells the story of a woman who pours everything she has into a magnificent meal for her friends. I make no such grand claims about this repast before us, but hope you find it acceptable. Please, eat!

"However, there is a story I must recount that concerns this meal. We all know, the French are reputed as masters of fine cuisine, but this was not always so. During the 1500s, France underwent a great period of turmoil, mostly because of wretched Protestants." She turns her head to wink at me.

"Catherine de' Medici ruled the country with great strength and cruelty. I consider her a true inspiration for any woman who wishes to thrive in this world. At any rate, one of her sons was Henri III, a weak willed individual, most likely homosexual. Catherine even ordered him served meals by attractive naked women in hopes of changing his persuasion, but this failed utterly. Henri surrounded himself with a sycophantic group of young men who fawned over him and became known as *les mignons*, which means the dainty ones or cuties.

"Now, with France so frequently in a state of civil war between religious groups, food became scarce for common people and even royalty experienced difficulty finding a cow that hadn't been worked half to death. Such beasts naturally tasted like shoe leather. The vile English, of course, took as much advantage of this situation as they could and entered a period of relative prosperity. Their upper classes slaughtered healthy cattle and dined on meat like what we consume tonight."

Babette pauses, taking a large bite of steak. She washes it down with two sips of wine and continues, red stains down the side of her mouth.

"So, it came about that when a group of English nobles visited Catherine de' Medici's court, they imported beef to share for an evening's banquet. Everyone else had gone so long without consuming decent meat, they fell all over themselves with compliments. The English laughed and said 'Yes, our cutlets are indeed tender. One might even say they are as tender as *les mignons*!'

"Well, many French courtiers found this observation hilarious and soon called an especially good cut of meat a filet mignon, literally a cut of cutie! The English for their part, considered Henri's little playmates rather unappealing and adopted the word for themselves into minion, so under Anglophone usage, the French cutie becomes a mindless obeyer or drone. It is amusing how these things happen, *oui*? Well, you must admit you have learned something tonight– and for no extra cost!"

The table bursts into laughter. Brian elbows me in the ribs. "Does Dr. Ellsworth ever run out of these stories?" he asks.

I set down my fork. "No, this is pretty much how she is all the time. Just like a history faucet."

Andreas gestures at his plate. "Everything is so wonderful. It's like I've died and gone to heaven."

Angela dabs her lips with a pink and white serviette. "I'm already full, but haven't tried everything yet. Maybe just one potato– they look so good, could you pass those, Rosalyn?"

Brian leans back and stretches. "God, I can hardly move. Someone may need to kick me during the movie if I pass out."

While our guests consume final portions, I clear away empty dishes and rinse them in the sink. My limbs hang heavy from wine and rich food. With a sponge, I scrub each piece of the beautiful Spode Bluebird service and set them in the drying rack. The metal pans take longer, where teriyaki sauce and meat particles have baked onto the bottom. I give up and leave them soaking in soapy water. From the other room, chairs creak as students rise to follow Babette upstairs. Soon dialogue from the introduction of 'Babette's Feast' filters down. Just as I finish washing up, my professor appears in the doorway. She beams at me.

"Thank you for your help, Wrahs, I really feel dinner tonight was a success."

"No problem. Yes, it did seem like everyone enjoyed themselves. Aren't you going to watch the film with them?"

"Oh, I have seen it so many times. But I come asking a favor since I am now weary. Would you please fetch a book from the basement? It is called A Distant Mirror by Barbara Tuchman. Andreas, that Greek student, is interested in the late Middle Ages and I recommend her work as an excellent treatment of the period."

I nod and dry my hands. "Sure, give me a second."

My boots clip downstairs to the library. The gas fireplace flickers away and soft orange light bathes every surface. My professor leaves it burning all winter long to prevent moisture. I scan past the extensive Roman history section until titles look promising. The Invention of the Crusades ... Women in the Middle Ages ... The Land of the Cathars ... I must be close. At last my eyes land on A Distant Mirror. I pull out the hardback and return to find my professor seated at the cleared dining room table. She nods and casually flips open the title page. With a cry, she drops it as if the pages were flames.

"Ah! No! This won't do. Wrahs, Wrahs, find me a pen, something quickly!"

"Calm down, I have a permanent marker in my pocket. Here, is that ok?"

Babette takes the black Sharpie and hunches over her book, scribbling madly. I recognize a familiar stamp on the front page. It adorns most every tome in the house and reads: "From the library of Albert Ellsworth." My professor crosses out the first name with thick strokes and writes ELIZABETH above it in large capital letters.

"There!" she crows. "Now it can be properly lent out. I will rejoin the others upstairs now, oh, but first, Wrahs, there is a scheme I have contemplated these last few days. Do you know whose birthday comes in two months?"

I frown. "Uh, lots of people! That's way too vague."

Babette's lips crack wide. "April 20 is Hitler's birthday. Can you imagine my plan? I will have a mass said for Adolf Hitler!"

I clap a hand to my forehead. "Can you just request that at church? I don't know what the procedure is, but surely someone would object!"

"Oh, you can have mass said for anyone!"

"Right, but, do you think St. Agatha's might rather perform it in the middle of the night, when no one is paying attention?"

"You may have a point. I know! ... I will have mass said for Adolf of Linz, after his hometown in Austria. That may keep people from asking too many questions. I don't know why it has taken me so long to discover your true purpose in life, but it is truly crushing my dreams!" Babette waves her arm dramatically and moves toward the staircase. I follow.

"So, you're still fine with Rosalyn helping tomorrow on the tour, right?"

"Yes, she will come along. It is my Mt. St. Helens trip. Honestly, I do not look forward. This cold weather is unbearable early in the morning and even on a heated bus, my bones never warm up. But that is enough complaints. Thank you again for assistance with dinner. Go have fun tonight. Rosalyn and I should return late afternoon tomorrow. I shall see you then, dear Wrahs."

She turns and walks up the stairs, steps hesitant. I return to the kitchen and finish drying the dishes with a towel. Colorful plates and bowls clatter together as I stack them away in the china cupboard. Serviettes, dishrags and table cloth whisper down the laundry chute. Downstairs in my quarters, I throw on a thick olive drab jacket and toss toothpaste, toothbrush, deodorant and clean underwear into my satchel. Through casement windows, white frost coats rhododendron leaves that tap against dark glass. As I exit the house, Babette call out a muffled comment from above, and her students burst into peals of laughter.

Chapter 39

"What do you think, my lord, of all these wonderful events? … It all ends up like a regular tragi-comedy … But, after all, it is not so surprising perhaps as it seems at the first glance–since the theatre is only a copy of real life."

Theophile Gautier. Captain Fracasse. 1861.

The next morning I wake beside Zoya on the beige carpet of Dawn's apartment in northeast Portland. Her dreadlocks, smelling faintly of tobacco and almond oil, splay across my rolled-up jacket under our heads. I stretch underneath the stained pink quilt covering us and my feet poke out into cold air. They rattle against crumpled beer cans. The floor is also littered with plastic cups, jeans, undershirts, several sparkly wigs, a leather belt and long string of blue and green beads.

I sit up, yawning. Dawn and Salazar are sprawled by the television, where Blanche yells something at Sophia while Rose looks befuddled. Why they are watching more Golden Girls episodes I cannot imagine. A wall clock reads almost two in the afternoon. Zoya stirs and pulls the quilt tight around her.

"You getting up?" she mutters.

"Yeah, it's late. I've got homework."

Her eyelids flutter, then shut again. "Ok ... I sleep more ... call me later …"

I extricate myself and tuck the blanket back around Zoya's chin, then plant a kiss against her smooth brown cheek. She smiles. I shiver as a chilly draft upbraids my bare torso. There are black trousers crumpled nearby, hopefully mine. Outside, rain patters against foggy windowpanes. I pick through party detritus until pants, mechanics shirt and boots turn up. My hands gently lift Zoya's head and replace the jacket with a sofa cushion.

Salazar looks over, red eyed. "Going?"

I nod. "Yeah, did you two ever pass out?"

Dawn groans. "Somewhat. It's all a blur. This was probably my best party ever. I think everyone dressed up ... except you, Ross!"

"Sorry. I had a dinner party to prepare. I'll make a better effort next time. Anyway, gotta go catch a bus, see you guys later."

I exit Dawn's apartment into a pelting rain shower. The side pocket of my jacket contains a black stocking cap and wool gloves with the fingers cut off. I slip these on and walk east toward 39th Avenue. Fortunately there are several covered stops at the Hollywood light rail transfer station. A forlorn looking waif who pulls her dark hoodie around narrow shoulders and two gutter punks with well-worn butt flaps share the glass enclosed shelter. They reek of shag tobacco and body odor. I lean against one support post and pull out my most recent Babette recommendation, Endymion by the nineteenth-century British Prime Minister Benjamin Disraeli. Water droplets run down transparent side panels with a fury as overhead clouds tear apart. Liquid shadows dribble along each page.

Before long, a southbound #75 pulls up, wet brakes squealing. I take a seat near the rear and continue my book. The bus rolls along, wipers in constant motion, left-right-left-right-left-right. Condensation shrouds each window and I wipe a circle clear with the back of my hand to monitor street signs and landmarks. We pass Division Street, then Powell Boulevard and Trader Joe's until finally Woodstock nears. I yank the stop cord. Upon standing, my boots slip on the wet floor. I grab a vertical support to remain upright. One of the punks snickers. I ignore him and step out the back door as several young Reed students with book bags clamber in the front.

The rain has paused finally, yet thick drops tremble and fall from naked tree limbs along Tolman Street. Our neighbor's pickup truck still has a small dent around the rear wheel well where Babette backed into it last time. The driveway sits empty as expected. The Mt. St. Helens tour is a long one. My professor and Rosalyn shouldn't return for a while. I can tidy up more from last night entertaining, then maybe get some homework done.

I walk up the front steps, wipe my feet and unlock the door.

Every light burns and no letters wait under the postal slot. *Strange.* Mail usually comes early on Saturdays. I move into the dining room. A fresh copy of Maclean's is on the table. Now I pause, uneasy. From the kitchen comes a faint murmur, then something squeaks on linoleum. I turn the corner, heart pounding. At the kitchen table sit two women. I recognize Rosalyn; yet the other seems oddly familiar– with oval glasses and long gray hair coiled in a bun. I look from one to the other, and they stare back, faces grim. My mouth opens. There is something I should ask but I don't know how.

Rosalyn speaks first. "Ross, Elizabeth died this morning. She had a heart attack."

I drop my bag on the floor. Voices continue, but no longer intelligible. Language splinters apart and shards cut every direction. Even pain feels muffled as I try fitting sharp pieces together.

The woman who isn't Rosalyn stands and approaches. I focus on her face. It is lined and pale with intense violet eyes. Her mouth moves, the words precise.

"I'm sorry Ross, sometimes ... life … happens. My name is Sandra Baily. I work at the PCC records department. You came through my office last year about transfer credits. Are you all right? Do you want to sit down?"

My head throbs and hands tremble. Sandra leads me toward the table and pulls out a chair. I sink into it. Rosalyn turns her head, gaze steeled. The meek facsimile of my professor has vanished.

"There are things you should know, Ross," Rosalyn begins. "Let's be completely truthful with one another."

I lower my eyes. "Well, I'll go first. A confession. Every e-mail you got from Babette, I typed. She just dictated them."

Rosalyn's mouth curls into a tight smile. "Oh, I always knew that. But your honesty is appreciated. So I will tell you who I really am. It requires traveling back in time, the year 1946 when Albert returned home to Yakima from France. You see, Albert never met his birth mother, Mildred Sweet, before. You can imagine this strange homecoming, he a worldly young man of seventeen and she a simple rural woman, then only in her mid-thirties. There's no easy way to say it ... they had sex. Albert never got along with her husband, Albert Ellsworth, Sr. and almost immediately fled to Portland. What he didn't realize is Mildred became pregnant. The resulting child was me." Rosalyn sits back, lips thin.

Behind us, cheese molders away under the glass bell, rind dark around a pasty white core. Outside, a crow dips its beak into the concrete bird bath. Intermittent raindrops fleck the surface. I rub my forehead.

"So ...then you are Babette's sister, like she said, but... daughter also. Shit ... sorry, when did you discover this?"

"Several years ago. I hesitated contacting Elizabeth for quite some time. A lost brother? A father? Then to find perhaps a mother? What could I even say? How do you begin the conversation? But as you know, I eventually did. This wasn't the best reunion, but it was all we could have. It's all we had time for ..." Her voice trails off.

"But, what happened ... today? This morning? Babette ..."

Rosalyn clears her throat and sniffs. "We woke early. Right from the beginning Elizabeth didn't feel well. I said to cancel the tour, but she refused. We had a little breakfast, just oatmeal, though she hardly ate. Then I drove us down to the Sylvania Campus parking lot. Elizabeth still felt sick and cold, oh, the way it hurt her was dreadful. I stayed in the car with her, heater running until everyone boarded. We climbed on, but once Elizabeth reached the top step she collapsed, right there in front of forty students."

"It was just that sudden?" I ask, shuddering. "Could she speak?"

"No, not a word, she just ... dropped. I was right behind her and thought maybe she only tripped. Someone with a cell phone called 911. Elizabeth was barely breathing when the ambulance arrived. They put her in back and took me along. I sat holding her hand, holding it until she just ... let go. I think she knew her teaching career was over. She could tell and just gave up. I held her hand and talked to her ... Ross, that's all I could do ... I told her she'd be ok, I told her she wasn't alone ..."

At this Rosalyn's voice cracks. Sandra reaches across the table and clasps her hand. "You're being so strong," she says quietly, then looks at me.

"Rosalyn didn't know what to do, Ross," says Sandra. "She

knew Bobbie trusted you completely, but couldn't get a hold of you. There was no one else. So the school contacted me for assistance in this unusual matter. You see, I married Albert a short while after Billie's death. We were close friends for decades and contemplated spending our final years together, but as the reality of his decision to become a woman set in, I realized things couldn't work. It was just ...well, too weird. I'm a grandmother, for crying out loud! And I ... well, I'm not ... a lesbian. We divorced in 1994, just after his sex change. At any rate, Rosalyn hoped I could reach Bobbie's relatives. In fact, I did. Two of her daughters from Washington are en route, they should arrive in less than an hour."

"Oh no! NO!" I leap to my feet. The room spins. Orange enameled pots blur with whimsical nautical wallpaper through mists of panic. The women stare at me, stunned.

"You were right!" I cry, "I do know exactly what Babette wanted. She was VERY specific with me. No family at all. In fact, she said if they came to the house, I should call the police!"

Sandra frowns, her face pained. "I'm sorry, I didn't know. It seemed the best thing. Are you sure she that's what she said?"

"Yes! She spelled out every word, and very recently, almost as if she knew. She made me promise. This is awful!"

Sandra shakes her head. "Well, it's too late to stop them. I guess if Bobbie wanted police involved, that's your decision."

A sheen of sweat spreads across my brow. I take a deep breath. "This is all off script now. I'll just have to make it up from here and follow her wishes as best I can."

Rosalyn pushes a lock of grey hair back from her temple. "Well, I can't say I'm looking forward to this reunion either."

My eyes focus on her, an ordinary woman who could blend in seamlessly at any church social or PTA meeting. Suddenly, I feel a wave of sympathy. At least I voluntarily stayed in Babette's pantry and shared her adventures. Poor Rosalyn lost all chance of escape the day Mildred Sweet and young Albert reunited in 1946; ever since shackled through blood to a story more bizarre than any ancient UFO theory.

Antique clocks tick away. I stare at the telephone. *Bonnie Church should have been alerted, not Babette's family. Would Rosalyn and Sandra mind if I started burning Canadian papers right now? Maybe I could ask them for help. It's only to cover up some kind of shady international finances over who controls a fake Benedictine convent!* At this I almost laugh, but turn it into a choked cough.

Sandra raises an eyebrow. "Are you ok?"

I sigh. "No, not really. This is just absurd. It's so perfect in some ways. Babette wanted to teach until the end ... and she did. She loved shocking everyone and with a final act like that, no one will ever forget her. But now the people she liked least are almost here and, you know, I don't think I can just slam the door in their faces. They do have more of a right to be here than me now. How could I call the police anyway? The family obviously has priority. I'm just a weird subculture kid from the basement. Maybe if I'm lucky they'll give me twenty minutes to clear out."

Rosalyn's eyes widen. "I'm sure they wouldn't do that! You helped Elizabeth so much!"

I look away. "Maybe. I guess we'll find out soon enough."

The light outside is dimming. It's half past five. Despite no sustenance in my belly since a succession of cheap beers last night, I can't imagine eating. Outside, the rain has picked up again. It drums against every window with relentless fury. I rub a chipped corner of the red Formica countertop. Forty-five minutes later the doorbell rings. Sandra and Rosalyn look at me expectantly. I walk down the hallway, take a deep breath and open the door. On the porch stand six figures, heads wreathed in mist from the cold.

"Hi, I'm Ross, the basement dweller. Come inside." I invite. The group moves past and circle awkwardly. There are two women who must be in their mid-fifties, one stout, with dark bobbed hair, the other taller, who looks around curiously through horn-rimmed glasses under grey bangs. The shorter one fixates on me, gaze serious.

"Hello Ross. I'm Joyce. This is my sister Ethel." She gestures toward the taller woman, then squeezes the arm of a pudgy man who nods at me, lips berry bright within a clipped white beard. "My husband Allen." This fellow removes a hand from his jacket pocket and shakes mine, expression solemn. Drops of rain spatter his plaid scarf.

Ethel wipes her glasses and sniffs. Beside her slouches a

skinny fellow with prominent cheekbones and balding pate. He straightens up, pumping my hand. "Jeffry," he rasps. "I'm Ethel's husband. Sorry, bit under the weather. Caught the cold going around, y'know." His eyes rove about the entryway, from my professor's photograph in her Santa costume to rusty Mauser rifle.

Beside a hefty bearded man around my age, I recognize Babette's granddaughter who surprised me the day I moved in. She removes a black beret covering blonde hair and grins at me.

"Hey Ross, nice to see you again. Sorry I startled you that one time ... was afraid my grandpa might run out into the street all ñaked and cause a scene. Anyway, I'm Lauren .... this is my boyfriend Robby. Mom called us up a few hours ago, that's how we heard the news." She glances sidelong at Joyce. "I live in town these days, but thought we should wait until her and the fam showed up before coming over. So, as you can imagine everyone is curious, what's going on?"

Each of the three unmistakable Ellsworth faces stare at me. Their male partners shift uneasily from foot to foot.

I clear my throat. "Well, there are some people you should meet. Come this way."

Everyone follows me into the kitchen. Sandra and Rosalyn are still seated around the small table but rise and greet them. I retreat to lean against the counter. Rain spatters steamy windows and pans from last night's dinner party soak away in the sink. Tiny black webs of mold spin across Babette's cheese under its glass bell and my stomach revolts. I choke down sour bile as conversation fragments float around me.

"A heart attack! ... Right in front of everyone? ... Those poor students...such a shock! ... Wait, Sandra, you were Dad's second, no, third wife? ... Oh, Rosalyn, what an ordeal, thank you for sharing everything with us..."

Dazed, I study the physiognomy, shadowy imprints of my professor, passed down through generations. Ticks from every clock ring out like hammer blows, vibrations rattling me boots to bones. Voices fall silent at last. Now Joyce turns toward me. My heart seizes.

"Well," she asks, "what do we do now? It seems you probably know what my father wanted more than anyone."

This is it.

"You're right," I admit. "I do know exactly what Babette wanted. She told me that when she died, I shouldn't have contact with any relatives and if her family showed up at the house ...well … not to let them in." I look down. The linoleum tiles are tracked with mud residue from so many shoes. Three brown skeletonized leaves lie flattened in sharp relief near the recycling bin. Silence stretches.

Jeffrey emits a short cough, it might almost be a laugh. "Sounds just like old Albert, doesn't it?" He snorts.

The others nod slowly. My heart begins beating again. Sandra makes the next move.

"It's been very meaningful providing what help I could today," she begins, pulling a wool jacket around her narrow shoulders, "but I think my usefulness here is done. Bobbie's death means the passing of a dear friend. I will always remember her fondly. I know Albert wasn't a perfect parent, but try not to hold onto resentment now he's gone." She buttons the collar up to her chin. "I wish you all well and goodnight. I can find my way out."

She leaves the kitchen. Moments later the front door slams shut and a brief draft rushes past us. Ethel pats her husband's shoulder and looks around.

"Well, I don't know about the rest of you, but I'm starving. It seems we aren't welcome here. Let's find a restaurant and get some food. Rosalyn and Ross, you can both come out with us."

I look away. "That's generous, but I'm not hungry."

Rosalyn bobs her head. "Actually, I'll join you. Who knows when I might ever be in this part of the country again? And … you're family."

Lauren shoots me a concerned glance. "Are you sure? It's really no problem. You don't have to be a recluse."

My eyes focus again on the floor. "No, I'm fine. I don't want company right now. Go ahead without me."

Rosalyn reaches for a thick sweater on the back of her chair and buttons it up. "I think we all understand you need some space."

The group turns away. Footsteps fill the hallway and winter air flows around me once more until the door firmly shuts. A whiff of decaying leaves and wet pavement fills my nose. The wall clock reads minutes after seven. There's no more time to waste. I open Babette's alphabetized phone directory. Her handwriting is terrible. *Church? Hopefully this isn't the local Catholic parish hotline. No, it can't be, with an international country code.* I punch in the number. It rings and rings. My boot squeaks against the floor.

Finally a voice breaks in, tinny and distant, but familiar.

"Hello?"

"Oh, Bonnie, I'm so glad you're home!" I take a full breath. "Babette died this morning at school. She had a heart attack. I only found out a short while ago. Her family already knows. There was no avoiding it. The administration got her daughters involved, they came by the house just now."

Bonnie is silent a moment, then collects herself. "... Ok, Ross, don't panic, I know exactly what to do. Has her attorney been contacted?"

"Not by me. You're the first call, that's what she said."

"We're still good then. It's late now, but I can jump on this first thing tomorrow. How long until you're supposed to let the lawyer know?"

"Babette said four days, but her executor is a colleague and I'm sure everyone on the faculty has heard by now. It would look suspicious if I delay."

"Right, right, eh? But I won't need long to get things initiated at least. Just give me one business day head start, let's see, it's still Saturday. Can you wait until Tuesday morning?"

"Sure. Also … there's more. Her sis ... well, long story. A relative is staying here. I'll tell you more about that later. Anyway, she's supposed to fly home tomorrow. I can't destroy any Canadian papers until that lady's gone for sure."

"Right, I understand. Do what you can. But I'm so curious, what happened when Babette's daughters showed up? From the things she always told me about them, I'm surprised you aren't calling from a payphone with your things in cardboard boxes!"

"Yeah, I know. But here's the thing, they were really decent. I'd expected an order to pack my bags and clear out, but as soon as I told them Babette didn't want family in the house, everyone just left. I couldn't believe it. But for all I know, the lawyer will tell me I have no right to be here. Plus even if I'm not evicted, there's only

$65 in my bank account, that won't cover bills around here."

"Ross, if you're really hurting for money, I can help."

"Thanks, Bonnie. I hope I don't need it. Piss, there's so much at once. I have a full load of classes right now too. Babette wouldn't want me bailing on that."

"Well, just let me know, eh? I want you on top of things down there. Oh, God, Ross, this is heavy. I need a drink. You hang tight, ok? We'll keep this plan on track."

"Sure, Bonnie."

"Goodnight then."

I hang up. My stomach growls. The sensation is so sharp I almost jump. Just a short while ago any thought of food made me nauseous. Now even my professor's rotting cheese looks nearly edible. I open the refrigerator and scan its shelves. There are a few roasted potatoes leftover from last night wrapped in plastic. Beside them is a carton of 2% milk, an unopened bacon package and toward the rear, Thai food in a box from some time ago. That one I should probably throw out.

Babette's forbidden fruit jar still sits untouched; slices of peach, mango and cherry in clear syrup. With one rapid motion, I reach inside and unscrew the lid ... it pops as suction releases. I inhale three deep breaths. Ambrosia. No wonder she was protective. I take a fork and skewer one of the round yellow cherries. It crushes between my teeth in a fructose explosion. Next I stab a mango slice. Unbelievably delicious. I probe for another cherry, then lance a peach. The sugar electrifies my mouth from gums to throat. Within minutes the entire container is empty. Well, not quite. I tip it back and swallow a deep gulp of syrup. Sweetness courses through my blood, jolting every brain synapse into conflicted spasms.

Both knees buckle. I sink down to the floor, jar still clenched tightly. The kitchen spins, whimsical sailors and orange enameled pots in mutual pursuit. Distant sensations are tightly wound wires that might snap or warp delicate clockwork ... runaway gears stripped away inside someone else's body.

This is when my eyes should erupt with tears. I'll sob for Babette, who will never eat her fancy fruit, never scandalize another parishioner or dent the neighbor's truck again. Her classes will remain unfinished and tours cancelled. Shaniko, the high desert, southern Oregon; all abandoned. I set aside the jar and brush a fist against my cheek. The knuckles come back dry. Everything freezes in place as the tide subsides, textured linoleum firm beneath me.

I blink, stand up and dump out the remaining syrup. It disappears down the drain, gurgling away in a viscous spiral. With tense fingers I dial the House of Many Pleasures.

"Hello?" Salazar answers.

"I need Zoya, is she there?"

"Oh, hi Ross. Perhaps, let me check."

A Lene Lovich record screeches in the background. Then Zoya picks up.

"Ross? What's up?"

"Babette died this morning. She had a heart attack in front of forty students right before the Mt. St. Helens tour … right on the bus."

"Oh my fucking God! That's terrible, well ... I mean, it's exactly what she would have wanted, isn't it? Are you ok? Do you want me to come over?"

"I don't think I can handle company right now. My brain is kinda going crazy. Hopefully it'll settle down by tomorrow ... I think I just had a panic attack, I don't even know what that's supposed to be like..."

"Ross! Seriously, I'll catch the next bus over if you need me to."

"No... Thanks, I'm ok now though, just give me tonight by myself. I only wanted to tell you right away. I mean, I love you ... it's a big deal, y'know?"

"Ok, maybe you're right. Take it easy and get some sleep, you sound pretty out of it. I love you too, silly. Call me tomorrow, alright?"

"Ok. I'll do that. Good night then."

I hang up. One task still remains. The wooden Black Forest clock ticks away in the dining room, long weights and chains almost fully extended. I make sure each arm is correctly positioned, then wind its mechanism. The long pendulum swings back the forth, oblivious that different hands perform the nightly ritual. I stare for a moment at the timeworn face, then slowly walk downstairs. In the pantry everything remains still, miniature Canadian National rail cars on circular track and canned goods lined up, row after row. I undress, switch off the lights and lie down. Darkness presses all around, weighty with Babette's expectations. Every muscle is weary with fatigue, yet sleep won't come. A thousand worries infiltrate each thought. *Will the family come back tomorrow and kick me out? If my professor's Canadian affairs are illegal, might I become an accomplice?* Anxieties fester with each heartbeat.

After two uncomfortable hours, I detect a soft thump from above as the front door closes. Rosalyn's footsteps creak into the kitchen. There is a liquid rush through pipes as she draws water. Silence. Then her tread moves faintly upstairs. I hear nothing more and somehow, eventually fall asleep.

Chapter 40

"We'll spy relentlessly on the dead: we'll open their letters, we'll read their journals, we'll go through their trash, hoping for a hint, a final word, an explanation, from those who have deserted us – who've left us holding the bag, which is often a good deal emptier than we'd supposed."

Margaret Atwood. The Blind Assassin. 2000.

I wake in a panic, alarm clock blaring. 9:00AM. For a moment I stare at the numbers, confused. It's Sunday, isn't it? There's no class today. Why am I up so early? Almost immediately the answer materializes like a boot to the face. Babette dead. My promises derailed. There's no time to waste. With feverish speed I dress and rush upstairs. On the kitchen table my professor's day planner lies open beside her key ring. There is a handwritten inscription for February 16th.

Dear Ross, Thank you for your hospitality. I truly do appreciate your patience and understanding and for being Elizabeth's friend and confidant. You can find her car parked in the upper Sylvania campus lot. It meant so much coming here. I'm off to catch my flight home, but keep in touch and take care.

– Rosalyn

I pocket the keys. My stomach decrees the immediate priority. I scramble three eggs and heat up a couple leftover roasted potatoes. It feels strange eating alone at the kitchen table without lively commentary on world events or random apologies for Hitler. Once my hunger is satisfied, I flip through the phonebook and dial. A woman answers.

"Wilhelm's Funeral Home."

"Hello, I'm calling about the death of someone who set up an account with you."

"My sympathies. What is the deceased's name?"

I pause. "Elizabeth Ellsworth. Maybe. Or Albert Ellsworth. You might try Bobette Ellsworth too."

The woman sighs heavily. "Sir, I don't believe you have the correct number."

"No really!" I plead. "This was a client of yours who underwent a sex change operation. I know there's an account. I'm serious ... um, also, she might have gone by Babette Bonnefont."

The woman sniffs. "Repeat those again?"

I recite the list once more.

"No," she returns after a minute, "we don't have any record. I'm sorry. Goodbye now."

"Wait, wait!" I cry. "Can you just look under Ellsworth? With an address on SE Tolman Street? Please, one more time!"

I hear the click of keys. *This is ridiculous. Why didn't Babette tell me what name she used?*

After a moment the woman comes back. "Ah, we do have an account for A.J. Bobbie Ellsworth on Tolman Street. Is that who you mean?"

"Yes, that's right. She was taken to Legacy Meridian hospital yesterday morning. There should be an obituary on file and plans for mailing her ashes to Canada."

Keys click again. The woman makes a droning sound with her lips as she types. "I see ... crematory of remains paid in full but nothing beyond that. No obituary, nothing about Canada."

"Oh, no!" I think quickly. "Is mailing ashes out of the country difficult?"

The woman clears her throat. "It is an unusual request. I'll consult with my colleagues. We probably can, but expect some red tape. Do you have the Canadian address?"

"Not in front of me. I could find it, though."

"All right, well, I recommend locating that. Call back tomorrow afternoon. By then we should have recovered and processed the remains."

"Ok, thank you, thank you so much."

She hangs up. The phone doesn't leave my hand. I punch in

Zoya's number and wait. After three rings she answers, voice raspy.

"Hello?"

"Hey you, it's me."

"Ohhhhhhhhhhhhhh...such an early one you are!" She yawns. "So, how are you doing? I almost came over last night anyway. You really sounded beside yourself."

"That's so sweet. I'm ok now though ... or as fine as I'll likely be anytime soon. It feels good to be up and taking action."

"What do you mean" I hear a faint whisk of flint as Zoya lights a cigarette.

"So, that lady Rosalyn I mentioned before is gone. She flew out early this morning. God, there's so much to tell you– about her and everything. I already called the funeral home. It looks like that may be kinda problematic, but at least the process is started. Anyway, unless the family shows up today with cops, there's a chance I'll still have time for burning Babette's Canadian papers."

Zoya exhales in a rush of static. "Never mind. Now you just sound completely insane. Sorry, I didn't get the memo that my fiancé needed to worry about police and international document destruction. What the hell's going on?"

"You're right, I'm sorry. How about I explain everything in person? Babette's car is still parked at school. I gotta pick that up. Can I drop by your place on the way back? We can talk and I'll bring you over here, if you like."

There is a terse pause as tobacco crackles. "Ok. See you in a little bit."

"Alright then, see you soon."

I hang up the phone and grab my olive drab jacket. It's still warm enough inside a t-shirt feels comfortable. Without Babette's complaints about ice-water in her veins, there's no point keeping her house tropical. I turn the thermostat down from 88 degrees to 74.

Minutes later I stand in a light drizzle at the Reed College stop on Woodstock. A handful of chattering students walk past toward their dormitories. They seem incredibly young and lighthearted, backpacks slung over their shoulders on the way to classes. Soon wide headlights penetrate foggy dimness and the #19 pulls up. Two transfers later the Sylvania campus comes into view. Its long sloped parking lot is nearly empty and Babette's blue Toyota jumps out immediately, stranded in an ocean of concrete. I smile, remembering my first sight of it stopping traffic on Killingsworth Street, Babette confused as usual behind the wheel. Now it sits abandoned, alone beneath grey skies on a Sunday afternoon at the college that gave her purpose for so many years.

I exit into gusts of frigid air and approach the car. My boots splash through puddles that pucker with rain drops. I unlock the door and climb inside, surrounded by my professor's perfume once again. Hibiscus washes over me in a thick wave. She must have splashed on a whole bottle yesterday morning. I turn the key and with a roar, air rushes from every vent as the heater kicks on full blast. I turn the control knob down. Babette's stereo is still tuned into her classical station, and Brahms swirls around my cold ears. I swallow hard and pull out of the parking lot.

Twenty-five minutes later I find a spot across Burnside from the Civic apartments and press Zoya's buzzer. It rings and rings. There is no response. At last I walk down below her window.

"Zoya!" I cry out. There is nothing. "Ay, Zoya!" I try again. "ZOY-AH!" An old home bum across the street snickers loudly and pantomimes my shout.

"Zoy, ah, Zoy ah, Zoy aaaaahhhh!" he hoots through stained teeth. Abruptly the window opens. My fiance's sleepy face peers down.

"Oh, already? Sorry, the buzzer hasn't been reliable lately, I'll come let you in."

I return to the front door. Soon Zoya appears, wrapped in a long floral bathrobe. The hallways reek of sour milk and fungal rot. She pulls me inside for a tight hug. Muscles along her spine tense under my fingers through thick terrycloth. We walk arm in arm to her doorway and enter. Salazar's large rotund form snores atop his elevated mattress. My boots clatter against beer cans and Mountain Dew bottles on the way into her chamber. Zoya takes my hands.

"Sorry I snapped at you earlier, I know you've been through a lot."

"I'm fine. Or at least I can fake it for now. Everything still feels out of control. It's just so fucking stressful not knowing if I'll have a home beyond tomorrow. I wish I could call her lawyer and get answers but I promised Bonnie Church in Canada to wait until Tuesday morning."

"That's the convent lady, right?"

"Yeah. Somehow Babette bought a half share of the convent and then tricked Mother Superior into thinking it would revert to her when she died. They had some kind of conflict, maybe because Babette tried seducing her. Anyway, I'm supposed to go through the house and destroy everything Canadian. But I found out a whole bunch more information last night, it's all so ... beyond bizarre. I can't really take it all in, not yet."

Zoya nods slowly. "So, Bonnie and you are part of a giant posthumous revenge scheme because a counterfeit nun turned down Babette's counterfeit vagina? Now she's gone, why's that your problem? This could be some major international crime. Are you willing to spend years of your life in Babette's pantry and then do jail time for her after she's dead?"

I sigh. "As long as I'm still living in her house I should do what she asked. Who can say if her Canadian business is illegal, though it's definitely shady. Everyone knows how secretive Babette was. If papers never turn up there's no way to prove I destroyed them. I know this must sound totally ridiculous" I offer a helpless grin.

Zoya smiles back. "Well, if being a loyal friend is your main fault, then it's a good one to have. Ok, let me change and throw a few things together. I've got the next couple days off work at the daycare. We can have some quality time, sift through French-Nazi artifacts and commit a felony or two."

Once she is ready, we drive back to Babette's house and I fill her in on the remaining details. Rosalyn's true origin. The dramatic climax in front of forty students. Sandra Baily's strange role and my meeting with the family.

Zoya frowns in disbelief. "Wait, did you really tell them Babette wanted the police called?"

I drum my fingers on the steering wheel and take a sharp right off McLaughlin Boulevard that loops up Bybee Street. "No. I didn't have the heart to tell her daughters quite that much. They got the point either way. It can't have been pleasant hearing."

Zoya reaches over and squeezes my leg. "God, I don't envy you."

I pull into the driveway and park. The weather has calmed for a moment and faint curved lines of a rainbow stretch in the distance. Inside, Zoya sets her backpack down and looks around.

"You've kept the clocks running." She observes. "That's nice. It feels reassuring. I think Babette would approve."

"Yeah, probably so. I've only wound the daily one so far. The others will need it tonight. So, are you hungry or shall we jump right into this?"

Zoya's eyes sparkle. "Let's eat later. I'm up for an exploration."

I pull her close for a brief kiss. "Thanks. I didn't want do this all by myself. Well, I guess let's start with her bedroom."

We head up the creaky stairs into my professor's sanctum. Dust motes silently dance in a column of sunlight through parted window curtains.

"God, what a weird feeling," Zoya whispers. "It still smells like her. This perfume is awful!" She sifts through cosmetic bottles and makeup tins on the black vanity while I move the metal toy tanker truck from atop General Bonnefont's large wooden trunk and raise its lid. Inside are numerous cardboard boxes. I lift several of these out and set them on the carpet. The first contains binders of stamps, mostly Canadian and American. The next is filled with older European post marks, there must be thousands. The last several boxes hold yellowed French newspapers from the 1930s and '40s. Zoya looks over my shoulder.

"Find anything interesting?"

"Yeah, but not what I'm searching for."

I place each box carefully back in the trunk and turn my attention to a large dresser by the window. Its top drawers hold socks and underwear, the middle sweaters plus many shoehorns of various sizes and Babette's antique field glasses she showed me so long ago. The bottom drawer contains several framed photographs. Zoya picks one up.

"Is this Babette's sister?" she asks.

"No, these are all Billie Shoemaker."

Zoya removes two more. "You could have fooled me. They

might as well be twins." Her eyes widen. "Check out Billie's blouse. That black and white patterned one. It's what Babette wore the first time you brought me over here. And this yellow sweater she had on too! Look, its hanging up in the closet!"

I stare and shake my head. "She loved that sweater. She wore it all the time."

"Damn," breathes Zoya, "after Albert had the sex change, he didn't just become any woman, he turned into his dead wife! That's almost beautiful ... but still creepy as hell."

We set Billie's portraits back and rummage through the nightstand. It contains little except pill bottles and prescription information. I look under the bed but only see stacks of French political magazines. Then Zoya draws out the lowermost drawer and emits a chirp of surprise.

"Oh! Ross, look here!"

"What?"

"I found Babette's ... well, special collection!"

She points where three glass dildos sit by a half empty tube of K-Y jelly.

"Wow!" My eyes widen.

Zoya grabs a silk handkerchief and wraps it around her hand. Carefully, she extracts one of the dildos. It is thick and clear, a gentle curve at one end with slight grooves along the other. She squints and looks closer.

"But look at this, it's broken."

I lean in. "Yeah, there are deep cracks all through the thing."

Zoya taps it against the metal bed frame with a clunk. "This shit is solid. What the hell was she using it for? I know Babette had a synthetic vagina but they didn't pour it out of concrete. This is the kind of sex toy damage I'd expect if someone used it to jack up their car or something. Plus check out the others, all cracked as well."

"Weird." I slide the drawer shut. "Hey, let's investigate her closet next. I know there's another trunk."

We step inside the large walk-in space and Zoya shudders. "It's creepy, all those mannequin heads just staring at us."

I scan along Babette's hairpieces to where the last Styrofoam dome sits bald and vacant, then read their labels out loud. "Sunday,

Monday, Tuesday, Wednesday, Thursday, Friday ... All here except Saturday."

Against the back wall is a large metal trunk painted green with brass fittings along each edge. I grab a leather handle. Zoya helps push and together we slide it beside the bed. I twist the snap below a built-in lock but it doesn't budge.

Zoya points at Babette's vanity. "There are some keys in the top drawer."

I investigate and find a small ring with several old-fashioned skeleton keys. At least three look about the right size. My first try is a failure but the second slides in smoothly. With a muted click, the lock releases. I raise the lid. Papers. Reams of papers, some loose, others stuffed in binders or manila envelopes.

Zoya examines a binder. "Ok, so these are all relatively recent statements from Wells Fargo. Her account here is pretty healthy. I guess I was expecting millions or something. Maybe a few gold bricks stashed away."

"Well, Judge Shoemaker left serious money when he died but Billie and Babette had a lot of time to blow through it. She talked about them traveling often, and it wasn't all school tours. Then there was her sex change. I'm sure that didn't come cheap."

Zoya digs further into the trunk. "Ah, here's something Canadian. Looks like property records."

I glance at these and set them aside. "Nice! Oh, this whole other folder labeled Canadian Assets, we'll delete that for sure."

Zoya filters several stacks into piles to burn. I pick through medical bills and uncover a small folder. It contains two sheets of paper.

"Hey, listen to this!" I cry out.

Re: Albert Ellsworth
Date of Birth: October 28th, 1928

To Whom it May Concern:

This is to verify that Albert Ellsworth has completed all the surgical procedures required for male-to-female sex reassignment on June 21st, 1994 at Oregon Health Sciences University. Legal

status should therefore be changed to female. If you have any
questions, please feel free to call.

Toby R. Melzer, M.D.
Assistant Professor of Surgery
Division of Plastic and Reconstructive Surgery

Zoya raises an eyebrow. "Well, that's considerate."

"Yeah, but it gets weirder. The second sheet is an official name change report dated January 3, 1995. It says here Albert James Ellsworth is now A. J. Bobbie Ellsworth."

Zoya takes the document. "You'd think it would have been Babette. Or Elizabeth at least."

"Exactly. And why keep Ellsworth? It means worthless in Old English! She hated that! I'd have expected Bonnefont once more."

Zoya shrugs. "Maybe it was professional reasons. The school, her tours and all that"

I nod. "Oh, right. Yeah. Once mayors began consulting her, she didn't want a different name getting lost in their Rolodexes. Well, it's all odd anyway. "

Zoya laughs. "Ya think? If we expect anything to make sense we'll be disappointed! I mean, strange names, sex changes, lost family members, burning papers for a fake Benedictine convent ... fractured dildos."

"True, but..." I pause. "Here's a theory about that."

"What do you mean?"

"So, imagine Albert in late June of 1994. His whole life wanting to be a woman and, hallelujah, it manifested at last. But the surgery was pretty intensive, we're talking major operations, a long recovery time, plus all kinds of hormones. Then of course, mid-sixties is a rather advanced age for this kind of thing. The healing process must take forever. All this hardship and money for equipment that won't be usable for months at least. I'm sure as soon as Babette could walk she went down to some sex shop and bought their most expensive dildo set. I mean, blow tens of thousands of dollars for a custom vagina, you don't want to cheap out on what you put in it."

Zoya cackles. "Exactly."

"And you know how impatient Babette was," I continue. "Those toys must have mocked her forever. Now, I'm guessing by the time she was ready to rock and roll, winter came around. I'm sure Doctor Melzer provided a date, probably circled in red on the calendar. So the big night arrived, she put on some Wagner, lubed up with K-Y and gave it a shot, but hell no, too cold! Unacceptable! She ran downstairs, tossed all three in the microwave and blasted them on high for ten minutes. Well, as we can see, they cracked up. But, I'll bet she used them the same night anyway."

Zoya frowns. "I can't think of what else would cause that kind of damage."

"Yeah. Well, enough lurid speculation. C'mon, let's get this Canadian stash downstairs."

In the kitchen, I flip open the calcinators lid and toss in several crumpled papers. There are long wooden matches nearby. I strike one, lean through the sulfurous cloud and drop it down the dark cavity. Flames shoot up, almost scorching my hand. I drop the metal lid. Fiery red glows through vent holes and then dies down. I open the top again and stuff more paper into the device. After a few minutes our entire stack is reduced to ashes.

Next we enter Babette's study on the main floor. Her television, after years belching nonstop international news, now lies sullen and silent. Dusty file boxes behind the writing desk contain decades-old marriage certificates signed by Judge Shoemaker as well as his old notary embossing stamp. Nothing Canadian turns up except my professor's giant wall map of the Northern Territories.

Zoya gestures at this. "You going to cram that in the calcinator?"

I roll amused eyes. "I'd need an axe to break it down small enough. The best route from Whitehorse to Yellowknife probably isn't classified information. So, it's already a bit after noon. I'm hungry. Shall we stop and eat?"

"Totally. What have you got?"

"Ha! Everything. The basement freezers are full plus we have a thousand pounds of canned goods. I could some defrost chicken to cook later. There's also salami and everything we need for sandwiches."

"Yeah, let's do that. I need food now. Here!" Zoya takes my hand and presses it against the soft curve of her belly. I squeeze back, then draw her against me. She wriggles with pleasure, then pushes me away. "Later, you! C'mon, go grab some bird to thaw. I'll start on sandwiches."

After a satisfying lunch, we descend to the basement. In the main area between my pantry and the library stand eight tall file cabinets packed full of papers, some itemized or labeled and others crushed together with no obvious categorization. Between them, cardboard boxes almost reach the ceiling. There are rolled up geographical surveys, two slide projectors and a reel-to-reel tape recorder. Every corner holds more possibilities.

Zoya coughs as dust billows up from a large political map of 19th century China. "I don't know. We could spend our whole lives down here. How thorough did Babette really want you to be?"

"She said destroy whatever I could find on Canada and the rest would sort itself out. I guess the basement is a bonus adventure. Those property documents in her room I'm pretty sure were the main things. I mean, she didn't want her family getting a hold of the library but that doesn't mean I'll torch it."

"Right. Hey, speaking of torches, I need a smoke, come on outside."

We walk upstairs and step out onto the front porch. Broken grey clouds overhead allow checkered glimpses of blue sky. Water drops sparkle from rhododendron leaves and tufted fern clumps in the garden. Zoya takes out her pack and sparks up a Capri 120. I stand behind her and squeeze full hips. The mossy gnome watches us with bemusement. She leans back into me, a cool breeze raising goose bumps on my arms.

"Do any neighbors know?"

"Don't think so. I should inform the old lady next door. She's always been nice to me. Not many others were really close with Babette. Except the guy whose truck she always backed into. God, I've never known a worse driver. She ..." my voice catches, "she could hardly operate a fucking motor vehicle. It's amazing she didn't die in flames before I moved in."

Zoya reaches her free hand around to stroke my neck. "You

took good care of Babette. No one else could have done it. Hell, she would have driven me crazy. It was her good fortune you met just at the right time."

I step back, take out a handkerchief and blow my nose. Salty tears run down both cheeks. Zoya exhales a cloud of smoke, then turns and pulls close, body against body. I unleash sobs into her menthol scented hair, shaking as she holds me. Two crows flutter beside the tall acacia tree, curious beaks at work where thick roots twist deep into the ground. Through bleary vision, their dark feathers distort and shimmer as patches of sunlight break through. After several minutes my chest stops heaving. The birds have moved further away, now pecking at debris around a neighbor's trash bin. Zoya stubs out her cigarette butt in a Canadian National Railway ashtray and traces crusty tracks beneath my swollen eyes with warm lips.

I sigh and kiss her smooth forehead. "I'm sorry, I just don't know what's going to happen. This is so much stress."

She strokes my chin. "I know. We'll figure it out step by step. You know, you're not alone."

We return inside and move onto the library. I look over stacked historical journals on top of a bookshelf, then glance down. The ancient history section stretches below me. Albert Schweitzer, Ernest Renan and S.G. F. Brandon ... the titles stretch on forever ... Works of Flavius Josephus, Historical Atlas of the Holy Land and A Guide to the Thought of St. Augustine. I pull out Jesus and the Zealots. Brandon's face glares up at me with familiar severity. My fingers reach into the dark gap left behind but feel nothing. I remove several more books but discover only a mummified spider amidst dusty cobwebs. Babette's suicide stash, the two brown bottles are gone. Just then Zoya's voice echoes from inside a large cabinet.

"Ross! Look at this!"

"What'd you find?"

"It's a box of photos. God, I don't know from when. These are color, but pretty grainy."

I look over her shoulder. In the first picture young Babette poses in cat's-eye glasses and a dishwater blonde wig. Her coquettish gaze angles to one side. Cone-shaped breasts project underneath her white sweater and a long gold chain dangles between them. I flip to the next print. Here she stands before an imitation wood background; now wearing a sheer black top. Her makeup is more pronounced, scarlet lipstick darker and heavy blue rings around each eye.

Zoya turns through more photos. "It's so sad. She's all alone. I don't know for sure, but notice the background. Looks like she's always in some cheap motel. I'm assuming she took these with a tripod and timer. Hey, here's one in front of a church. Do you think she attended mass in that terrible drag? How could it fool anyone?"

"Seriously." I pick over the remaining stack. "Oh, check this, she's finally not alone." In the next series of pictures, Albert and Billie pose beside a sign for Seaside, an Oregon coastal town. I flip further and stop dead. Zoya raises an eyebrow. I laugh.

"Well, here's everything you don't want to see."

She snorts and takes the photo stack. "Don't be a tease ... oh, wow, they were really busy!" Her wide eyes lock on Billie and Albert, naked in bed, their pudgy bodies intertwined and middle-aged faces wild with passion.

I turn several more over. "Yeah, and look at the dates printed here. They're all from 1967. That's four years before Albert got divorced. If Helen found these, it's no surprise she kicked him out."

Zoya hands me the rest. "Pretty low abandoning her family for someone new with money. I mean, love or not, that's how it broke down. So, what shall we do with these? It's not Canadian material."

"Yeah, but I doubt she'd want her family finding them. Honestly, no one should see pictures like this of their parent."

Upstairs we drop photo after photo into the calcinator. Flames rise and consume Babette in her ill-fitting costumes. Black lace nighties and angora sweaters writhe on glossy paper that bubbles into oily smoke. Crimson blossoms burst through my professor's round face and strip gaudy outfits to ashes. Billie and Albert's portly nude bodies shimmer under red light for a moment before heat melts them together one final time. Proof of their coastal liaison flutters apart, now mere cinders in a hot swirling draft.

Chapter 41

"It often happens that the sex of the soul does not at all correspond with that of the body, and this is a contradiction which cannot fail to produce great disorder."

Theophile Gautier. Mademoiselle de Maupin. 1836.

The next morning I leave Zoya sleeping in bed downstairs and dial Babette's attorney. She answers after the second ring.

"Deborah Gray."

"Hi, I'm Ross Eliot, I live in the pantry of your client Dr. Ellsworth."

"Ah, yes, Bobbie has mentioned you."

"Right ... well, I'm calling to let you know she passed away. It happened last Saturday. Sorry this is delayed information, things have been crazy."

A sharp intake of breath cuts across like static.

I explain Babette's heart attack on the bus, her family's arrival and my failure at keeping them out of the house. After a few moments, Deborah Gray speaks.

"Well, don't feel bad. It sounds like her relatives took the news better than could be expected. I doubt I could have just slammed the door in their faces either. Anyway, it's good you called this morning. I see in my day planner Bobbie had an appointment tomorrow about changing her will again. Too late for that. So, what I need from you is all her important papers. Bank statements, financial documents, identification materials and the like. Do you know where she kept those?"

"Yes."

"Good. That's a starting point. There are other items I'll require later but if you can bring Bobbie's paperwork to my office today that would be excellent. I'll contact her executor, I believe he handles the remains."

"Oh, I took care of that. In fact, she's probably already cremated. I'll call the funeral home later and most likely pick up her personal effects from them this afternoon."

"Ok. Come by after that. It'll give me some time to look over what papers she left with me. Goodbye..."

"Wait," I break in, "there's more! I have questions, like ... uh, what's my ... status here? Now Babette is gone, can her family make me leave?"

"Actually Ross, I want you right there. That house is a maze. I'd never find anything so please stay put. If anyone gives you trouble, have them call me. I will create a trust account for utility bills and existing expenses."

"Oh. That's a relief."

"Glad to put your mind at ease. You were – and are – important. See you soon."

I hang up. A great weight lifts off my chest. Tattooed sailors broadcast semaphore signals from the wallpaper and new streaks of mold run across Babette's cheese under the glass bell. Thick fuzz coats its sides. I remove the heavy cover and gag. Only one human in Portland might have found it halfway appealing and she is likely burned to a crisp. I dump the putrefied sludge into a garbage bag and tie it shut.

Upstairs in my professor's bedroom, I remove Wells Fargo and Washington Mutual bank documents from the green trunk. Underneath are American property records and materials related to the house. I cram these together with tax information and various other papers into a leather satchel from the closet. That should satisfy her lawyer for now. On my way out, I pause before the wall-mounted holy water dispenser. Jesus stares at me, bloody head crowned with thorns and wounds frozen in plastic. I dip two fingers into the shallow dish. They come up dry.

After making a quick call, checking that Babette is indeed cremated, I step outside and start the Toyota. It takes only a few minutes to reach Wilhelm's funeral home up on Milwaukee, windshield wipers in furious motion. Despite passing nearly every day on the bus, the old distinguished building never captured my attention. Now I walk by manicured shrubs around the small front garden and enter a large elegantly furnished room, wet boots squeaking against slick marble. Its antique furnishings rival Babette's French Second Empire collection. A receptionist with short curly hair and rings on every finger examines me closely but doesn't request identification.

"Ellsworth? Ah, yes, I just spoke with you on the phone. We do have personal items for you."

She passes over a heavy black plastic bag and sets my professor's purse on the counter.

"So, do you know anything yet about mailing ashes to Canada?" I ask.

The woman bobs her head. "Ahem, yes, we did some investigation. It looks like that is possible. If you wish, we can pursue the necessary permits. I don't yet know what additional costs apply."

"Well, it's what she wanted. Just let me know. Oh, here's where I'd like the remains sent."

I hand over a scrap of paper with Bonnie Church's address. She takes it and nods.

"We will contact you as soon as we have more information."

"Ok, thanks a lot."

The sack swings in one hand and outside, I heft it onto the passenger seat. Water droplets smear the shiny black surface and run off, absorbed by blue upholstery. I shut the door. Rain patters against every surface. I sit still for a moment amidst the tiny symphony for metal, plastic and glass. The bag huddles beside me, shriveled and wet. It must contain shoes that carried Babette's last steps ... whatever sweater my professor picked out that morning ... perhaps a jacket and scarf. Even her favorite black thigh-high stockings that horrified so many students? At that image I can't help but grin.

Next I drive to the lawyer's home office. It isn't far, just another ten minutes south. I park before her house on a nondescript residential street and approach the door, leather satchel and purse in hand. At my first knock Deborah Gray answers. She is about five and a half feet tall, with deep-set eyes under a shock of grey-tinged dark hair.

"Come in, come in! Get out of this weather," she invites.

I follow her to a comfortable room dominated by office

furniture and legal literature. She points toward a chair and sits down behind her hardwood desk. I open the satchel, laying out my collected paperwork.

Deborah Gray scans over a couple folders, then smiles with satisfaction. "So, this is everything I asked for?"

"Yes, it's as best I could do."

"Looks like a good start. Thank you so much."

I unsnap the closure on Babette's purse and rummage through its contents. "The funeral home just gave me this. It should have her driver's license. Oh, and passport too."

Deborah Gray takes these and slips them into a manila envelope. "Wonderful. So, do you have any more questions?"

"Well, just like we discussed on the phone, I want to make sure I still have a place to live for the moment since I'm not well-fixed financially. There's probably no concrete time frame you can give me, right?"

The lawyer shakes her head. "Not a date. But you will be given fair warning when or if that becomes necessary. For the moment don't worry. I want you there as my safari guide since Bobbie's house is such a jungle."

"Ok, I'm glad to hear that."

"So, please stay where you are. Come by in a couple weeks and bring the bills that have accumulated."

"No problem. So, did you know Babette very well?"

Deborah Gray purses her lips. "Only the past few years and just professionally. She invited me over for lunch on a couple occasions. That's how I know it's fortunate you live there. Bobbie often mentioned your helpfulness."

I gulp back a sudden knot in my throat. "Oh! Well, I'm glad then...it's good hearing."

The lawyer stands up. "Then I think we have enough covered."

I rise and follow her to the front door. It clicks shut behind me. Outside, rain has stopped falling but water drops tremble on blades of grass and evergreen needles. Steam rises off soaked lawns and the Toyota's hood as sunlight breaks through scattered clouds.

Back home I find Zoya in the study, a floral bathrobe

wrapped around her. Canadian television flickers on the satellite channel once more.

"Come here quick!" she exclaims as I enter. "It's a Kokanee commercial where there's this funny ranger. He's chasing a Sasquatch who steals all the beer! It's so cute! Oh, damn, you missed it! Hey, what's going on? I woke up and you were already gone. Is everything ok?"

"Yeah. Good news actually. I talked with the lawyer and visited her just now. She said I can stay here. Well, for now at least. No move out date anyway."

"That's great! So, now we have the place to ourselves. There's a hot tub and enough food for the Royal Canadian Mounted Police! Things are looking up! Say, what's in the bag?"

"Oh, that's from the funeral home."

I turn it upside-down. Clothes tumbles out onto the carpet. A red plaid jacket, long dark scarf and purple skirt lay on top of the pile. Zoya reaches down and moves those aside, exposing a thick beige sweater. As she lifts the knit fabric, it unfolds and Babette's grey wig leaps free. It lands, bristle-backed, at my feet. Involuntarily, I lean down and pick it up. Stringy fibers rotate under my fingers. Rancid perfume mixed with Babette's scalp ointment wafts upward. There's wet adhesive on the rim and my stomach churns. With a convulsive shudder I drop it.

Zoya's eyes widen. "I forgot about that."

"Yeah, me too. Babette's wig was a part of her. You saw the old pictures. Before the operation, wigs were what made Babette female, especially for a bald guy. It's as if they burned her as a man. She would have hated that."

"Well, they couldn't send her boobs home in a baggie. She got to keep them and her vagina to the bitter end. That might have been some consolation."

"Yeah, true."

"So, what'll you do with this stuff?"

"Oh, Babette's clothes I'll stash in her closet. That wig is bound for the calcinator."

"It is kind of unnerving."

"Yeah, I don't want it around. Her ones upstairs are ok but that thing gives me the creeps."

Zoya takes my hand and fixes me with a serious gaze. "Hey, I want you to know this is really special for me. We'll probably never afford a fancy house in some nice part of town, so let's enjoy ourselves while this lasts, even though it's because of something so sad."

I pull her to me and plant several kiss along a thinly plucked eyebrow. "I know. It means a lot we can have this time here. Just not being alone through everything has been such a help."

Zoya squeezes me back. "I'm glad. Ok, next mission. Let's clean up your mess here and burn that wig!"

On a frosty afternoon, two weeks later, I drop by Deborah Gray's office, utility bills for gas, telephone and electricity plus garbage and recycling in hand. She takes the stack of unopened envelopes from me and smiles gently.

"You did mention a money shortage before, correct?"

"True. Before long I'll find work, though with a full load of classes, that won't be fun."

Deborah Gray blinks. "Well, I examined the bank statements you brought in and discovered Bobbie put your name on a Wells Fargo account. It contains $2,000. I don't know how the rest of this will play out long term, but with joint accounts, any surviving party owns it entirely."

"How amazing! I can survive on that quite a while."

Deborah Gray hands me a thick white envelope. "Here is information for it. Also, I have something else." She passes a pink-tinged document with engraved blue borders across her hardwood desk. "This is Bobbie's death certificate. I picked up several copies and think you should have one. It may come in useful."

I take the paper, fold it in half and slip it into my cargo pocket. "Thank you. Thanks for everything. You've been such a help."

Later that afternoon I sit at the kitchen table when Zoya comes in the front door. An orange smear streaks across her white blouse. She leans down for a kiss.

"What's that? Work-related injury?" I ask.

"Yeah, one of the rug rats tagged me with a crayon. Little monsters. So, whatcha got there?"

"Babette's death certificate. The lawyer gave me a copy."

"Damn." She sits down across from me.

"For real. Look at this thing. It lists her birthplace as Yakima on October 22nd, 1928. That fits with the story and pictures. Mother was Mildred Sweet-Holm and father was A.J. Ellsworth. But check this out. It says her spouse is William! That's obviously Billie, even though Sandra Baily was her more recent wife. I don't know how that kind of information is collected, pretty bizarre."

Zoya wrinkles her brow and unslings a backpack.

"I wonder if they can't list someone having a same-sex spouse in official paperwork." She takes the document from me. "Ok. Cause of death is acute myocardial infarction. I believe that's a heart attack, just like we were told. It also says she had coronary artery disease, ischemic heart disease, systemic hypertension and chronic lymphocytic leukemia. Shit, that's a lot to go wrong with someone."

"Yeah. Also, I have good news. Babette put my name on one of her bank accounts, and its two thousand bucks. So I don't have to work right away and can concentrate on graduating."

"Excellent! Or just buy me a diamond engagement ring!" Zoya embraces me, cheeks aglow with mirth. I laugh and hug her back.

Around early March, Babette's executor, a school colleague I've never met, calls me with news that Deborah Gray has resigned all involvement in my professor's legal affairs. A new lawyer named Richard Sandersen requests my presence at his urban office.

Not eager to park downtown, I wait for the bus at my usual stop by Reed College. Swollen clouds temporarily withhold rain and a few students hurry past up the sidewalk, bundled against winter chill on their way toward early classes. A light odor from decaying leaves by the curb rises, mixed with car exhaust.

I exit on Washington Street and locate the address of a multi-story professional building. An elevator quickly rises to the eighth floor. The door opens, revealing a sign engraved on glass. It reads: Sanderson & Associates - Attorneys at Law. I enter a waiting room, the atmosphere crisp with apple scented air freshener.

"Ross Eliot" I announce to the middle-aged blonde secretary, who frowns at my army jacket and patched cargo pants. "I have a 9 o'clock appointment."

She types on her computer keyboard. "Ah... there you are. Please wait just a moment. Mr. Sanderson will see you shortly."

I sit down on a firm sofa and cross my legs. Illustrated sports journals and Hollywood gossip magazines fill a rack nearby. I reach into my satchel and remove a Charles Paul de Kock novel. The old fashioned binding is still intact and each leaf requires an incision from my pocket knife before turning. After just two pages, the secretary clears her throat. I look up and see a lanky business suited man with thin gray hair and sideburns. He approaches, hand outstretched.

"Ross? Good to meet you. I'm Richard Sanderson."

I click the knife shut, fumble for a bookmark and shake his hand. "Likewise. I heard you wanted a meeting with me as soon as possible."

"Absolutely. Please, come along. Would you like some coffee? Tea?"

I stand up and follow him. "Oh, no thanks, I'm good."

We enter a spacious office with tall windows. Sanderson circles behind a large wooden desk and gestures at two upholstered chairs before it.

"Pick a seat then. Thank you so much for coming down in person on short notice. I always find it worthwhile having personal contact with parties involved in cases and honestly, this situation is one of the most unusual ever. Things only get stranger and stranger and we haven't neared the end yet."

"Definitely not news here. So, what happened with Deborah Gray?"

Sanderson strokes his chin. "Well, matters of Dr. Ellsworth's estate became more than she was prepared to deal with. The more stones I turn over, the more understandable her position becomes. This is far from a simple disposal of assets. I wish I could be more open, but as you are a potential beneficiary, speculation is improper."

I shift in my seat. "Do I still have a place to live? That's my main concern."

Sanderson bobs his head. "For the moment, yes. You will be

given adequate time if or when you are required to quit the premises." He pauses. "Do you really live in the pantry?"

I grin. "Oh yes. For the last three years almost. It's not a tiny closet. Actually quite sizeable, but yes, also where all the dry goods are stored. Plus a huge model train diorama. The house is pretty big, but my professor turned the other upstairs bedrooms into a parlor and guest room. The one on the main floor was her study. Really, there's no way I could have made it through college this far without Babette's pantry."

"I see. You met Dr. Ellsworth as a Portland Community College student then?"

"Yes. I moved in shortly afterward since she needed live-in help. If plans work out, I should complete my history degree at Portland State this quarter, though with everything lately, schoolwork has definitely suffered."

Sanderson leans back in his chair. "That's a shame. I'll certainly do what I can on my end to make this as stress-free as possible. So, do you mind if I ask more about your relationship with Dr. Ellsworth?"

"No. Go right ahead."

"Thank you. So, to be clear, the professor paid you no wages for caregiving. There wasn't an oral or written contract?"

"Not a contract certainly. We had an understanding about her needs, although they did change over time. I was a chauffeur, housekeeper, gardener, that kind of thing. In return, she didn't charge rent and fed me. Actually, better than I'd ever eaten in my life. We also traveled together extensively and she always covered that. So, my work was rewarded, but no money changed hands."

The lawyer raises an eyebrow. "Where did you two travel?"

"Oh, all over the Northwest. As far as Canada a couple times. We did take a train through California once. Mostly central and eastern Oregon. Babette really loved the high desert, God, she could lecture about it for hours."

"How fascinating! I rarely visit that part of the state. So, did you have much chance over the last years to observe Dr. Ellsworth's relations with her family?"

I stare behind him, through a plate glass window. Tiny cars and bicycles make their way across the city streets, grey pavement dark from moisture.

"To a certain extent, yes. I know her granddaughter lived in the house before me for some time, but they argued a lot. Babette asked her to leave just before I moved in. The daughters had occasional contact, but it seemed clear they weren't very close. That's why she spent her last Christmas with my family in Seattle. I had very specific instructions on dealing with them when she died. She actually said I should call the police if they showed up."

Sanderson leans closer. "I see. So, Dr. Ellsworth provided instructions in the event of her death?"

"About the family, yes. I couldn't just leave them standing on the porch in the cold after driving from out of state, so I did let them in. It was hard enough to say they weren't welcome. I'm just thankful they didn't order me out that night. I hate badgering you about this and understand you probably can't say for sure, but do I have just weeks... or more like months left at the house?"

Sanderson frowns. "Well, don't quote me, but most likely months. This really is a complicated situation. Don't worry, I'll keep you in the loop as much as I can."

"Thanks. Let me know how I can help."

"Oh, I understand you've provided much assistance already. Dealing with her cremation, for instance."

"Well, it wasn't a big deal. I knew what she wanted. Say, should I bring household bills here now?"

"Yes, that would be excellent. Deborah Gray created a trust fund to pay those expenses so you shouldn't have issues with services. If there are, call me and we'll get things straightened out."

"Ok."

"Great, great. So, I mostly only wanted to make your acquaintance and confirm a few details. Thanks so much for coming down. Hopefully this will be relatively painless. Oh, one final thing I wanted to ask..." Sanderson smiles cheerfully. "Have you come across any legal papers dealing with Canada?" His eyes fix me with an appraising stare.

"Canada? Ahhh, no."

He shrugs. "Probably not important. Well, thanks again. It was a pleasure meeting you. Let's talk soon."

We shake once more, and I exit the building. Pedestrians

bustle down wet sidewalks, to-go coffee cups clutched in hand. Four Hare Krishnas stand on the corner, hems of their orange robes hanging beneath thick parkas. I walk across Washington Street to catch my bus home.

Two weeks later I'm in the kitchen, study texts for a history final scattered across the red Formica table. Outside, rain thunders down with dense fusillades but indoors a cozy pot of water heats on the stove. Condensation frosts each window with tiny white droplets. I pick through tea packets, searching for rooibos. As I tear a package open, the phone rings. High Pitched. Urgent. My heart jumps. The caller ID pulses bright red with every tone. 999-999-9999. Water bubbles over onto the electric burner, hissing angrily. I pay it no heed, eyes locked on the device.

999-999-9999. My hand stretches out and touches the receiver. 999-999-9999. I pick it up.

"Hello?"

The line goes dead immediately. Silence. Only sharp crackles emanate from the stovetop. Numbly, I switch the burner off. My tongue feels thick and dry. I turn, inspecting the caller ID. It now reads UNKNOWN. Babette would have changed it back immediately but I resist, every nerve shaken.

"This is a perfect time for some tea." I announce out loud. No sound responds, except the ever present tick of clocks. There is a Union Pacific Railroad mug ready on the counter. I drop in my rooibos bag and pour water. Aromatic steam rises. I lift the cup to inhale tranquil, earthy wisps. Babette always declared there really is no exit, just illusions on the wall of a room with no doors or windows. The afterlife has no cellular connection. There's no way we can ever speak again, even if the devil is an Englishman. Just then the phone rings once more and I almost spill scalding water down my shirt. This time letters on the caller ID spell out SANDERSONANDASSOC. I set the cup down and answer.

"Hello?"

"Ross? This is Richard Sanderson. How are you?"

"Oh, fine. I'm buried in school projects, but it looks like I'm still on track for graduation this spring."

"Ah, good, good. Glad to hear it. So, ah, there have been

some, well, interesting developments. Are you sure Dr. Ellsworth kept no papers about Canada?" Maybe that mention Nanaimo? Or even just British Columbia?"

I look down and tap a boot heel against the linoleum.

"Sorry, I've pretty much gone through the entire house. There's nothing like that here. Wish I could be more helpful."

The lawyer sighs. "We have a serious problem. It appears the professor wrote two wills in two different countries. It's very irregular. Did she ever speak about such things?"

I take a tiny sip of tea. It burns my tongue, still too hot to drink.

"She really was very secretive, even with me."

Static breaks through as Sanderson exhales heavily. "Yes, everyone mentions her ... penchant for privacy. And as an attorney I do know many people often take little consideration for their affairs after death. Funny thing about that. Well, thank you anyway. We'll get this straightened out."

He hangs up with a click. I take my railroad cup and walk down the hallway. Babette smiles mischievously from her Father Christmas portrait.

"Hope you knew what you were doing," I comment. She stares back, rosy cheeked amidst a false white beard.

As I stand in contemplation, boots clatter up the front steps and Zoya bursts inside. I catch a rush of cold wet air before the door slams. Her hoodie is soaked. I reach out and help remove it.

"Damn girl, let's get you warmed up!"

She shivers and embraces me. "It's a long bus ride. Plus three blocks in this weather is three too many."

"Sorry. I'm glad you keep coming over, I don't know how I'd manage things alone. Does Sal mind you more or less moving in since Babette died?"

Zoya laughs. "He misses me but appreciates entertaining gentleman callers without interruption." She raises icy hands to my cheeks.

"Yikes! You're frozen! Wait a minute!"

"Careful! Don't spill that and scald us!"

I sample the tea. "It's drinkable now, no worries. So, here's something. I just talked with the new lawyer."

"Oh yeah, what's up?"

"More obstruction of justice on my part. I feel bad making his job harder. They discovered the convent. He specifically asked if I knew about Nanaimo."

"What did you tell him?"

"Claimed ignorance. Canada? Where's that? Anyway, just before there was a weird phone call that kinda spooked me. In fact, you almost caught me talking to Babette here." I gesture at the festive holiday picture.

Zoya turns, then leans in closer. Her lips purse.

"Ross, that is not Babette."

"What?"

"It's Billie! Take a good look!"

I unhook the frame and squint. "I don't know, are you sure?"

"Pretty certain. Let's compare!"

From underneath a stack of delicate saucers, I find the Chinese plate with Albert and Billie lacquered to its center. My eyes rove back and forth.

"Goddamn, I think you're right."

Zoya nods. "Yeah, the faces are similar, but they wear slightly different glasses. Same with the jaw. It's very subtle though."

I shake my head. "All this time. She even mentioned dressing up for that picture once, God, totally laughing inside that she fooled me. All the lies and fantasies. Oh, plus it seems she wrote two wills, one American and one Canadian. I should call Bonnie Church and check in."

"Aha," says Zoya. "The plot thickens. Well, you take care of that, I gotta change into something dry." She heads downstairs.

I return to the phone and dial Bonnie. She answers almost immediately.

"Hello?"

"Hey, it's Ross. So, the jig is up. I talked with Babette's new lawyer today and he knows about the convent. Poor guy had no idea what he was getting into. Did I stall enough for you?"

On the other end Bonnie cackles. "Oh, don't worry. Everything is finished. I knew the lawyer would find out soon anyway."

"How's that?"

"Mother Superior probably contacted him. Oh, is she ever pissed!"

"Did you meet her? What happened?"

"Lord no! I sent my attorney to deliver the news. With money from Babette's Canadian assets I bought out Mother Superior's share of the convent. We just presented an eviction notice for her plus all the other nuns. It's a fantastic location. I think I'll turn their place into a rental."

"Mother Superior must curse the day she met Babette."

"True. No, I don't have enough courage to face the woman myself. I drove by once last week and saw her at work in the garden– oh, a face of pure hatred."

"I guess that makes sense. Maybe this whole thing is just elaborate revenge for not putting out when Babette wanted some hot illicit nun sex."

"Perhaps. She really bore a grudge against that place and never said exactly why. I just followed instructions. This has been so amazing, eh? Just a year ago I was close to bankruptcy and now everything changed. She helped me so much!"

I laugh. "Well, me too. I only had sixty-five dollars when Babette died. Turns out she left me a bank account with a couple thousand bucks that saved my ass. Or at least my chances of graduating from college on schedule."

"Oh God, Ross, that's nothing. You'll get her house I'm sure."

"What? Oh, I don't know about that. Maybe the library."

"Babette wouldn't cut you out completely. She really loved you. She always told me how much you meant."

"Thanks, but since there are two wills, it might void everything."

"Well, I'm no legal expert, but there's one thing. If you do inherit Babette's property, just remember I'd love some of her antique furniture, eh, you know, in the guest bedroom upstairs?"

"The French Second Empire stuff?"

"That's right. I have the perfect room to set it up properly here.

"Don't count on it. Things could go any way still."

"Oh, I'm sure Babette made sure you'd be taken care of."

"We'll see. Hey, did you know she made an appointment to change her will with the original lawyer? It was for just a few days after she died."

"No, I can't say what that was about. All I know is everything went according to plan up here."

I take a gulp of tea. "Anyway, speaking of Babette, you got her ashes just fine, right?"

Bonnie laughs. "Yes, thanks for that! After a lifetime traveling, she now spends her days in a fancy urn on my mantelpiece. I'm going to wait until better weather comes along and the nuns have left before spreading them in Mother Superior's garden. Seems like a good activity on some nice sunny day."

I grin. "That's probably the most appropriate conclusion for this whole adventure."

"Seriously, eh? Well, keep me updated if anything else happens, ok?"

"All right Bonnie, we'll talk soon then."

As I hang up, Zoya enters the kitchen in thick slippers, sweatpants and an old Killing Joke t-shirt. She reaches over and grabs my mug, sips at it, then makes a face.

"Needs a little sugar. So, everything good in Canada?"

"Yeah, it sounds like Bonnie's got her business with Babette nailed down."

Zoya smiles softly and runs long fingernails across my neck. I pull close, hands on her hips as we spin slowly in a tight embrace. The house circles around us, Mauser rifle, fine china, and French Second Empire furniture. I bury my face amidst menthol scented dreadlocks.

On the morning of April 15th, less than two months before my graduation is scheduled, Richard Sanderson calls again. His voice is raspy and low.

"Ross? We figured everything out. At last." He clears his throat.

"What's that?" I ask.

"Oh, sorry, I've been a little sick. This case has really kept me up. So, here's how it all boils down. Professor Ellsworth wrote two wills, one for the United States and one for Canada. This greatly confuses the issue because a will automatically supersedes any previous document regarding the deceased's possessions. However, whether legally or not, her Canadian assets have already been dispersed which throws everything into turmoil.

"What I have the power to do is make a simple judgment in this case and settle it once and for all. So Ross, you are now the owner of everything in Dr. Ellsworth's house. That includes her library, furniture, appliances and personal property– her car also. Pretty much everything that isn't bolted down. The house itself goes to her daughters who will most likely sell it and divide the money. They likewise inherit Dr. Ellsworth's American investments, real estate and finances. So, do you have any questions?"

My brain flickers through fuzzy pictures. Babette smiles, her round face beaming. The kitchen shudders and patterns dance on the red Formica. Tattooed sailors flash joyous semaphore signals and wallpaper whales cavort along wave tops. Downstairs, the library rumbles, thousands of authors ... millions of pages, muttering together; S.G.F. Brandon, Blasco Ibanez, Barbara Tuchman ... now all of them ... mine.

"Ross? Are you still there?"

"Yeah, sorry, this is a little overwhelming. How much time is left then? Do I need to be out soon?"

"No, this process will still take a while. There isn't a firm date but I'm sure it'll be months away. My advice is plan ahead. Emptying that house will be a major project, whether you keep it all or sell things off."

"Understood. And thank you ... thank you so much for deciding in my favor this way."

"Well, it was a tangled mess. This seemed the fairest way to honor Dr. Ellsworth's intentions and keep everyone relatively satisfied. So, is there anything I've forgotten?"

"No, I guess that's all for now."

"Excellent. Well, let's keep in touch."

I set down the phone. My stomach floats, light and tingly. Every object, from orange-enameled pots on the wall to antique clocks and empty cheese bell appears new, viewed through a prism of possession. The library, Babette's prized collection, now my responsibility. As I blink back tears, Zoya pads down the hallway, a towel wrapped around her sleek form. Water droplets from the shower still speckle each shoulder.

"Babette's lawyer just called," I begin, "everything in her house goes to me. The house itself will be sold probably."

"Oh my God, so they finally figured out the wills?"

"I don't think so. It was more like nobody could make sense of the wills, and he just made an executive decision."

"And he had the authority? The relatives can't challenge it? Hmmm. I don't know anything about this stuff but it seems almost too simple. Did he give you a deadline?"

"No. It looks like I still have a while. Good, 'cos with final projects I'm swamped."

Zoya releases her hair from a top knot. The locks swing down low, past her neck. "Seriously, what's going to happen?" She looks up at me.

I exhale slowly. "Well, I've gotta sell off a lot of things. There's enough furniture here for three ordinary houses. Bonnie Church wants the antique set upstairs."

"Really? That's quite a gift!"

"She's been a huge ally. Plus, what would we do with such nice stuff? Our gutterpunk friends would tear them up just sitting down, then spill beer on the wreckage. I'd rather treasures like that find a good home than stay with us and get destroyed. Anyway, there are enough other things I can raise money with to cover storage. Someday maybe we'll have a house and shelves for millions of books."

Zoya reaches over and takes my hand. "This will be a lot of work."

In mid-June, Bonnie drives a rental truck down from Canada. Its brakes squeal as she pulls up and I step outside for an embrace. Late afternoon air surrounds us, warm and still. Wide green leaves overhead shade Tolman Street from a hot summer day. I help carry several bags inside and set her belongings down in the kitchen.

"Margarita?" I ask.

Bonnie nods, wavy brown hair tied back. She dabs at her

forehead with a handkerchief. "Thanks! I need one. Such a drive!"

"I'm sure! Well, glad you made it. This should improve things, just wait a moment. " Liquor splashes into the blender with mixer and ice. Whirling blades churn up light green froth.

Bonnie picks up a bottle, the Spanish label old and cracked. "This looks ancient. And it's mescal!"

"Judge Shoemaker probably picked that up at some Tijuana grocery store around 1914. It makes a fine margarita in my opinion."

I pour the slushy mixture into two glasses and pass her one. She takes a sip. "Thanks. Enough highway traffic for one day. So, looks a bit different here, I see a few things are gone."

"Yeah, now that I've graduated from school, there's been time. The piano was a headache. I gave it to my friend Sal. Took a whole crew of people getting that thing moved. Soon I'll have an estate sale and after that, rent a storage unit for what's left. My parents passed me down their old Volkswagen bus, the blue one parked outside. It helped a lot since I gave Babette's car to Naomi. Just taking inventory was a project. It turns out we have four Victrolas here! I'll just keep the crank-powered one. Then there are three complete china services. I could start a catering company!"

Bonnie grins. "Oh, I almost forgot. Congratulations on your graduation!" She lifts her glass.

"Yeah, thanks. It feels good. Speaking of long trips." I smile. We clink our rims together.

So, where are you going? Will you move in with your girlfriend, what's her name?"

"Zoya. No, her place is too small. I'll stay with friends in a house on the eastside who have a room open."

"Well, I'm grateful for the furniture." She takes another drink of her margarita. Outside, a neighbor's lawnmower roars into life. Open windows allow breeze through, cooling beads of sweat on my brow.

"Seriously, it's a relief getting that all outta here."

"I did bring one item in return." She picks up a paper sack on the floor and extracts something brown, rectangular and plastic.

I squint at it. "Whatcha got there?"

Bonnie pushes her package toward me. "This is the urn

Babette's ashes were shipped in. It contains half of them. I know she wanted to be spread in Nanaimo, but I think you should have a share."

I take the plastic box and open a catch that releases the lid. Inside sits a clear plastic bag. It contains dense grey ash flecked with dark clumps.

"Wow! Thanks. I'll have to think of something appropriate for this." I tip back the margarita and fragments of ice crush between my teeth.

"You'll come up with a good plan. You knew her best."

"Perhaps." I examine the box. "What's this metal disc taped here? It's stamped 336994."

Bonnie brightens. "Oh, that's her toe tag. Each deceased gets issued a file number that corresponds with a metal tag clipped to their toe. That stays with each body until cremation. Once the ashes cool, attendants sweep them into a bag, place it inside an urn and tape the tag on top. Just a way we keep things organized in my industry."

"So, how are things up north? Any Mother Superior drama?"

"No, the nuns packed up. They left for God knows where. I cleaned the house and rented it out weeks ago. You know, I did find some interesting things. Babette left quite a bit of paperwork with me, mostly financial and property related, but there was one thick manila envelope she said never to open. In fact, she declared in the event of her death it should be incinerated. Always so dramatic, of course! Well, I'm only human. Last week I followed her instructions and burned the envelope, but couldn't resist peeking inside first."

"What was it?"

"Oh, materials from her sex change. You know, she really didn't skimp on that operation. Her surgeon was named Dr. Toby Meltzer. I did a little research and discovered he's famous, probably the best in his field. Plus there were several before and after photographs. You know, Babette mentioned once she was born with a penis, but some tiny thing, almost unusable. My God, Ross, what a liar! Albert Ellsworth had a huge cock!"

Chapter 42

"By the year three-thousand everyone would have forgotten my name, by the year five-thousand the marble column would have turned to dust, the cemetery would have disappeared under a wheat field. . . .Even this second annihilation would not be the end. Then the sun would lose its heat, the earth collide with another heavenly body or explode, and Michelangelo's statues and Beethoven's symphonies would be flung after me into Nirvana.

George Faludy. My Happy Days in Hell. 1962.

On August 10th, 2002, I leave the Tolman Street house for good. Every room stands empty, yet as my boots tread from doorway to doorway they fill again. In Babette's former bedroom, only the crimson carpet and striped velvet wallpaper remain, beside a lingering perfume odor brought out by summer heat. I can almost hear her low voice rumble over the R in my name. A crucifix shaped witness mark on the wall traces the outline of her holy water dispenser.

I walk downstairs, and they groan with each step. No ticking clocks distract me, each one packed away weeks ago in storage. Even the living room windows stand naked of drapes and sunlight pours through in a torrent, every vacant inch bared beneath the golden glow. Carpet depressions memorialize couches, end tables, ottomans and china cabinets. Some of these objects have been sold, but a few adorn the small room I share in a house with several roommates near the Hawthorne district.

At last I descend into the basement where footsteps ring out loudly on bare concrete. Every freezer and refrigerator whose constant hum lulled me to sleep have been sold. The library is desolate and rows of built-in bookshelves along the walls yawn empty, volumes now stacked away in endless liquor boxes. For a moment I reach to turn up the gas fireplace one last time but then hold back. This room feels spent, something no longer necessary. Outside the day beckons and with a light heart, I walk back upstairs, lock the front door and leave my professor's house behind.

Chapter 43

"People say the dead aren't safe in their tombs; even the burial
sites, even the pyres are rifled for remains."

Apuleius. <u>The Golden Ass.</u> circa 158 CE.

"Say, here's an idea for Babette's ashes," I call down from
atop Sal's elevated bed in the Civic apartments. October rain beats
against steamy windows and so close to the ceiling, Zoya's
cigarette smoke spreads out in a dense fog. She sits before a mirror,
Capri 120 between purple tinted lips as quick fingers twist blue
extensions into her dreadlocks. His own hair bundled under a black
beret, Sal sits at Babette's piano. He squints up at me, final notes
of a Kate Bush song fading as he presses the sustain pedal.

"What's that?"

I hop off the bed and my boots snap several pieces of plastic
fast food cutlery scattered across the floor.

"Babette always loved visiting Yakima, where she was born.
Some of the best times we had were at the local symphony. I want
to drive out there again, maybe catch a classical music performance
at the Capitol Theatre, then scatter her remains on the train tracks.
What do you think?"

Sal nods. "Seems appropriate."

Zoya exhales smoke through her nose and flicks ash into a
glass jar on top of the stereo speakers.

"Babette would have liked that. But, is this something you
gotta do alone?"

I grin. "Absolutely not! We should plan a trip together. How
about next month?"

My friends voice their agreement, and Sal strikes up a jaunty
musical improvisation, fingers skipping gaily across the keyboard

On the late evening of November 7th, I park my Volkswagen

bus across Burnside from the Civic and holler up through Zoya's window. She lets me in, and we saunter down befouled hallways to her apartment. Sal is nowhere to be seen.

"Are you two ready for tomorrow?" I ask. "Let's get an early start, like, before noon. Yakima is a good three hours away or more."

"Oh, almost. Sal probably not. He's been gone all afternoon. What about you, is everything set?"

"Yeah, pretty much. I didn't bother with hotel reservations. We won't need them, it's always deserted this time of year. Plus, I don't know what performances are at the theatre right now. So, sorry, my plans are a little haphazard. I did remember the guest of honor though. This is a trip fifty percent of Babette shouldn't miss."

Zoya runs a finger across my forehead. "What's that on your face? You play in a sandbox or something?"

I laugh. "No, today was my last swing shift at a concrete plant down south in Clackamas. I swear, that temp company gives me the shittiest jobs. Glad that one's over. Anyway, like you can see, I could really use a shower. Do you have clean towels?"

Zoya nods. "There's one on the wall."

"Thanks, I just need a quick rinse."

In the bathroom I undress and lay my clothes on the toilet seat. Empty beer cans, cigarette packs and hair dye jars cover almost every surface. I peer inside the shower stall to discover it filled with pans and dishes. I turn on the faucet. Once the water is hot enough I step inside. Something pricks my toe. I bend down and lift a crumpled bathmat. The curved edges of a Cuisinart blade glitter up at me.

"Goddamn!"

"What?" comes Zoya's muffled voice through the door.

"I just found your food processor. It almost processed me!"

"Oh, sorry. The sink plugged up so I've been doing dishes in the shower."

Her voice continues, but now the stereo outside blares abruptly and I can't hear anything else. Water flows over my head in a warm torrent. Once every particle of grit is removed from behind my ears, I shut off the faucet and fumble along a wall for the towel. Excited voices now rumble and punk rock reverberates with a staccato beat.

Dried and dressed, I open the door but within inches it jams. A large cardboard box slides away with some effort. The perpetual odor of mold mixes with something sweet I can't identify. Every square foot of floor is now occupied with gutter punks who dangle legs off the elevated bed and hoist forty-ounce bottles of Pabst. Zoya pushes her way through.

"Ross! Look at this! Sal brought home a ton of chocolate his friends dumpstered tonight from the industrial area." She points at the box. My fingers pick out a small brown brick and raise it. With cautious teeth I nibble a corner.

"What do you think?"

"Ok. A little dry, though. It's cherry flavored, how odd. Quite a score, hey!"

Now Sal is beside me, eyes excited. "So, who's up for croquet?"

He hoists a wooden mallet high and the gutterpunks cheer. We file outside, occupying a nearby park with nocturnal merriment. Our challenging course leads across concrete, gravel, grass and even incorporates children's playground equipment. Around midnight, a police cruiser briefly spotlights us but the officers merely laugh and drive away. Hours into the early morning, our last ball rolls beneath the final wicket. Weary and cold, we call it a night.

At 9AM Zoya's alarm sounds, and I wake with a start. We lie curled in her nest, thick blankets draped across our bodies. She reaches out, presses a button and the racket ceases. I rub crusted eyes.

"What time is it?"

"Time to sleep more." She strokes my arm.

"Piss, we should get up and hit the road. I can't believe we stayed up so late."

Zoya yawns. "Don't worry about it. C'mon, you said yourself this wasn't planned well. Take some time, find out when there's a good music performance, and we'll go then. You're not on a schedule, Babette won't get any more ashy."

"True ... you're right. I gotta move my bus though; parking

enforcement around here really nails you without a zone permit."

"Ok. Hurry back where warm lives! It's freezy out there!"

I dismount the bed and pull on clothes. A single thin golden ray penetrates tightly drawn blinds. Shivering, I exit into cold sunlight. Untied bootlaces skitter over the concrete sidewalk down Burnside, then across on 19th. Just half a block up, keys jingle in my hand when I pause. *This is too far. Last night I found a closer spot.* I turn back and forth in confused stupor as realization sinks in. Just across from the car wash lot, a silver Volvo station wagon is parked where my blue Volkswagen should be. It reflects morning glare with painful clarity.

Back inside the apartment, I flip through a phone book. Its delicate pages don't turn easily, gummed with sticky residue, hopefully just spilled beer. Zoya stirs and lifts a blanket as I dial her bedside phone.

"Come here ...what's going on?"

"My bus is gone. I'm trying to find out what tow company the city contracts with. Maybe I parked illegally somehow. I sure hope ... oh, hold on, hello, I'm calling to see if you towed an '84 Vanagon last night or this morning from 19th street downtown, just off Burnside? ... No? ... Would any other outfit move vehicles in that area? ... Really? ... Well, that's lame...ok, thanks for the info then."

I place the receiver down and turn to Zoya. "Shit! My bus wasn't towed. They recommended filing a police report. It must have been stolen."

She stretches and blinks, clumps of mascara caught in dark eyelashes. "Damn, Ross ... I'm so sorry, that's awful. You were all ready for the trip too. Was your stuff in there? Oh my God, was SHE in there?"

"Yeah ... talk about bad timing."

"Pow!" Zoya mimes a pistol to her head with two fingers, then pulls a robe around her naked body and heads toward the bathroom as I punch in numbers for the police non-emergency line. When she returns several minutes later, I lean glumly against the elevated bed. She envelopes me in a sleepy embrace. I clutch her back.

"The cops took a brief report on the phone," I say. "They'll send an officer over for additional details at my place on the eastside. Not until after noon, though. You should sleep more. I'll take a bus home, then call later and let you know what's up, ok?"

"Alright. Tell me if there's anything I can do." She climbs back into bed and closes her eyes. I pull the covers up, kissing each smooth cheek. Zoya smiles faintly as I turn and leave.

One bus transfer later I step off along Hawthorne Boulevard and walk south toward Grant Street. A cold breeze swirls around my ears. Unlike Babette's posh locale, this is a working class neighborhood with unkempt lawns and recycling bins on sidewalks full of empty beer bottles. The two story house I share with three others sits halfway down the block. Its driveway lies empty. The roommates must all be at work.

Inside, I hang my jacket on a wooden rack and set water for tea boiling in the kitchen. A framed Canadian National railroad print adorns one wall. One orange-enameled pot rests by the stove. I enter my bedroom and sit down behind Babette's writing desk. A long bookshelf occupies one end, the titles comprising my favorite selections: Ancient history to WWII, religious theory to novels. Nineteen thick volumes of Elisee Reclus's The Earth and Its Inhabitants almost take up an entire lower level. Napoleon III's bust glares sternly from the windowsill above General Bonnefont's chest, now filled with boots and cassette tapes.

Almost two hours later, a knock sounds at the front door. I open it to see a uniformed policeman, medium build and trim, with cheeks pink from the cold.

"Good afternoon. I'm Officer Helzer. Are you the one whose vehicle was stolen?"

"Yes, that's me. Would you like to come in?"

"Thanks." He moves past me, eyes roving about. They come back and rest on me. "So, this won't take long. We just gotta verify things. I have here your plate number, last known location, time of disappearance and insurance information. Is this all correct?"

I look over his paperwork. "Yeah, that's right."

"Did you make sure it wasn't just down another block? Maybe a friend borrowed it?"

"Unlikely. Nobody else has keys. I did look around, but it was definitely on 19th last night."

"Were there any items of value in your vehicle? Any weapons?"

I sigh. The officer rolls his eyes.

"Look guy, if you stashed your dimebag there, I really don't wanna know."

"Oh no, not like that. No weapons either. Well, this probably sounds a little weird. I left an urn in back filled with the ashes of a dead friend."

His countenance clears. "Oh, that is something." He scribbles in a small notebook. "Well, I'll file this and get back to you if anything turns up. Here's my card, please call if you think of anything else that could be helpful. Have a good day."

Officer Helzer turns and lets himself out. I head toward my room and sag behind Babette's writing desk again. The old Macintosh sits on top now, instead of her typewriter. Beside it is a small framed portrait depicting young Albert in drag, round-faced above his haphazard fake bosom. I take a final sip of thoroughly cold chai tea and settle back with a collection of essays by Michel de Montaigne. "Oh, he was an absolute genius!" I can still hear my professor declare, her enthusiasm palpable even after death. "Do you know Montaigne wrote that one of life's greatest joys is not achieving political power or sex with some beautiful partner, but a satisfying bowel movement?"

I have scarcely finished the first chapter before another knock sounds. I answer the door and see Officer Helzer once again. He steps inside, grinning widely.

"So, new one for me here. I talked on the radio with some people down at the station about your situation and it turns out under Oregon law, remains of a deceased individual retain many civil rights no matter their condition, including post-cremation. Therefore, my question is, would you like to file a kidnapping report?"

My jaw drops. "Yes! Absolutely!"

The officer takes out his notebook. "All right, what was the name of the deceased?"

"Oh, well, that's complicated. My friend underwent sex reassignment surgery and became known as Babette or Elizabeth Ellsworth. Before that she was Albert Ellsworth. Sorry, it's a little convoluted. I believe her official name change was A.J. Bobbie Ellsworth. Plus she sometimes used the last name Bonnefont."

The policeman's pen stops.

"Could you spell that?"

"B-O-N-N-E-F-O-N-T."

"Do you know her date of birth?"

"October 22nd, 1928."

"And when did this sex change take place?"

"1994."

The notebook snaps shut. "All right, that should be enough information for now. I'll let you know if we get any leads." He looks me over with a slight smile. "Sounds like a very interesting person, your friend. Bye now."

I close the door behind him and can't help but laugh. Back in my room I pick up the old drag portrait. "Well, Babette, talk about being kidnapped often enough, it might actually happen! Bet you didn't see that one coming!" The image stares silently back at me through cats-eye glasses, pudgy cheeked and serious.

Ten days later an impound yard in Northwest Portland calls. My Volkswagen turned up abandoned, illegally parked just blocks from the Civic apartments. Anxiously, I catch a bus down and reluctantly pay $75 for its release. An attendant in stained coveralls leads me through a barbed wire fence where rows of vehicles are lined up on gravel. There, between a Mazda with broken headlights and an early '80s Toyota, sits my bus. I circle it cautiously, examining the exterior. Ok so far. There are no new dents or even paint chips. I next open the sliding side door. Several empty Tecate beer cans roll out with a clatter. The front passenger seat is shoved far forward, a large gap underneath where the battery formerly resided. My rearview mirror is also missing, but in the rear, shiny brown plastic glints under a bench seat. Flush with relief, I pull Babette's urn toward me and snap the lid open.

Empty.

Completely empty. Not so much as a speck of ash.

The residual smell of cheap alcohol blows away as chilly wind gusts through the open door. I throw my head back and laugh again. Babette's final journey was never one I could select, for her soul bore no more appropriate epitaph than a question mark. This is the best sendoff, and wouldn't she be absolutely delighted? My professor's travels; endless now, free to continue without conclusion. Half of her remains in Canada, yes, but the other portion? Everywhere and nowhere. A life too expansive for bounds of nationality and religion– even gender... has broken from terra firma into the unknown. One final mystery even here. It couldn't be more perfect.

Chapter 44: Coda

"The past did not exist. Not at all. Not in things, not even in my thoughts."

Jean-Paul Sartre. <u>Nausea</u>. 1938.

"In Geography and Geology I find the physical world is transitory, in History I discover that the past vanishes hopelessly ... in Philosophy I find that all hope is delusion. But perhaps the most important element is that I love music passionately. Music allows immense daydreams. It makes one imagine a beauty greater than beauty itself, it creates exaltation and sublime passions or at other moments it is extremely tender and is a balm to the heart, and it melts the soul."

Albert J. Ellsworth. "Counseling: A Frame of Reference."
Summer, 1963.

It is spring of 2011 when I finally read Jean-Paul Sartre's <u>Nausea</u> aboard a commercial longliner in the Gulf of Alaska. During daylight hours we pull halibut from the sea and drop their heavy bodies onto layers of ice in the hold. When the northern sun sets and our last skate of rope is coiled away, our crew cleans blood and slime from safety orange rain gear and hangs it on hooks before entering the pilothouse. We pack hot meals into our bellies, then collapse, exhausted. Warm at last under thick wool blankets, I curl up on my bunk in the foc's'le and turn page after page until sleep overcomes me.

A decade after my first attempts, the relevance strikes hard. Sartre's protagonist strives to understand a Napoleonic era diplomat and write his biography. However, the past eludes and frustrates him with bile-inducing consequences. Every paragraph resonates with my own work documenting the past. When I recount adventures spent with Babette, I'm troubled by collisions between perception and reality.

What is memory? Are my journals reliable? If the feeling of Babette's damp panties under my hand where she hung them to dry on cut glass doorknobs lives only inside my mind, can I trust this image, these sensations?

Sartre's frustration with history penetrates every sentence I write. Babette claws away inside me, nearing escape with every word. My weary fingers type her story; at the end of heavy workdays, while we buck through stormy water toward different fishing grounds, and in port after unloading our catch.

September 2nd, 2011 is a gloomy southeast Alaskan evening toward the end of trolling season. I'm exiting the Sitka public library when my cell phone vibrates. Brandon, another fisherman on our partner boat *Hallie Lee,* has sent a text: *At the P-bar/come over.* The Pioneer Bar is a local dive close by the docks where old timers while away summer afternoons and young deckhands sometimes blow whole paychecks in a drunken weekend. I walk through Sitka's small downtown, past furriers, Native art stores and an old Russian Orthodox church until tourist shops give way to harborside fish processing plants.   In my pocket, Babette's crematorium toetag jingles on a key ring.

"You fucking, cheating bastard!"

I enter the P-Bar and scan for familiar faces.

"Suck my dick, asshole!"

Every inch of wall is covered with photographs of boats—some hauling gear, others stuck on rocks. The jukebox plays a country hit, but all heads turn toward the rear pool table where two large men yell obscenities. Their faces darken with anger and one throws an ill-timed punch, swinging and swaying like an oversized marionette. The other dodges and slugs him back hard in the belly.

"Hey, hey, hey, guys, come on, ENOUGH!" An even bigger fellow with two other men assisting grabs the pair and hustles them out a back exit.

Hands raise from a rear booth as Brandon waves at me. A slender, blonde youth, he sits with several other crewmates; bottles and tumblers strewn before them. I buy a can of Rainier and join in. The bar slowly fills as more members of the fleet join us. We discuss ocean storms that currently trap us in port, groan about salmon dock prices, and compare living conditions aboard different vessels.

One young newcomer, back from his first commercial trip, takes a shot of whiskey. He slams the glass down and squints hard. "I know some of you have it rough," he announces, "but check this. Just last week we're trolling for silvers down south off Forester Island, and I take a minute to admire the sunrise. Ain't got shit on my lines, the water is clear, and it's goddamn beautiful. How could I not look? Well, captain comes out on deck all pissed, says 'Hey, what are you, some kind of fag? Gotta eyefuck scenery all day? Get back to work!' Anyway, that's what I've lived with all season."

The others murmur angrily.

"Hell, that's uncalled for." Brandon observes.

I take a deep swallow of beer. "Yeah, what a prick." I'm about to comment further but then my gaze flicks toward the entrance.

A black man has entered the bar, something unusual for Sitka. He wears a loose-fitting dark suit, and long dreadlocks fall past his shoulders. Small oval glasses reflect neon above a bushy beard. He surveys the room briefly, then strolls past our booth. My eyes open wide in shock, and I jump up.

"Awadagin Pratt!" I cry, touching his arm.

"Yes?" He turns.

"My name is Ross Eliot. I'm a fan of your work. The show here tomorrow is something I'm really looking forward to. In fact, it's quite a surprise I can attend at all since this is Coho season. My boat should be out on the water, but terrible weather kept us in port."

I extend a hand, but just as we clasp—BOOM!—an explosion sounds nearby. Smoke drifts from the bathroom and a strong odor of gunpowder fills our nostrils.

"Holy shit!" Brandon shouts. He half stands and almost knocks the table over. Everyone reaches frantically to steady their drinks. Several people run past us out the back door. Pratt looks around with alarm.

"What was that?"

I cough, embarrassed. "My guess is somebody lit off a seal bomb or two in the toilet."

"What's a seal bomb?"

"Oh, small explosives we use to keep sea lions from eating fish off the lines. They take our catch and could get tangled up so it scares them away. Just big firecrackers with lead weights and waterproof wicks."

"Why would somebody light one indoors?"

I laugh. "Probably because they're drunk– and also idiots."

Pratt smiles. "I understand."

"So, I've actually seen you before. Once in Yakima, about ten years ago."

Pratt raises his eyebrows. "Yakima? Yes ... I remember that performance. And then here? How on earth did it happen you should come to multiple shows in such out of the way places?"

"Well, the short version is I spent several years living with a devotee of yours in Portland, Oregon. We saw many classical music concerts and once drove all the way to central Washington when you played there. You signed a CD for her. She claimed she was kidnapped from Yakima and raised in France during World War II before her sex change and later becoming an atheist nun."

I stop, biting my lip. *What the hell?* Pratt will surely think I'm drunk or crazy, maybe both. If I'm lucky this famous musician couldn't hear me over the jukebox.

Pratt nods, his brow furrowed. "Quite unusual indeed." He looks past me where others beckon from a nearby booth. "I must join my friends, but do you have a ticket for tomorrow?"

I shake my head. "Not yet. I didn't know until recently the storm would keep us here. Why, is it sold out?"

Pratt bends closer. "I don't know, but you are welcome to come as my guest. I could put your name at the door. Ross Eliot, correct?"

"Yes. Oh, thank you, that would be quite wonderful." We grip hands once more and rejoin our separate tables.

The next evening I arrive at Sitka's Performing Arts Center just before show time and give my name at the will-call desk. As promised, a ticket waits for me. I accept it and enter. The hall interior is paneled in deep orange, with red upholstered seats and a long scarlet curtain. There's a full house tonight. Patrons lean back and browse stapled programs. I take a seat about ten rows back, on the right, just in from an aisle. The space to my left is empty.

On the schedule are four Brahms works for cello and piano. A black Steinway grand is positioned center stage. Flowers arranged in a large vase accent the far side. House lights dim and silence stretches. Someone nearby clears their throat. Then Pratt and cellist Zuill Bailey enter together. Pratt wears a black shirt spangled with red and white geometric shapes. He seats himself on a thickly-cushioned bench resembling an ottoman. Bailey carries his cello and sits facing the audience. He positions this instrument before him, dark shoulder-length hair falling around his long pale face. The two pause a moment, then unfurl the initial movement of Brahms' sonata No. 1 in E minor.

A sudden shock passes through me in the darkened theatre. The *allegro non troppo* hits at gut level and penetrates like a sharp blade. There is no warning, no preparation can save me from this grief. I weep as the empty seat on my left fills with a vortex thirteen years deep. Without protest or will I topple into the abyss. Germaine and Robert Brown stare up at me, their lips forever sealed with captive secrets. The cello wails, its cry that of a lonely child cast into existence on the cold winter plains of Central Washington. Images from sepia prints rush together as Pratt's fingers march along, black and white keys lined up for review in SS uniforms.

A well of sorrow overflows inside me as the *allegro quasi menuetto* begins. Albert Ellsworth snaps a self-portrait in some cheap motel room, his round face painted and portly figure bound up with lace, awaiting some unknown rendezvous. Judge Shoemaker welcomes him home with open arms. Billie Shoemaker looks on, her countenance set with stern authority. *Sannyasins* wake for their day's labor at the Rajneeshpuram compound, and counterfeit nuns cultivate a vegetable garden under sunny skies. Notes rise and fall with cascades that lift heartfelt prayers to heaven.

The final *allegro* stirs into substance, and tears run freely down my cheeks. I see Babette when we embraced, cold and miserable outside a train station on the way to Portland, then envision her as a slender teenage youth with the same one-way ticket from Yakima over fifty years before. I feel Annakiya's soft skin and Buenaventura's lips press against me. Dora's sweet face dissolves into Hitler's photograph slipped between pages of a Bible and Felix Yusupov executes Rasputin again and again. Brahms' music becomes phosphor bombs, incest, broken dildos, civil wars, fake tits and genocide. The wet salt in my mouth is thick with ashes from burned documents and illicit photographs. Now every sound subsides, yet neither piano nor cello completely hide muffled anti-aircraft fire. When the final notes fade– I leap to my feet.

The End

Citation and Notes

Chapter 1.

Jean-Paul Sartre. <u>Nausea</u>. New Directions, Norfolk, 1938. (1959 edition). 130.

Albert J. Ellsworth. "Counseling: A Frame of Reference." Summer, 1963. (author's collection)

Chapter 2.

Benjamin Disraeli. <u>Endymion</u>. Belford, Clarke & Co., Chicago. 1881. 92.

Chapter 3.

Vicente Blasco Ibanez. <u>The Shadow of the Cathedral</u>. E.P. Dutton & Co., New York. 1919. 180.

Chapter 4.

Octave Mirbeau. <u>The Diary of a Chambermaid</u>. HarperCollins Publishers, New York. 1900. (2006 edition). 44.

Chapter 5.

Francis Rabelais. <u>The Works of Francis Rabelais.</u> Rarity Press, New York. 1932. (orig. 1534). 366.

Chapter 6.

Max Aub. <u>Field of Honor</u>. Verso, London. 1943, (2009 edition). 52.

Chapter 7.

Emile Gaboriau. <u>The Widow Lerouge</u>. Charles Scribner's Sons, New York. 1873. 120.

Chapter 8.

Alphonse Daudet. <u>The Evangelist</u>. Little, Brown, and Co., Boston. 1883. (1899 edition). 203-4.

Chapter 9.

Charles Paul de Kock . <u>Little Lise.</u> The Frederick J. Quimby Company, Boston. (1904 edition). 34.

Chapter 10.

C.A. Sainte-Beuve. <u>Portraits of Celebrated Women</u>. Robert's Brothers, Boston. 1868. 95.

Chapter 11.

Octave Feuilette. <u>Monsieur de Camors.</u> Current Literature Publishing Company, New York. 1867, (1910 edition). 120.

Chapter 12.

Anatole France. <u>The Revolt of the Angels.</u> Dodd, Mead & Company. 1914 (1925 edition). 9.

Chapter 13.

Petronius. <u>The Satyricon.</u> The New American Library, New York. 1959. 52-3.

Chapter 14.

George Faludy. <u>My Happy Days in Hell</u>. Forever Kiado, 1962, (2003 edition). 203.

Chapter 15.

Emily Carr. <u>Hundreds and Thousand.</u> Clarke, Irwin & Company Ltd., Toronto, 1966. 26.

Chapter 16.

Lucretius. <u>On the Nature of the Universe.</u> Penguin Books, Baltimore, 1960. 60.

Chapter 17.

Honore de Balzac. <u>Father Goriot</u>. The Gebbie Publishing Co., Ltd. 1835. (1898 edition). 48.

Chapter 18.

Francois Villon. <u>The Complete Works of Francois Villon.</u> Covici, Friede, New York, 1931. 217.

Chapter 19.

Charles Paul de Kock. <u>The Barber of Paris Vol. II.</u> The Frederick J Quimby Company. 1826. 23.

Chapter 20.

Honore de Balzac. <u>Father Goriot.</u> 48.

Chapter 21.

Anatole France. <u>The Revolt of the Angels.</u> 109-10.

The only known evidence connecting Albert Ellsworth to the East German government is a 1963 letter from Sigrid Schwieger, an official with the *Gesellschaft fuer Kulturelle Verbindungen mit dem Ausland*, an agency that maintained international cultural contacts, about an American named Denis Mosgofian who attended Berkeley and earlier visited the GDR. She hoped Ellsworth would contact this young man and share a collection of propaganda films which might inspire student affinity groups. In February of 2010, I corresponded with Mosgofian, then a retired labor activist, but he recalled no communication between Ellsworth and himself ever taking place.

**Glasgow Courier, Thursday, September 5, 1974. 7A

Chapter 22.

Francois Villon. <u>The Complete Works of Francois Villon</u>. 43.

Chapter 23.

Octave Feuillet. <u>Monsieur de Camors.</u> 39.

Chapter 24.

Henri Rochefort. <u>Mademoiselle Bismark</u>. G. P. Putnam's Sons, New York. 1881. 296.

Chapter 25.

Max Aub. <u>Field of Honour</u>. 143.

Chapter 26.

Alain Rene Le Sage. <u>Gil Blas</u>. A.L Burt Company, New York. 1715. 72.

Chapter 27.

Theophile Gautier. <u>Mademoiselle de Maupin</u>. 416.

Chapter 28.

Evelyn Waugh. <u>Brideshead Revisited.</u> Penguin Books, Middlesex. 1945. (1981 edition). 295.

Chapter 29.

Alain Rene Le Sage. <u>Gil Blas</u>. 161.

Chapter 30.

Lucretius. <u>On the Nature of the Universe.</u> Penguin Books, Baltimore, 1960. 163.

Chapter 31.

J.K. Huysmans. <u>Against Nature.</u> Oxford University Press, Oxford. 1884, (1998 edition). 85.

Chapter 32.

Alain Rene Le Sage. <u>Gil Blas</u>. 109.

Chapter 33.

Petronius. <u>The Satyricon.</u> The New American Library, New York. 1959. 105.

Chapter 34.

Theophile Gautier. <u>Mademoiselle de Maupin</u>. 120.

Chapter 35.

Emile Erckmann & Alexandre Chatrian. <u>Waterloo</u>. Scribner's Sons, New York. 1865, (1869 edition). 116-7.

Chapter 36.

Hendrik van Loon. <u>The Story of America</u>. Garden City Publishing Co., Inc., New York. 1927. 463.

Chapter 37.

Octave Feuilette. <u>Monsieur de Camors</u>. 150-51.

Chapter 38.

Charles Paul de Kock. <u>The Barber of Paris Vol. I.</u> 89.

Chapter 39.

Theophile Gautier. <u>Captain Fracasse</u>. P.F. Collier & Sons, New York. 1861. (1902 edition). 357.

Chapter 40.

Margaret Atwood. <u>The Blind Assassin</u>. Anchor Books, New York. 2000. 494.

Chapter 41.

Theophile Gautier. <u>Mademoiselle de Maupin</u>. 341.

Chapter 42.

George Faludy. <u>My Happy Days in Hell</u>. 112.

Chapter 43.

Lucius Apuleius. <u>The Golden Ass.</u> Yale University Press, New Haven. 2011. 35.

Chapter 44.

Jean-Paul Sartre. <u>Nausea</u>. 130.

Albert J. Ellsworth. "Counseling: A Frame of Reference."

Heliocentric Press is a Portland, Oregon based independent press
that believes in treating its writers as equals. It encourages
freedom of self-expression without censorship or dictation of
content and allows authors full creative control over their works.

Visit us on Facebook or for more information, write:

heliocentricpress@yahoo.com